AF560746

EMPIRES IN INDIAN HISTORY AND OTHER ESSAYS

EMPIRES IN INDIAN HISTORY AND OTHER ESSAYS

DIETMAR ROTHERMUND

MANOHAR
2013

First published, 2013

© Dietmar Rothermund, 2013

All rights reserved. No part of this publication may be reproduced or transmitted, in any form or by any means, without prior permission of the author and the publisher.

ISBN 978-93-5098-13-2

Published by
Ajay Kumar Jain *for*
Manohar Publishers & Distributors
4753/23 Ansari Road, Daryaganj
New Delhi 110 002

Typeset at
Digigrafics
New Delhi 110 049

Printed at
Salasar Imaging Systems
Delhi 110 035

Contents

Preface 7

Acknowledgements 11

1. Empires in Indian History 15

2. From Chariot to Atom Bomb: Armament and Military Organization in South Asian History 36

3. The State Society in India from Ancient Times to the Present 63

4. Akbar and Philip II of Spain: Contrasting Strategies of Imperial Consolidation 85

5. Gandhi and Nehru: Two Visions of India 100

6. The Rural Roots of Jharkhand 120

7. The Self-consciousness of Post-Imperial Nations: A Cross-national Comparison 136

8. The De-Industrialization of India 163

9. Mumbai: From Fishing Village to Metropolis 178

10. Nation Building in India under British Rule 200

11. Max Müller's Science of Language and Religion 220

12. Rajghat: In Memory of the Mahatma 239

Bibliography of Dietmar Rothermund 247

Index 251

Preface

After serving as Professor of South Asian History at Heidelberg University for 33 years, I retired in 2001. I could then concentrate on writing books and articles, following up many themes on which I had worked earlier and exploring some new ones. In 2006 I published the *Routledge Companion to Decolonization* and in 2008 *India: The Rise of an Asian Giant*. In addition I contributed to the fourth and fifth editions of *A History of India* (2004, 2010) whose chapters on ancient and medieval history were written by Hermann Kulke. But I also wrote papers for conferences and for volumes edited by other authors. I have selected 12 papers for the present volume. For details I refer the reader to the acknowledgements. In this preface I only wish to outline the topics of the 12 papers and explain in which way they are related to each other.

The first three papers are concerned with three different approaches to the study of political organization in Indian history. The first deals with empires as the most prominent instances of state formation. Since military organization and armament are essential elements of state formation, the second paper is devoted to that subject. The state is embedded in the society which supports it. The 'state society' is therefore discussed in the third paper. Some repetitions could not be avoided, because these three papers are devoted to a common theme.

The fourth paper offers a comparative study of two remarkable rulers: Akbar and Philip II of Spain. The two mighty rulers were faced with similar challenges but met them in very different ways. The methods they adopted were deeply related to their personalities. The impressive buildings which they constructed mirrored these contrasting personalities.

The fifth paper on Nehru and Gandhi contains the gist of a book I published in German in 2010, *Gandhi und Nehru: Zwei Gesichter Indiens*. I had two long interviews with Nehru in January 1961 and since then had plans to write a book on him. Many other projects intervened, but finally the suggestion of a German publisher that I should write a book on Gandhi and Nehru enabled me to do what I had planned long ago. In this book I also covered Nehru's work after Gandhi's death. In the paper presented here I have only concentrated on their interactions while Gandhi was still alive.

The sixth paper reflects my earlier research interests in Indian agrarian relations. When I was asked by Nivedita Mohanty to contribute a paper to a volume on Jharkhand, I studied the history of tribal rebellions in this region and linked this up with my earlier work on the Chota Nagpur Tenancy Act of 1908 and on zamindars, mines and peasants in Dhanbad District.

The seventh paper was originally a keynote address of a conference at the German Historical Institute, London, in September 2008. When preparing this text, I consulted several colleagues in European countries (Great Britain, The Netherlands, Belgium, France, Portugal). I also included Japan in my study. I noticed that there have been similar patterns of 'self-conscious' reflections on the colonial past in all these countries, but there have been no cross-national comparisons of these experiences. I hope that my paper will stimulate such comparative studies.

The eighth paper is a contribution to the ongoing debate on the 'De-industrialization of India'. I have tried to widen the scope of the debate which has usually been restricted to the effect of British colonial rule over India in the nineteenth century. I have also dealt with the partial industrialiation of India in the late nineteenth century and the lack of linkages which prevented comprehensive industrial growth. My contribution on 'The Industrialization of India: Technology and Production' to a volume on the economic history of India edited by B.B. Chauduri is far more comprehensive (see reference in Acknowledgements). Its inclusion in this volume of essays was impossible because of its size (55,000 words). The present paper is based on a lecture at a meeting of the Asiatic Society, Mumbai, in 2008.

The ninth paper was my keynote address to a conference on Urban India held at the Jawaharlal Nehru University in March 2012. I then contributed it to a Festschrift for Mariam Dossal whose work has greatly influenced me in the study of Mumbai. In my earlier research work I had rather concentrated on agrarian relations in India. This 'urban turn' in my work is a new experience. If time permits, I shall pursue this new line in more detail.

The tenth paper owes its origin to a request by an American colleague, Sally Paine, to write on nation-building for a volume edited by her (see Acknowledgements). The British had certainly not conquered India in order to build an Indian nation. For a long time they did not even think of India as a nation, but referred to it as 'congeries of nations'. However, the unintended consequences of their rule contributed to nation-building. In the fields of education, jurisdiction and legislation, etc., British rule had a decisive impact. Moreover, the constitutional reforms introduced by the British shaped the course of agitation adopted by the Indian freedom movement.

The eleventh paper is devoted to Max Müller. It was originally the text of a lecture delivered under the auspices of the Max Müller Bhavan, Mumbai, in 2008. It was then published in a German journal (see Acknowledgements). Max Müller himself referred to the 'Sciences of Language and Religion' and he tried to connect them. At a time when the natural sciences were triumphant, he deliberately staked a claim for the humanities which he wanted to see established as 'sciences' in their own right. I conclude this paper with a detailed review of the *Sacred Books of the East* edited by Max Müller and provide information about the authors whom he inspired to share this monumental work with him.

The twelfth paper was my contribution to a conference on 'Places of Memory' held at Cumberland Lodge, Windsor Palace, by the German Historical Institute, London in 2006.

I hope that this collection of essays will be of use to my readers and I thank my publisher, Ramesh Jain, for his support. I have worked with him for about forty years and I have always enjoyed his encouragement.

DIETMAR ROTHERMUND

Acknowledgements

(1) EMPIRES IN INDIAN HISTORY

In 2010 I participated in a conference on 'Imperien und Reiche in der Weltgeschichte' convened by Professors Robert Rollinger (Innsbruck) and Michael Gehlen (Hildesheim) at Hildesheim University. My paper (in German) dealt with Indian empires from the Guptas to British India. Hermann Kulke presented a paper on the Mauryas. He kindly permitted me to draw upon this paper for my outline of 'Empires in Indian History' which is not a translation but an entirely new text. The Harappan empire was not discussed at the conference.

(2) FROM THE CHARIOT TO THE ATOM BOMB

This was my contribution to Jos Gommans and Om Prakash, eds., *Circumambulations in South Asian History: Essays in Honour of Dirk H. A. Kolff*, Leiden: Brill, 2003, pp.325-51. I thank Dirk Kolff for contacting the publisher who has no objection to the reprinting of this paper.

(3) THE STATE SOCIETY IN INDIA

Professor Rila Mukherjee organized a conference on the state in South Asia at the University of Hyderabad in October 2010. She is editing the conference volume and has kindly permitted the reprinting of my contribution to this conference.

(4) AKBAR AND PHILIP II OF SPAIN

Professors Irfan Habib and Shireen Moosvi organized a conference on 'Reason and Tolerance in Indian History' sponsored by the Indian Council of Historical Research in New Delhi, October 2006. Shireen Moosvi, who edits the conference volume, has kindly permitted the reprinting of my contribution to this conference.

(5) GANDHI AND NEHRU: TWO VISIONS OF INDIA

This essay has been written for this volume. It is based on my book *Gandhi und Nehru: Zwei Gesichter Indiens*, Stuttgart: Kohlhammer, 2010.

(6) THE RURAL ROOTS OF JHARKHAND

Nivedita Mohanty is editing a volume on Jharkhand to which I contributed this paper. The publication of this volume has been delayed. I am grateful to her for permitting me to reprint this paper here.

(7) THE SELF-CONSCIOUSNESS OF POST-IMPERIAL NATIONS

Keynote address for a conference held at the German Historical Institute, London, in September 2008. Published in *India Quarterly* (Indian Council of World Affairs) 67(1) March 2011. I am grateful to the editor for the permission to reprint this paper.

(8) THE DE-INDUSTRIALIZATION OF INDIA

Unpublished manuscript of a lecture delivered at a meeting of the Asiatic Society, Mumbai, 2008. I have dealt more in detail with this subject in the chapter on 'The Industrialization of India: Technology and Production', in B. B. Chaudhuri, ed., *Economic History of India from Eighteenth to Twentieth Century* (History of Science, Philosophy and Culture in Indian Civilization, vol. VIII, part 3) New Delhi: Centre for Studies in Civilizations, 2005, pp.437-523.

(9) MUMBAI: FROM FISHING VILLAGE TO METROPOLIS

In March 2012, a conference on Urban India was held at the Jawaharlal Nehru University in collaboration with the South Asia Institute, Heidelberg to celebrate its 50th anniversary. I was asked to contribute a keynote address to this conference and I wrote the present paper for this purpose. I was then asked by the editors of a Festschrift for Mariam Dossal, whose work on the history of Mumbai has inspired me, to contribute this paper to the Festschrift. They have kindly permitted me to reprint this paper here.

(10) NATION-BUILDING IN INDIA
UNDER BRITISH RULE

Originally published in *Nation Building, State Building, and Economic Development: Case Studies and Comparisons*, ed. S.C.M. Paine, Armonk, NY: M.E. Sharpe, 2010, pp. 13-29. Copyright © 2010 by M.E. Sharpe, Inc. Used by permission.

(11) MAX MÜLLER'S SCIENCE OF
LANGUAGE AND RELIGION

A lecture delivered under the auspices of the Max Müller Bhavan, Mumbai, 2008. Originally published in *ORIENTIERUNGEN: Zeitschrift zur Kultur Asiens*, Munich: edition global, vol. 21, no. 1, 2009, pp. 1-21 (www.edition-global.de). Reprinted here with the permission of the edior of the journal.

(12) RAJGHAT: IN MEMORY OF
THE MAHATMA

A lecture delivered at a conference on 'Places of Memory', London, 2006. A German version 'Rajghat: In Memoriam Mahatma Gandhi' has been published in *Zeitschrift fur Weltgeschichte*, Nr. 9/1, 2008.

CHAPTER 1

Empires in Indian History

THE STRUCTURE OF EMPIRES

Empires are systems of governance which control a large space over several generations. Their central area of intensive rule may be restricted, but they have a much greater outreach in terms of military intervention and long distance trade. They may decay due to internal tensions or 'imperial overstretch'. However, their style of governance and their cultural manifestations may continue to influence subsequent realms. The Roman Empire shows this very well. Indian empires have had a similar impact on their successor states.

In this paper only a few major Indian empires will be discussed. Recurrent features of imperial consolidation will be highlighted, but the individual characteristics of different empires will also be taken into consideration. The means of military power which were crucial for these empires will be mentioned only in passing as a subsequent paper is devoted to this subject.

Empires were not only of political importance, they also stimulated cultural developments. They drew upon cultural traditions for their legitimation and invested a great deal in monuments which remain a testimony to their splendour. They gave rise to forms of art and to the evolution of language and literature. They depended on the existence of state societies in which their systems of governance were embedded and they contributed to the evolution of such societies. Again, this context of imperial rule will only be touched upon in this paper, because a subsequent paper will deal with state societies in detail.

Particular historical constellations favour the emergence of empires. In this paper an attempt will be made to explore such constellations. Similarly, the structural elements which are conducive to the decay of empires will also be studied. The history of Indian empires contributes much to the analysis of the rise and fall of empires in a global perspective.

THE HARAPPAN EMPIRE: HARNESSING A MIGHTY RIVER

The state of the Indus civilization is usually not classified as an empire. But due to its vast expanse and its longevity, it certainly deserves to be mentioned in this context. The reason for its exclusion from the study of empires is the lack of knowledge of its system of governance. There are only indirect clues for the reconstruction of its history. Moreover, among the material survivals of the Indus civilization, royal palaces and tombs are conspicuous by their absence. This may have been an empire without an emperor, controlled by an elite which set norms and standards for a vast realm. The existence of such an elite could have guaranteed the existence of this empire for about a millenium, much longer than that of empires depending on dynastic succession. The structure of the Indus cities provides evidence for this kind of polity. These cities have citadels divided into two parts. One part contained a large tank, probably for ritual baths, the other half had residential quarters which may have been destined for a priestly class. Among those priests may have also been experts who knew how to predict the floods of the Indus and could design the drainage required for making the land suitable for agriculture. They would have also standardized the weights and measures which showed an amazing uniformity throughout the 'empire'. Even the bricks used for the construction of houses and fortresses had the same dimensions in all of the Indus cities.

The Harappans did not build dams to harness the mighty Indus. However, they managed to cultivate the enormous flood plains of the Indus. It was not flood control but the productive use of the fertile silt spread over large areas by the annual floods of the Indus which was the essence of their economy. 'Settled agriculture' in the usual sense of the term was impossible in the flood plains. The peasants had to move in and out of the plains in a seasonal rhythm. This is why no village sites have been found around Mohenjo Daro, the city which dominated the lower Indus valley. Earlier settlements of the precursors of the Indus Civilization are located on the periphery of the flood plains. Only the 'Mature Harappans' (*c.* 2600-2000 BC) ventured out into the plains, which must have appeared to be a dangerous territory to their precursors. The Indus carries twice as much water as the Nile and its floods are awe inspiring. 'Harnessing the river' then meant developing a strategy of the deployment of thousands of peasants in this vast area and planning their seasonal advance and retreat. The surplus produced by those peasants supported not only the elite of an empire but numerous artisans whose products fed the thriving internal as well as the long distance trade.

The numerous delicately carved steatite (soapstone) seals found at all the sites of the Indus civilization are characterized by a repetition of patterns (animals, symbols). They were probably used for the identification of traded goods. Many of the animals depicted on the seals carry burdens indicated by a type of saddle with bags attached to it.[1] Such loads were probably also standardized and the figures on the seals would then indicate the quantity of grain or other goods dispatched under the respective seals. The long distance trade of the empire extended as far as Mesopotamia where the kings had interpreters who knew the language of the Indus merchants. There was a term, Meluhha, which the people of the Indus civilization used when referring to themselves.[2] In later Indian languages this term changed into 'mleccha' which refers to an impure foreigner. It seems that the Aryan immigrants when they encountered the people of the Indus civilization picked up this word and used it to distinguish them from their own 'pure' people.

The rise of the Indus civilization and the potential for state building was probably due to climatic conditions. There is paleobotanic evidence for the increase of rainfall and the spread of various plants, beginning in the third millennium BC. A special type of wheat which could flourish in a hot climate supported the ancient green revolution on which the Harappan empire depended.[3] African millets were adopted later on and helped to extend agriculture to Gujarat and adjacent regions of western India where wheat would not grow.[4] Cotton was also grown by the peasants of the Indus civilization and cotton textiles were obviously part of its long distance trade with Mesopotamia. The other export articles were precious stones. Lapis Lazuli was procured by the Indus merchants from distant places such as Badakshan (Afghanistan). The profits from international trade also led to the penetration of Gujarat by the Harappans. Dholavira, probably the largest city of the Indus civilization, covering about 100 hectares, was a busy port which may have owed its rise in the late second millenium BC to the trade with Mesopotamia.[5]

The decay of the Indus civilization and of its 'empire' was again due to climate change. Rainfall receded and there may also have been tectonic upheavals which affected the Indus river. It is presumed that the Yamuna, which now flows to the east and joins the Ganges, earlier flowed to the west and ran parallel to the Indus. There are numerous settlements of the Indus civilization around Ganweriwala, a city which may have rivalled Harappa and Mohenjo Daro. It had about the same size as Mohenjo Daro (80 hectares). Ganweriwala has not yet been excavated and there have only been preliminary explorations of the settlements in this region, i.e. the Cholistan Desert of Bahawalpur (Pakistan). The cities of the Indus Civilization seem to have been abandoned around 1900 BC. The subsequent centuries are referred to as 'Late Harappan' by most authors. In this period many traits of the material culture of the preceding 'Mature Harappan' have been retained. But long distance trade as well as the central control of norms and standards obviously disappeared.[6] The 'empire' had disintegrated. The theory that Aryan invaders destroyed the cities of the Indus civilization has been discarded. Various environmental factors contributed to its decay. 'Imperial overstretch' due to the military conquest of a large territory does not seem to have been the cause of the decline of the Indus civilization. It had so to speak spread by contagion and had gradually incorporated several different regions. It was probably not dominated by a single capital but was controlled from several centres which shared the same system of governance. The distance between the two large cities in the north (Harappa) and the south (Dholavira) of the 'empire' was about 1,000 km. Harappa was the 'gateway city', dominating the trade with the northern regions[7], while Dholavira was the 'gateway city' for the maritime trade. There was another port city, Lothal, on the other side of the Kathiawar peninsula, which was much smaller than Dholavira. Neither horse nor elephant which played a crucial role in later empires were available to the Harappans who had to rely on bullocks. Extending its sway over such a large area for about one millenium, the Harappan empire was one of the most impressive in world history.

ASHOKA MAURYA: THE GRAND DESIGN OF AN IMPERIAL MISSION

More than a millenium passed before another Indian empire emerged in the east. The base of this new empire was the fertile Gangetic plains of Bihar and Bengal where rice grew in abundance. The hills adjacent to the plains harboured rich deposits of iron ore, and in the forest were plenty of elephants which could be caught and trained for transport and warfare. Brahmins considered this territory to be impure and hesitated to go there. Therefore heterodox religious movements freely spread in this area. Mahavira, the founder of Jainism, Gosala, the master of the Ajivikas, and Gautama Buddha, the founder of Buddhism were contemporaries and attracted numerous followers in the fifth century BC. The Ajivikas believed in radical determinism, denied the existence of a free will and also the responsibility of human beings for their actions. Gautama Buddha was the most trenchant critic of the Ajivikas and stressed the moral value of human actions.

In the years from 424 to 321 BC the Nanda dynasty ruled a large empire with its main base in the eastern region but extending throughout northern India.[8] In 327 BC Alexander the Great invaded the Punjab but had to withdraw as his soldiers were unwilling to march further to the east. He thus never encountered the mighty Nanda army. But a young warrior, Chandragupta Maurya, who probably participated in the fight against Alexander, subsequenly usurped the Nanda throne and established the Maurya dynasty. It is said that he owed his success to his teacher Kautilya, the author of the *Arthashastra*, the ancient Indian text which surpasses Machiaveli's doctrine of statecraft. Kautilya is supposed to have belonged to the Ajivikas, this would explain his indifference to a moral order. Chandragupta, however, was a pious follower of Jainism. He was a great conqueror and penetrated southern India where he finally ended his life by fasting unto death, a practice sanctioned by Jainism. His son Bindusara who ruled from 298 to 271 was a follower of the Ajivikas. He further expanded the empire and left an impressive heritage to his son, Ashoka, who then conquered Kalinga. This bloody conquest burdened his conscience so much that he became a devout Buddhist.[9] He mentioned this change of heart in his inscriptions which he installed in all parts of his empire.

Buddhism actually taught how man could free himself from the cycle of rebirths so as to enter *nirvana*. This was not a suitable foundation for a universal political ethics, but Ashoka managed to interpret the Buddhist *dhamma* in such a way that it could ensure his peaceful rule over an enormous empire. As a lay brother of the Buddhist order (*sangha*) he could claim some influence on Buddhist missions and he used them very well for the consolidation of his empire. He dispatched *dhammamahamatras* (inspectors of right conduct) to all parts of the empire and they were probably Buddhist monks. But Ashoka did not make Buddhism a state religion of his empire. He distilled the principles of right conduct from Buddhist doctrine. This also implied a preference for vegetarianism and the prohibition of animal sacrifices. Those who followed the principles advocated by Ashoka were otherwise free to follow their own religious practices. The Ajivikas who had been patronized by Ashoka's father also enjoyed Ashoka's patronage even though he was a Buddhist.

In his rock inscriptions in distant Afghanistan he 'beamed' his message of goodwill also to his neighbours. He informed them that he had sent ambassadors to the West, mentioning the kings by name whom he had assured of his benevolent intentions. His foreign policy was thus in tune with his domestic policy of peaceful imperial consolidation. At first sight, the borders of Ashoka's empire seem to be marked by those distant inscriptions. But this would mean to mistake the outreach of imperial intervention for the actual control of territory. Probably the fertile Gangetic plains were the centrally administered parts of the empire, beyond this imperial heartland the control of trade routes was more important than territorial domination. In the east and south these trade routes followed the coast and extended to the present state of Karnataka around Suvarnagiri where a whole cluster of inscriptions has been found.[10] Another important route crossed the Deccan plateau and reached the west coast. Probably the most important route was the one which connected Pataliputra with the provincial capital at Taxila and extended from there to Afghanistan. In addition to the inscriptions, the spread of punch-marked silver coins marked the extension of the trade-based empire.

The Persian empire founded by Cyrus the Great (*c.* 559-530 BC), which was destroyed by Alexander, may have inspired Ashoka in his imperial vision. The lion capitals which crown the pillars bearing his edicts show distinct traces of Persian art.[11] But this concerns the outward manifestation of Ashoka's imperial style whereas the ideology of his imperial mission showed his personal imprint. But this great individual contribution also marked its limitation. His emphasis on 'right conduct' was not universally appreciated by his subjects. After his death many of them may have shrugged it off. The later Mauryas ruled a declining empire whose memory has only been preserved by Ashoka's magnificent edicts carved in solid rock.

THE GUPTA EMPIRE: SETTING AN INDIAN ROYAL STYLE

The Gupta empire relied on the same regional resource base as the Maurya empire. It could also use the rice production, the iron ore and the elephants of Bihar and Bengal. The first prominent ruler of this dynasty was Chandragupta I who married a Licchavi princess. This clan was famous even in Buddha's times. The dynastic charisma of the Licchavis helped the Guptas who were 'parvenus'. The precious Gupta gold coins stressed this dynastic connection. Samudragupta (335-75), the empire builder, called himself 'son of the Licchavi' on his coins. His capital was Pataliputra (Patna) which had also been the capital of the Maurya empire. But the context of Gupta power was very different from that of the Mauryas. While Ashoka extended his empire by 'imperial mission' and did not encounter rulers who dared to challenge him, Samudragupta embarked on a great tour of conquest. He fully documented this tour in the Allahabad inscription on one of the old Ashoka pillars.[12] His war elephants carried his army to south India where he vanquished many kings whom he then reinstated as tributary rulers. Only in northern India he 'uprooted' kings and annexed their realms. The difference between the extension of imperial governance and the outreach of military intervention is clearly demonstrated in Samudaragupta's account. The mighty Vakataka dynasty of central India is not mentioned in the Allahabad inscription, Samudragupta must have known the Vakatakas, but he seems not to have been able to vanquish them. His son, Chandragupta II, then married his daughter Prabhavatigupta to the Vakataka king Rudrasena II who died five years after this marriage. Prabhavatigupta then ruled this kingdom which thus became an integral part of the Gupta empire. It is therefore often called the Vakataka-Gupta empire.[13] After her death (*c.* 443) the relations of the two dynasties were not always harmonious.[14] The reign of her brother Kumaragupta (415-45) is considered to be the best period of the empire. He was not a great conqueror but consolidated the empire inherited from his ancestors and presided over its cultural efflorescence. An elegant urbanity prevailed in the cities of the empire.[15] Classical Sanskrit poetry reached its zenith at that time. The great poet Kalidasa, the author of *Shakuntala*, may have been a contemporary of Chandragupta II and Kumaragupta. Technology also showed great advancement at this time as attested by Kumaragupta's iron pillar which had no traces of corrosion. Kumaragupta issued beautiful gold coins which often show him as an archer portayed in a very lively style. The sculptures in the temples of the Gupta are also very attractive. They have set the pattern for subsequent temple art in India.

The most important contribution of the Guptas was their setting of an Indian royal style which was even 'exported' to South East

Asia.[16] This was the manifestation of royal power in all its splendour and its religious legitimation. The Guptas were Hindus, worshippers of Vishnu, but they also patronized Buddhist monasteries. The Huns obliterated their empire and destroyed many of their monuments and their flourishing cities, but their cultural heritage was revived by later regional kingdoms.

After the interregnum of the Hun kings in northern India had come to an end, King Harshavardhana of Kanauj (reign: 606-47) tried to establish an empire of the same dimensions like that of the Gupta empire. He was partially successful, but he could not subdue southern India. Like Samudragupta, he embarked on a tour of conquest of the south, but he was met halfway by the large army of King Pulakeshin II (reign: 610-42) of the Chalukya dynasty of Badami in Karnataka. Harshavardhana was defeated by Pulakeshin II .[17] This showed that by now the power of intervention of south Indian kings was strong enough to ward off northern empire builders. The age of regional kingdoms had begun.

Harshavardhana's realm differed from the Gupta empire not only in its power of external intervention but also in its internal organization. The *samanta* emerged as an important figure of a kind of 'feudal' regime. Originally *samanta* meant neighbour, but it then designated a tributary prince who had been subdued and then reinstated by the ruler who was at the centre of a *samantachakra,* a circle of tributary rulers, who had to attend the court of the central ruler of whom it was said that he enjoyed the reflected glory of the crowns of his *samantas.* Some *samantas* then occupied permanent offices at the court of the king and his prime minister was called *mahasamanta.* Hermann Kulke has referred to this as 'samantaization' of medieval Indian regimes. All this was already in evidence in Harshavardhana's realm. The Gupta royal style which pervaded all Indian regional kingdoms was thus combined with a new type of concentric state formation based on the incorporation of *samantas.*[18]

THE AMPHIBIAN EMPIRE OF THE CHOLAS

The Cholas of Tamil Nadu were originally rulers of a regional kingdom. Even Ashoka had noted them in his inscriptions. For many centuries they had lived in relative obscurity. But then Aditya Chola vanquished the last Pallava king in 871. After this decisive victory, the Cholas were able to conquer almost the whole of southern India.

However, they were soon rivalled by the Rashtrakutas of western India.[19] The greatest king of that dynasty, Krishna III, defeated the Chola king Paratanka, but soon after Krishna's death, the Rashtrakutas were overthrown by their vassal Taila. This enabled the Cholas to regain their power. Their kingdom acquired the status of an empire under Rajaraja I (985-1014) and Rajendra (1014-47). This was an amphibian empire as the Cholas also conquered Sri Lanka and the Maldives and built a mighty fleet which Rajendra deployed against the Indonesian kingdom Srivijaya in 1025. This naval expedition was caused by the obstruction of Chola maritime trade with China by Srivijaya. It seems that this intervention was successful. It was not aimed at territorial gain but was meant to teach Srivijaya a lesson. Before and after this naval battle the Cholas maintained good diplomatic relations with Srivijaya.

The Cholas had become powerful intermediaries in the maritime trade from the Persian Gulf to southern China due to a favourable constellation which emerged in this period. Mahmud of Ghazni had carried away the enormous treasures of northern India in 17 raids. He used this booty as political capital to finance his rise in the realm of the Caliph of Baghdad.[20] In this way the Indian treasures envigorated the maritime trade of the Persian Gulf. At the same time the Chinese Song dynasty shifted its centre of power from the middle of China closer to the southern coast. It also stimulated the cultivation of rice and with it the growth of the population in Southern China which thus became a magnet attracting maritime trade.[21] Rajaraja had sent an embassy to China advertising the goods which the Cholas could deliver. Almost all of these goods were not produced in southern India. This indicates that the Cholas were only intermediaries in this trade from which they obviously profited very much. For the control of this trade it was good to rule an amphibian empire at a strategic position in the Indian Ocean. The Cholas cooperated with the powerful guilds of long distance traders.[22] Income from trade must have been at least as important for them as the land revenue. But they also tried to improve agricultural production in their domain. For this purpose they even made use of innovations which had been introduced in Sri Lanka. Technicians who were in charge of irrigation systems of northern Sri Lanka had invented a new type of sluices which were then copied in Tamil Nadu.[23] In this way the amphibian kingdom also contributed to technology transfer.

The instruments of land warfare remained more or less the same from the Mauryas to the Cholas. But maritime warfare demanded innovations in shipbuilding and it seems that the Indians proved to be experts in this field. Marco Polo praised the Indian ships of his time, but it is interesting to note that he did not mention Pumpuhar (Nagapattinam), the great port of the Cholas, at all in his travelogue. It seems that by the time of visit of India the amphibian empire of the Cholas had long since disappeared.[24] Only the magnificent Rajarajeshwar temple built in 1010 by Rajaraja Chola remains a permanent monument of the grandeur of this dynasty. The inscriptions on its walls show that the temple and its servants were maintained by donations of the leading nobles of the empire. The temple was the central node in the network of ritual hegemony which encompassed the empire.

The decline of the Chola empire was a gradual process. It experienced a revival of its power under Kulottunga I who reigned from 1070 to 1120. Rajendra had married a princess of the Eastern Chalukyas who controlled the Krishna-Godaveri Delta. Kullotunga belonged to this dynasty but claimed the Chola throne as a relative of the Cholas. Kulottunga means 'head of the family'. This indicates that he obviously felt the need to legitimize his accession to the Chola throne by adopting this dynastic title.

The Chola empire finally came to an end under Kulottunga III who was vanquished by the Pandya king Maravarman Sundaran (reign: 1216-38). The Pandyas were an ancient dynasty like the Cholas, but they had also lived in oblivion for many centuries. Their heartland was the fertile basin around Madurai. Under the Cholas they had been forced into exile in Sri Lanka, but now they reasserted their power. However, their days were also numbererd. In 1311 the Pandya army was vanquished by Malik Kafur, the general of the Sultan of Delhi.

THE CAVALRY EMPIRES: DELHI AND VIJAYANAGAR

The importance of the cavalry for state building in late medieval India will be discussed in subsequent papers. Here it may suffice to point out that cavalry warfare determined the rise and the maintenance of two great Indian empires – the Delhi Sultanate and the Vijayanagar empire. It was significant that both empires did not bear the name of a dynasty but of their capital city. These capitals survived the rise and fall of several dynasties. Usurpations of the throne occurred frequently, but the usurper would capture the capital and endorse its importance.

Empire building by means of cavalry warfare ushered in a regime of military feudalism. Cavalry officers received revenue assignments (*iqta*) from which they had to support their military contingents. Conquering large tracts of settled agriculture by means of the swift cavalry was easy.[25] The man on horseback was a powerful revenue collector. Thus the cavalry ensured both a sufficient intensity of territorial domination as well as a great outreach of military intervention. The latter was demonstrated by the campaigns of the great general Malik Kafur. Originally a Gujarati Hindu, Ram Chand, he was a handsome, castrated slave, who attracted the attention of Sultan Alauddin Khilji (reign: 1296-1316). Converted to Islam, he quickly rose to a high position in the sultan's court. He served as a daring cavalry general vanquishing many Hindu rulers of the south who were not yet used to the methods of quick cavalry warfare. He returned to Delhi with an enormous booty including thousands of horses and elephants as well as gold and precious stones.

Alauddin was the most ruthless and efficient sultan of Delhi. He registered all his soldiers and their payscales. He also branded the cavalry horses so as to keep track of them. His reign marked the zenith of the power of the Delhi Sultanate which had been founded by the slave general, Qutbuddin Aibak, in 1206. Qutbuddin had conquered most of Northern India for his owner, Muhammad Ghor of Afghanistan. When his owner was murdered, Qutbuddin became a ruler in his own right. But he was not yet a sultan. This title had been first adopted by the Turk, Tögrilbeg, who conquered Baghdad and forced the Caliph to appoint him as his plenipotentiary (sultan) in 1055.[26] Since then the Caliph had bestowed this title on rulers who hoped to gain legitimacy in this way. The slave sultans of Delhi were very much in need of this legitimacy. Qutbuddin's son-in-law and successor, Iltutmish (reign: 1210-36) finally earned the coveted title. He had been a slave of Qutbuddin who soon recognized his merits. Not being his legitimate heir he usurped the throne and thus set a pattern which determined many successions in the Delhi sultanate. The distribution of military power in this empire meant that the 'colleagues' of cavalry commanders would check each other. Succession was difficult under these conditions. Only the most daring commander who seized power at the centre could become a sultan.

Iltutmish was such a daring commander and empire builder. He had to face many challenges of local rulers as well as of the Mongols who tried to invade his realm. His slave Balban became very powerful in the interregnum of weaker sultans after Iltutmish's death. He finally ascended the throne at an advanced age and ruled the empire with an iron fist (1255-97). He was cruel and murdered all his rivals, but he was also known for his stern justice.

Throughout the thirteenth century the Delhi Sultanate had remained a north Indian empire extending from the borders of Afghanistan to Bihar. The conquest of the south began with Alauddin who followed a strategy similar to that of Samudragupta who had defeated and then reinstated the rulers of the south. These rulers were supposed to pay tribute to him. When they failed to do so, they faced another attack. Even in its central domains the sultanate was a superficial 'platform state'. The headquarters of the cavalry officers were the pillars which supported the 'platform'. The Hindus were recalcitrant subjects. Alauddin complained about their insolence and tried to humble them. There was an uneasy truce between the superimposed state and its population. The sultanate was not only built on a fragile foundation, it also faced the threat of a Mongol invasion. It was Alauddin's great achievement that he successfully defended India against the Mongols who had overrun China and Mesopotamia and could have vanquished India, too.[27]

The Delhi Sultanate reached its greatest territorial extension but it also met the fate of 'imperial overstretch' under Muhammad Tughluq (reign: 1325-51). Muhammad had shown his military prowess already before he ascended the throne by vanquishing the Kakatiya kingdom in 1323. The Kakatiyas ruled most of what is now Andhra Pradesh. Their capital Warangal had been captured by Malik Kafur who left it with a rich booty. The Kakatiya king, Prataparudra (reign: 1296-1323), had reasserted his independence soon thereafter. His state was also a cavalry state on the pattern of the Delhi Sultanate. It was a well organized state, which resisted Muhammad's first onslaught but then succumbed to his second attempt. Prataparudra was taken prisoner and committed suicide. Muhammad's conquest of the south faced no further obstacle. However, he soon found out that he could not control the south from Delhi and shifted his capital to Daulatabad, near Aurangabad. The same move was made by Aurangzeb three centuries later, and both times this shift of the capital was the harbinger of 'imperial overstretch'. Muhammad lost control of Delhi and decided to retrace his steps. But when he returned to Delhi, the days of his empire were numbered. Under his cousin Feroz Shah (reign: 1351-88) the Sultanate shrunk to its earlier size and managed to survive as a Northern India realm. The great conqueror Timur then achieved what the Mongols had failed to do earlier. He vanquished the Delhi Sultanate in 1398 and his army sacked Delhi, slaughtering most of its inhabitants.

In the last years of Muhammad Tughluq's reign, two nayaks (cavalry officers) of the last Hoysala king, Harihar and Bukka, had laid the foundation for the Vijayanagar empire in 1346. They were masters of cavalry warfare and it is said that they had served under Prataparudra for some time. Harihara (reign: 1346-57) and Bukka (reign: 1357-77) conquered the whole of the territory to the south of the Krishna River.[28] They introduced the *amaranayaka*-system which remained the backbone of the Vijayanagar empire. *Amara* referred to a military landgrant, similar to the *iqta* of the Delhi Sultanate. The institution of military feudalism had thus spread throughout India. Just like the Delhi Sultanate, the Vijayanagar empire witnessed a sequence of several dynasties and usurpation was a frequent phenomenon. The empire reached its largest territorial extension under its greatest ruler, Krishnadeva Raya (reign: 1509-29).[29] Almost the entire east coast was under his control. Krishnadeva was a Telugu warrior and his rule over Tamil Nadu was not welcomed by the Tamilians. He tried to gain their loyalty by building a large number of temples in Tamil Nadu. Once again, temple building was used as a means of imperial consolidation.

In the territory to the north of the Krishna River several sultanates had been established after Muhammad Tughluq's empire had vanished. These sultanates were busy fighting among themselves and thus did not seriously threaten the Vijayanagar empire. But in 1564 they banded together and jointly defeated the Vijayanagar army at Talikota. The victorious army then sacked Vijayanagar. The empire lingered on for some time. Mighty *nayaks* established their own realms, but they retained their old designations, e.g. Tirumala Nayak of Madurai, commemorating the past imperial glory.

While the Vijayanagar empire was still enjoying its greatest splendour under Krishnadeva Raya, Babur, the Great Mughal, had laid the foundation for a new Indian empire. He defeated the last Sultan of Delhi, Ibrahim Lodi, in the battle of Panipat in 1526.

THE CHARISMA OF THE GREAT MUGHALS

Babur's victory over the much more numerous army of Ibrahim Lodi was based on the ingenious deployment of the Mughal field artillery. Mobile artillery was a 'disruptive technology' introduced in the late fifteenth century. In modern economics the term 'disruptive technology' is used for innovations such as the computer which make older technologies obsolete very rapidly. This was certainly true of field artillery which first proved its devastating effect on European battlefields, was then adopted by the Ottoman sultans and then reached India where Babur proved to be a master strategist in deploying it. At the same time European powers managed to turn this mobile artillery into naval artillery, but this the Mughals never did. They ruled a land based empire. The coordination of cavalry and artillery was the main problem which they had to solve. Their empire remained essentially a cavalry state, but their imperial weapon was the new field artillery. Akbar, the greatest Mughal, devoted some time in designing guns and their carriages. The manufacture of guns was a closely kept secret which the Mughals did not even share with their trusted allies, the Rajputs, who took more than a century to master this art so as to establish gun foundries of their own.

Unlike the Delhi Sultanate which was never ruled by one dynasty for any length of time, the Great Mughals were an imperial dynasty accumulating a great deal of dynastic charisma. This found its outward expression in the portraits of the Great Mughals who were adorned with a golden nimbus. Such portraits were 'unislamic' as such, and the nimbus indicating a quasi-divine presence was even more of an offence to orthodox Muslims, but it was more appreciated by the Hindu subjects of the Great Mughals. Hindu kings have often stressed their identification with a divine patron in their visual representations.

Babur's son Humayun (reign: 1530-56) was deprived of his empire by the Afghan Sher Shah. Humanyan fled to Persia and during his flight his son Akbar was born to him in 1541. Sher Shah's successors were weak rulers and Humayun defeated them in 1555 with Persian support. He died soon after this victory and Akbar (reign: 1556-1605) ascended the throne as a teenager. Since the characteristics of his rule will be discussed in subsequent papers, it may suffice to state that he trebled the size of his empire in his long reign. It reached from Afghanistan to Bengal and included Gujarat which gave Akbar access to the Arabian Sea. He prudently refrained from extending his sway to Persia or Uzbekistan although the rulers of those states tempted him with offers to join forces and share the respective other state between them. His grandson, Shah Jahan, was less prudent and embarked on great campaigns of conquest. He extended the empire to the south and sent his son, Aurangzeb, on a campaign to the west, aimed at recovering Fergana, the homeland of the Great Mughals, of which they had been deprived by the Uzbeks. Aurangzeb's campaign came to a halt at Balkh, Afghanistan.[30] This taught him a lesson, and after he ascended the throne he never again ventured on such a campaign and rather concentrated on conquering southern India.

Aurangzeb's long reign (1658-1707) marked the zenith of the empire but also the beginning of its decline. He had imprisoned his father, vanquished his brothers and seized the throne which he then occupied for nearly half a century. His empire decayed not only due to 'imperial overstretch' but also to 'generational overstretch' as he survived some of his sons and the one who finally succeeded him was an old man who then presided over the disintegration of the empire. Aurangzeb was an ardent Muslim. He broke with Akbar's tolerant policies and reintroduced the poll tax (*jiziya*) for non-believers which was detested by his Hindu subjects. But far more damaging was his distortion of Akbar's mansabdar- system, which had served as a 'steel frame' of the empire. This system of imperial ranks will be discussed in subsequent papers. The *mansabdars* did not constitute a hereditary nobility, they were personally appointed by the Great Mughal. But studies have shown that there was a considerable continuity of mansabdar families. The son of a mansabdar would not immediately get the same position as his father, but he was accommodated in the system and could rise if he proved his merit. In order to incorporate the elites of the conquered territories, Aurangzeb increased the number of *mansabdars* at the highest level.[31] The southern highlands, which he had conquered, did not yield much agricultural surplus, therefore it was imprudent to create 'expensive' *mansabdars* there. The burdening of the agarian base of the empire led to peasant revolts which increased towards the end of Aurangzeb's reign. He was also challenged by the turbulent Marathas, whose leader, Shivaji, had even dared to sack the Mughal port, Surat, in 1664. The Marathas harrassed the Mughal army with their light cavalry, adopting guerilla tactics. Shivaji died in 1680, he had remained a dangerous challenger for Aurangzeb throughout his life. His son Sambhaji then joined forces with Aurangzeb's rebellious son, Akbar, but Aurangzeb defeated both and then shifted his capital from Delhi to Aurangabad in order to control the south. Aurangabad is near Daulatabad, where Muhammad Tughluq had established his capital for the same reason. Aurangzeb had resided there earlier when he was Viceroy of the Deccan in 1653. Being a very austere man, Aurangzeb did not build a big palace in Aurangabad, and his roadside tomb under the open sky is the most inconspicuous of all Mughal buildings.

The vast Mughal empire required the constant personal supervision by the emperor. The Great Mughal spent about half of every year in camp, often in distant parts of his empire. A large detachment of the field artillery always accompanied him on these tours so as to demonstrate his power to everybody concerned. The maintenance of imperial power was very expensive and required a large land revenue income. The monetization of the revenue demand was an essential prerequisite of centralized power. Mughal monetary policy was very sound. The silver rupee whose intrinsic value was guaranteed by the Great Mughal greatly contributed to imperial stability.[32] India had no silvermines and depended on the imported silver which flowed into India due to its increasing maritime trade. In this way a kind of symbiotic relationship developed between the huge agararian empire and the European trading companies which brought American silver to India. The Great Mughals appreciated this relationship and never feared that the European traders would threaten India. The monsoon precluded an invasion of India by sea. The fortified European bridgeheads on Indian coasts seemed to be insignificant for a land based empire.[33] Nobody would have thought that a British trading company would finally build an empire in India.

THE BRITISH IN INDIA: AN 'EXCENTRIC' EMPIRE

The English East Indian Company established in 1600 did not look like an empire builder until 1757 when Robert Clive defeated the Nawab of Bengal on the battlefield of Plassey. For more than a century the strength of the East India Company was mainly based on its swift and heavily armed ships. In fact, after 1660 when the Company had closed its shipyard and adopted a policy of leasing ships, this powerful fleet did not belong to the Company but to private shipowners who vied with each other to build the best ships which they could offer to the Company for the passage to India and then also to China.

With the benefit of hindsight one could say that the leasing of ships was the first step towards empire building. It enabled the company to invest all its capital in the maintenance of its Indian bridgeheads and the financing of trade.[34] Another step towards empire building was the concentration on the trade in Indian textiles. This made it necssary for the agents of the Company to venture into the interior of the country in order to contact the producers. In this way they gathered not only commercial but also political intelligence. In the eighteenth century the British demand for Indian cotton cloth shifted to white cotton goods which were semi-finished goods used by the London cotton printers.[35] Bengal was the premier source for this type of cotton, but internal wars were endemic in this region at that time. The agents of the East India Company had to tap new sources of supply of suitable white cottons ever so often. The Company was thus very well informed about all parts of Bengal.

In the meantime the ambitious Governor General of the French colonies in India, Joseph Dupleix, had got involved in the rivalries of Indian princes and deployed Indian soldiers trained in European methods of warfare. The British copied this and soon had an Indian infantry at their disposal whose salvoes had the devastating effect of a machine gun in their encounters with the cavalry of Indian princes. However, Robert Clive's victory at Plassey was rather due to the treachery of the Nawab's general, Mir Jaffar, than to British military superiority. The powerless Great Mughal to whom the Nawab of Bengal had not paid his dues thought that the East India Company would be a more reliable partner and offered the Diwani (revenue authority) of Bengal to Clive. According to the Company's royal charter, territorial acquisitions would belong to the Crown and Clive wanted to accept the offer on behalf of King George III. The British prime minister, William Pitt, feared that George III, who had absolutist ambitions, would use the income from the revenue of Bengal so as to reduce royal dependence on Parliament. Finally the East India Company accepted the offer of the Diwani of Bengal. This is how empire building on private account took its course. In the nineteenth century the Company was deprived of its trading monopolies but still retained its territorial empire which had greatly expanded in the meantime. The shareholders of the Company still received their dividends.

An empire ruled according to the principles of shareholder value was certainly an 'excentric' phenomenon, but it was 'excentric' also because its centre was in distant London and not in India. Initially the 'men on the spot' could make their decisions on their own. Communications with the distant centre were very slow. But this changed in the nineteenth century. After the 'Mutiny' of 1857 the British Crown took over India. Technological progress then saw to it that London kept India on a tight imperial leash. The steamship overcame the vagaries of the monsoon. The Suez Canal cut the distance between London and India by half and the telegraph speeded up communications. It even supported imperial monetary policy as telegraphic transfers enabled the Secretary of State for India in London to control monetary transactions at any moment.

The 'Mutiny' of 1857 was a traumatic experience for the British. They had conquered India with Indian soldiers paid by the Indian taxpayer. These soldiers served under British officers. Initially these officers had spent their whole life in India and often had Indian families. Newer generations of officers were not as intimately related with India. For them serving in India was only a profitable career and they looked forward to retirement in an English countryhouse. Their relations with their Indian soldiers were those of master and servant. There was an imperial delusion that the British could issue orders and the Indians would always obey them. This was also true for the field of civil administration where a very thin layer of British bureaucrats controlled millions of Indian subjects. The 'Mutiny' not only showed to the British that they could not rely on their Indian soldiers, but that their whole edifice of imperial rule was very fragile. The 'excentric empire' seemed to be on the verge of collapse. But British rule survived this catastrophe and soon recovered.

British power had vastly increased in the first half of the ninetenth century while the Indian economy had languished under a prolonged deflation because the British had once more extracted the silver which they had pumped into in India in the previous century.[36] British population had multiplied, the Industrial Revolution had added to British prosperity. The power of Parliament was by now thoroughly entrenched. Queen Victoria was a constituional monarch with none of the absolutist ambitions of George III. With its consolidated strength the centre of the empire could reassert its control over India. In the imperial heyday from 1877 when Queen Vicitoria assumed the title of Empress of India to the beginning of the First World War in 1914 it seemed that the 'excentric' empire would last forever.

Before 1914 Great Britan could live on the interest of its exported capital of which, however, only 10 per cent had been invested in India. With its comfortable financial position it could maintain the international gold standard which secured its commanding position in the world market. All this crumbled in the First World War which Great Britain won only with American support – and indebted to the USA. With the centre so fatally wounded, the end of the empire seemed to approach. Young British people who had earlier coveted a career in the imperial service were no longer sure that such a career was worth pursuing. Prime Minister Lloyd George's famous speech of 1922 in which he called the Indian Civil Service a 'steel frame' which kept the empire together was not an instance of imperial bravado but a desparate attempt at recruiting young men for this service.

After the war, the Indian freedom movement led by Mahatma Gandhi gained strength. With his noncooperation campaign, Gandhi challenged British rule by transgressing unjust laws. This was a successful strategy because the British had stressed that they had established a rule of law in India and had in this way asserted their hegemony. The Great Depression of the 1930s [37]then added strength to the freedom movement by rousing the protest of the Indian peasants which was articulated by Gandhi and Nehru. Since another paper in this volume is devoted to their activities, there is no need to discuss them in detail here.

The Second World War then dealt a final blow to the empire. Again Great Britain won the war only with American support and emerged from it heavily indebted to the USA. However, Great Britain was not only indebted to the USA but also to India, because India had produced goods for the British war effort and was forced to accumulate the respective reserves in the Bank of England. India had even to sign a moratorium on the eve of independence, pledging not to touch these reserves immediately as this would have driven Great Britain into bankruptcy.[38] The great 'excentric' empire thus ended not with a bang but a whimper.

NOTES

1. George F. Dales and J. Mark Kenoyer, 'The Harappan Project, 1986-1989: New Investigations at an Ancient Indus City', in Gregory L. Possehl, ed., *Harappan Civilization* (2nd revd. edn.), Delhi: Oxford University Press, 1993, p. 509.

2. Maurizio Tosi, 'The Harappan Civilization Beyond the Indian Sucontinent', in Possehl, ed., *Harappan Civilization*, p. 369.
3. Vishnu-Mittre and R. Savithri, 'Food Economy of the Harappans', in Possehl, ed., *Harappan Civilization*, p. 216.
4. Steven A. Weber, 'Changes in Plant Use at Rojdi: Implications for Early South Asian Subsistence Systems', in Possehl, ed., *Harappan Civilization*, p. 292.
5. D.P. Agrawal, 'The Harappan Legacy', in Possehl, ed., *Harappan Civilization*, p. 448.
6. A. Ghosh, 'Deurbanization of the Harappan Civilization', in Possehl, ed., *Harappan Civilization*, p. 382.
7. Shereen Ratnagar, 'The Location of Harappa', in Possehl, ed., *Harappan Civilization*, p. 263.
8. Hermann Kulke and Dietmar Rothermund, *A History of India* (5th edn.), London: Routledge, 2010, p. 33.
9. Kulke and Rothermund, *A History of India*, p. 38.
10. Ibid., p. 42.
11. Ibid., p. 38.
12. Upinder Singh, *A History of Ancient and Early Medieval India*, New Delhi: Pearson, 2009, p. 477.
13. Singh, *A History of Ancient and Early Medieval India*, p.483.
14. Hans Bakker, 'A Theatre of Broken Dreams: Vidisa in the Days of Gupta Hegemony', in M. Brandtner and S.K. Panda, eds., *Interrogating History: Essays in Honour of Hermann Kulke*, New Delhi: Manohar, 2006, pp. 165-87.
15. Singh, *A History of Ancient and Early Medieval India*, pp. 497-9.
16. Kulke and Rothermund, *A History of India*, p.106.
17. Ibid., p. 73.
18. Ibid., p. 87.
19. Ibid., p. 76.
20. Tilman Nagel, 'Das Kalifat der Abbasiden', in Ulrich Haarmann, ed., *Geschichte der arabischen Welt*, München: Beck, 1987, p. 147.
21. Jacques Gernet, *A History of Chinese Civilization*, Cambridge: Cambridge University Press, 1985, pp. 322 f.
22. Meera Abraham, *Two Medieval Merchant Guilds of South India*, New Delhi: Manohar, 1988.
23. R.A. Leslie H. Gunawardana, 'Intersocietal transfer of Hydraulic Technology in Pre-colonial South India: Some Reflections Based on a Preliminary Investigation', in *Southeast Asian Studies*, 22/2 (1984), pp. 115-42.
24. Dietmar Rothermund, 'Der Blick vom Westen auf den indischen Ozean vom 'Periplus' bis zur 'Suma Oriental', in D. Rothermund and S. Weigelin-Schwiedrzik, eds., *Der Indische Ozean. Das afro-asiatische*

Mittelmeer als Kultur- und Wirtschaftsraum, Wien: Promedia 2004, p. 22.

25. For a discussion of cavalry warfare see the paper 'From the Chariot to the Atom Bomb' in this volume.
26. Nagel, 'Das Kalifat der Abbasiden', in Haarmann, ed., *Geschichte der arabischen Welt*, p. 149
27. Kulke and Rothermund, *A History of India*, p. 120.
28. Ibid., p. 133.
29. Ibid., p. 135.
30. Ibid., p. 150.
31. M. Athar Ali, *The Mughal Nobility under Aurangzeb*, Bombay: Asia Publishing House, 1966
32. Kulke and Rothermund, *A History of India*, p. 144.
33. Om Prakash, *European Commercial Enterprise in Pre-Colonial India*, The New Cambridge History of India, vol. II.5), Cambridge: Cambridge University Press, 1998.
34. Kulke and Rothermund, *A History of India*, p. 161.
35. Sergio Aiolfi, *Calicos und gedrucktes Zeug. Die Entwicklung der englischen Textilveredlung und der Tuchhandel der East India Company, 1650-1750*, Stuttgart: Steiner, 1987.
36. Kulke and Rothermund, *A History of India*, p. 190.
37. Dietmar Rothermund, *India in the Great Depression, 1929-1939*, Delhi: Manohar, 1992.
38. Dietmar Rothermund, *The Routledge Companion to Decolonization*, London: Routledge, 2006, p. 66.

CHAPTER 2

From Chariot to Atom Bomb: Armament and Military Organization in South Asian History

THE INSTRUMENTS OF WARFARE AND SOCIAL STRATIFICATION

Men must have fought with each other for millennia, but the rise of the professional warrior was a comparatively late phenomenon in human history. The warrior acquired special skills which ordinary people did not possess and he compelled them to work for his maintenance. The rise of a warrior class contributed to social stratification. The warriors emerged as a kind of 'nobility'. The instruments of warfare supported this development. The more difficult it was to master these instruments, the higher was the demand for skilled warriors who made warfare their full-time profession.

Initially the exaction of agrarian surplus from a fairly limited region was sufficient for the maintenance of small groups of warriors. But then the control of long-distance trade yielded higher returns in terms of a protection rent. There was a reciprocal relationship between trade and warfare. Larger empires provided more scope for long-distance trade and could afford more expensive instruments of warfare. In South Asia there have been several instances of this symbiosis of trade and empire, but in general the collection of land revenue from extensive territories was the main source for the maintenance of warriors.

State formation progressed along these lines of the rise of warrior elites. There is, of course, more to the state than the organization of warfare. The legitimation and manifestation of royal power draws on cultural resources which are not confined to the instruments of warfare, but these instruments are a necessary element of state power. The instruments of warfare discussed here include weapons as well as animals (war-elephant, war-horse). Discussing these instruments also implies paying attention to their tactical or strategic use. But the main emphasis will be on the social consequences of warfare and on the composition and the functions of warrior elites. Social rather than military history will be the mainstay of this essay.

The Indus or Harappan civilization should be the first subject to be discussed in this context, but unfortunately the evidence available is so meagre that it is impossible to arrive at any conclusions. At the most one can draw some inferences from negative evidence. This civilization obviously did not know the horse. Accordingly there was no 'man on horseback' at that time. The excavated sites show no traces of royal palaces or tombs, there were some elevated settlements and places of worship which would indicate that a kind of priestly oligarchy rather than kings and warriors dominated this society. Agricultural planning must have been the major task of this oligarchy. Venturing out into the annually inundated plains of the Indus valley was the essential achievement of the Indus civilization. This required various skills which went beyond those needed for subsistence agriculture in smaller valleys and plains. The Indus carries twice as much water as the Nile. The inundated plains are fertile, but in order to make use of the yield promised in this way, the people had to adopt new agricultural technologies, had to predict the arrival of the flood and plan sowing and harvesting. For all this the ruling oligarchy must have had specialists. The uniform system of weights and measures which prevailed for about a millennium in this vast region is evidence for the working of the minds of such specialists. They were obviously not warriors and did not need a king to lead them in battle.

Nevertheless, the massive fortifications of the main cities show that there must have been some kind of warfare. Traces of arson have been found at some locations. Probably there were raiders from the adjacent mountainous areas who wanted to plunder the rich harvests stored in the cities. Moreover, these cities were centres of long-distance trade in valuable commodities. Defence of this trade and of the grain stored in the cities must have been of great concern at that time. But perhaps there was no warrior elite but bands of peasant soldiers trained for this purpose.

The first professional warrior elite of South Asia is obviously that of the people who called themselves 'arya' (noble). Their main instrument of warfare was the chariot and we shall start our study of military organization with it.

THE GLORIES AND LIMITATIONS OF CHARIOT WARFARE

The evidence for this period of South Asian history is literary and not archaeological. The literature concerned was not reduced to writing until much later, it was transmitted orally for many centuries. But as it was learned and recited 'religiously', its transmission was even more reliable than that of written texts. This literature tells us a great deal about chariot warfare which was at the centre of 'Aryan' military preoccupations. But before delving into it, we must emphasize that the chariot entered South Asia as fully developed instrument sometime around 1500 BC or even somewhat later after it had been in use in Western Asia for quite some time. A Mesopotamian chariot is depicted on a seal dated between 1850-1650 BC. It shows two warriors standing in a chariot with spoked wheels running over a slain enemy.[1] The Hyksos conquered Egypt with their chariots and established the 15th dynasty (*c.* 1648-1540 BC). They came from Western Asia and were thrown out by the Egyptians who adopted the chariot and were henceforth ruled by a chariot-warrior elite.[2] Such an elite was also prominent in the Mitanni empire (northern Syria and northern Iraq) of the Hittites (around 1500 BC). Their chariot-based warriors were called *mariyannu* and it is stated that they were nominated by the king.[3]The Sanskrit sources refer to *ugras* (the terrible ones) as companions of the king[4] and it is very likely that they played a role similar to that of the *mariyannu*.

Chariot warfare depended on a number of essential elements. First and foremost was the availability of suitable horses. Their natural habitat were the Central Asian steppes and they had been tamed by about the fourth millennium BC. Then there was the lightly built and highly mobile chariot with spoked wheels. It was in evidence in Western Asia in the early second millennium BC. The chariot was mainly used for the swift transport of a skilled archer who could shoot arrows with a composite bow of great strength. This bow seems to have been invented in Western Asia in the fourth millennium BC, it thus ante-dated the chariot. The archer had to wear a mailed coat (made of rhinoceros-skin in South Asia), because he could not carry a shield.[5]

Next to the archer the driver of the chariot was of great importance. He was unarmed and according to Sanskrit sources he was naked to the waist[6] and would thus have been an easy target for the enemy. But the code of honour ruled him out as a target. The concept of *dharmayuddha* (righteous warfare) prevailed among the warriors who would not attack unarmed men. In terms of rank, the chariot-driver was placed lower than the archer, but there are references to his being a close companion of the archer. Some sources mention that the chariot driver was entitled to one fourth of the booty which the archer made in a war.[7] The king was expected to be a good archer and the *suta* (herald) who accompanied him everywhere was presumably also the driver of his chariot.[8]

The chariot-culture extended all the way to Greece and there is an ode of Pindar (522-446 BC) celebrating a chariot-driver who knows exactly how to guide the horse by restraining or whipping it at the right moment.[9] This was certainly also true of the chariot-drivers of ancient India. The best archer would be lost if he did not have such an expert companion. The division of labour was very pronounced, it seems that in general the one was not trained to master the skills of the other. But there are some exceptions mentioned in Sanskrit literature. In an emergency even a king could volunteer to act as a chariot-driver which implies that he must have learned this art, too. However, there seem to be no references to chariot-drivers turning into archers.

In addition to those who used the chariot, the maker of chariots (*rathakara*) was also a highly valued specialist. In Sanskrit sources he is mentioned as one of the jewels (*ratna*) adorning the king's court. The king had to visit him in the course of certain ceremonies and he seems to have inhabited about the largest compound in the small capital of such an early king. It is said that he had to house the guards of the horse to be sacrificed at the *ashvamedha* (horse sacrifice) and there could be 400 such guards according to some sources.[10] The *rathakara* must have been a very wealthy man if he could play host to such a crowd.

Chariot warfare appears to have been a chivalrous contest worthy of noble warriors. This would also explain why norms such as not shooting at the unarmed driver of the chariot were scrupuloulsy observed. This type of warfare was restricted to an open and even battlefield. Chariots were not suited for jungle warfare. Being very delicate, they could not cross difficult terrain but had to be transported on bullock carts. They were certainly awe-inspiring for soldiers on foot armed with simple weapons, because they were swift and the arrows of the archers were deadly. But chariot warfare was in general limited to small regions. Most of the early states were small and this type of warfare was adjusted to their needs. As soon as the war-elephants of large empires appeared on the scene, the chariots were lost.

The stratification of early 'Aryan' society was undoubtedly deeply influenced by this chariot warfare. It was a society in which a 'nobility' lorded it over the rest of the population. This 'nobility' was divided into a hereditary one from which the kings would be drawn and a lower one, probably appointed by the king because of its military skills. It was explicitly stated that this lower nobility could not be annointed (i.e. aspire to be king).[11] But the respect for the king's hereditary right did not necessarily protect him against internal rebellion. The de-throned king is a figure often mentioned in the Sanskrit sources.[12] It is also stated that the *ratnas* could give and take the kingship. This seems to imply that this entourage could "impeach" the king and drive him away.

The nature of this type of early kingship is reflected by the ritual preceding the *ashvamedha*. The king would let the designated horse roam freely for a year. It was accompanied by the guards mentioned above. Anybody who would let the horse pass would implictly recognize the sovereignty of the king. If he stopped it and challenged the guards, this was a declaration of war. This would presumably be conducted by the warriors on their chariots. The *ashvamedha* as a flexible test of sovereignty was well suited to the society of 'noble' warriors living in small states. If later on rulers of large empires celebrated the *ashvamedha* in order to manifest their status they did this without this flexible test as they dominated their territory by different means. They also did not use chariots any longer, except perhaps for ritual purposes. But the memory of the chariot was preserved for a long time. As late as AD 1012 a Cambodian king, Suryavarman I of Angkor, presented a chariot to the Chola king Rajaraja as a ceremonial gift.[13]

THE TRIUMPH OF THE WAR-ELEPHANT

While the chariot survived as a symbol it was literally stamped out as an instrument of warfare by the war-elephants of the great empires of eastern India which soon conquered the entire Gangetic plains. The elephants lived in the great forests of southern Bengal and Orissa. They could never be domesticated, but they could be tamed and made to perform all kinds of tasks. A tribal man from the forest where they had been 'recruited' usually accompanied them as their 'driver' (*mahout*). His skills were very different from those of the driver of a chariot and he could never aspire to the ranks of the lower nobility. Nor were the archers on the back of the elephant noble warriors. About ten archers could occupy the platform tied to the back of the elephant and it was the shower of arrows which they could direct at the enemy rather than the well aimed arrow of the elite warrior which mattered in this new type of warfare.

The war-elephant was, of course, also the appropriate mount for the king or emperor. Guiding his troops in a battle, he could have an overview of the battlefield from the back of his elephant. Being thus very conspicuous, he would inspire his troops – but also attract the attention of the enemy. The security of the king was of great concern. His fall would put an end to the battle. Accordingly the movements of the royal elephant were narrowly circumscribed. The game of chess which mirrors an Indian battlefield shows this very clearly. The king also mounted the elephant on ceremonial occasions – even British viceroys practised this later on.

War-elephants were expensive to maintain and it was not enough to have just a few of them. In medieval times the price of a good war-elephant was considered to be equivalent to that of 500 ordinary horses.[14] Several hundred elephants were required for an efficient army corps which could traverse long distances and overwhelm the enemy. The famous transfer of 500 elephants to Seleukos Nikator by Chandragupta Maurya clearly shows the dimensions of this kind of warfare. This transfer was made in the context of a peace treaty, it was thus not a generous gift. But presumably Chandragupta had at least 1,000 or more elephants left after he had parted with those which he sent to Seleukos. The enormous investment in war-elephants made sure that the great empires would expand and the smaller ones would go to the wall. The elephant had a centralizing function which the chariot never had.

Social stratification in such empires was very different from that of the earlier 'Aryan' kingdoms. Imperial officers rather than "noble" warriors were the new ruling elite. The control of long-distance trade became of much greater importance than ever before. Empires profited from this control, and the Mauryan one seems to have been a particularly good example. The pattern of distribution of Ashoka's famous edicts shows that while many areas of the interior remained more or less untouched, the Gangetic plains, the coasts and some trade routes running across the sub-continent were under the control of the emperor. The war-elephants extended the dimensions of military intervention enormously.

Imperial governors were posted throughout the empire. They also had to get Ashoka's edicts carved into rocks. There is evidence of this in a South Indian inscription which contains so to speak the covering letter of instruction in addition to the edict. The man who carved it into stone may well have been illiterate and simply copied everything contained in the paper or palm-leaf given to him.

The Mauryas were of low-caste origin, their officers presumably were also not 'nobles' but appointed by the emperor because of their valour and loyalty to him. Ashoka also used Buddhist monks as diplomats and imperial messengers. They also could not rank as a 'nobility'. A new social stratification appeared only in medieval times when small regional kingdoms copied some of the features of the ancient empires and also based their power on war-elephants.

The 'nobleman' of medieval times was the *samanta*. This term orginally means 'neighbour' but then came to mean the subdued neighbour whose realm had been conquered. He was reinstated by the victor but had to attend his court. He became part of a *samantachakra* (circle of neighbours). The gradient of power between *samanta* and king was presumably determined by the number of elephants which they possessed. The *samanta* in due course also attained a position in the royal administration. The chief minister of a king had the title *mahasamanta* (big neighbour) which was somewhat of a paradox, because he was certainly part of the entourage of the king. It has been stated earlier that in the ancient empires the war-elephant helped to sustain central power. On a smaller scale this was also true of the medieval regional kingdoms. But by that time there were competing centres. Elephant-power helped to articulate their importance.

The war-elephant retained its role in military affairs even after the cavalry reigned supreme in the thirteenth and fourteenth centuries. The Delhi sultanate maintained large contingents of war-elephants. When it was defeated by Timur in AD 1398 the sultanate could still put up 120 elephants which duly frightened Timur's army although their number was modest as compared to earlier times. [15] It was only when field artillery appeared on the battlefield that the power of the war-elephant came to an end. The Great Mughal Babur defeated the Sultan of Delhi, Ibrahim Lodi, with his guns, although Ibrahim had about 1,000 elephants on the battlefield.

THE 'MAN ON HORSEBACK' FROM SLAVE TO RULER

When the Delhi sultanate was established at the beginning of the thirteenth century its power was based on the swift cavalry which could cover long distances at a high speed. Just like the chariot which was developed in Western Asia and then introduced into India, cavalry warfare had emerged in that area, too. It had contributed to the rapid spread of Islamic rule. But unlike the chariot which gave rise to a nobility of free professional warriors, Islamic cavalry warfare depended on highly specialized slaves who were trained to ride and fight from their childhood. Promising boys could be literally caught young. As slaves they were bound to their ruler by stronger bonds than any noble warrior to his overlord. On the other hand there was an amazing social mobilty in such a slave society. A good fighter could quickly rise to become a general and if he was daring enough he could usurp the throne and become a sultan.

The war-horse by itself did not have a centralizing function, but the system of military feudalism based on the assignment (*iqta*)of revenue grants which were given to officers for supporting cavalry troops did have such a centralizing effect. The sultan usually saw to it that such grants were distributed evenly. Moreover, the holders of such grants were often shifted from one position to the other; by birth as well as by promotion they were usually strangers in the places where they served. Therefore they did not have the benefit of specific local support. They could not think of secession as their colleagues could easily put them down. If they were very ambitious they could only try to conquer the centre of power and replace the sultan. This strengthened central power as only the most daring commander would emerge victorious.

In one respect the war-horse also contributed to the centralizing of power: it was very expensive. The breeding of war-horses proved to be very difficult in India. The climate was not suited for horses and they succumbed to many illnesses, but there were no experienced veterinarians in India. However, the most important impediment to horse-breeding in India was the absence of adequate pastures which would provide the horses with good grass to eat and ample space to move about. The interior of the Kathiawad peninsula was one of the few places in India which provided such ideal conditions. Typically the local horse-breeders were semi-nomadic predatory tribes.[16] Such people were a great nuisance for agriculturists who needed no war-horses but peace and quiet. In due course both these tribes and the horses they bred disappeared. More orderly people would tend horses in stables, depriving them of the free movement which they needed so much and feeding them with fattening food which ruined their health. Thus good war-horses had to be imported into India at a high price. There were two major trade routes – one overland route from Central Asia via Afghanistan and the sea route from the Persian Gulf. The overland route was less expensive and there were fewer casualties among the horses. They could recover on their long march by spending some time in the vast pastures of Afghanistan.[17] But for places further down south like Vijayanagar, the sea route dominated by Persian horse-traders was the major one. The king of Vijayanagar paid for horses dead or alive, thus insuring the traders against the risks of sea transport.

The total volume of this horse trade must have been enormous. At a rough estimate there must have been more than 500,000 war-horses in South Asia for most of the period from the the thirteenth to the eighteenth century. Presumably one tenth of these horses had to be replaced every year.[18] Making some allowance for local breeds this means that about 30-40,000 horses must have been imported annually. This was a substantial burden for the budgets of the states which depended on such imports.

In assessing the relative value of war-horses a comparison of their price with that of cows and slaves will be useful. A good horse was worth about 30 cows in the Delhi sultanate around AD 1300 whereas an adult slave could be bought for the price of 4 to 5 cows. [19] A slave who was a good cavalryman was perhaps somewhat more expensive, but at any rate the horse would be more valuable than the rider. For every horse and rider there was at least one groom whose price was presumably much less than that of the cavalryman. Nevertheless a cavalry contingent of about 20,000 horses plus riders and grooms would represent an investment equal to the value of about one million cows. The sultans of Delhi often had more than 1,00,000 horses at their disposal. When Malik Kafur, Sultan Alauddin Khalji's great slave-general, raided southern India in 1310, he brought back 20,000 horses which had belonged to the Kakatiya king of Warangal. Such plunder deprived the enemies of the Delhi sultanate of any chance of resistance. It would take them a long time before they could replace such great quantities of horses.

All Hindu rulers of the south who had to defend their territories against the Delhi sultanate had to copy the cavalry system. However, they did not copy the institution of military slavery. Their cavalry officers (*nayak*) were free men whose loyalty they tried to preserve in a rather special way. Prataparudra, the Kakatiya king of Warangal, seems to have invented the institution of commanders of bastions of his capital's fortifications. There were 70 such bastions and each of the important *nayaks* of his kingdom was assigned one of them. Tirumala Nayak of Madurai who was originally a subject of the King of Vijayanagar but was practically an independent ruler in the seventeenth century still followed the same custom more than 300 years later. This shows the persistence of a new type of social stratification. The cavalry officer was literally the kingpin in the district which he commanded. Occasionally he could even become the founder of a new city, like Kempe Gowda, *amaranayaka* of the Vijayanagar kingdom, who established Bangalore.

The towns which served as centres of military feudalism all had similar characteristics. They were first and foremost the garrison of a large cavalry contingent and the captain of the cavalry was the highest political authority in the respective district. He controlled the collection of the land revenue and if the peasants were not paying it, he could send men on horseback to frighten them into submission. Earlier institutions of local government would wither away under cavalry domination. In this respect a certain uniformity prevailed throughout the subcontinent due to the exigencies of cavalry warfare regardless of the type of commanders. Whether an officer was a Muslim slave or a Hindu *nayak* did not make much of a difference as far as his military and political functions were concerned. Cavalry domination smothered all other forms of governance like a wet blanket. Enduring for many centuries, this system had a lasting impact on the polity of the subcontinent. The next stage of centralized military power based on field-artillery did not introduce much of a change at the local level where the cavalry officer remained in control, it only promoted a new style of empire building.

THE IMPACT OF FIELD-ARTILLERY

Heavy artillery of a stationary kind was known already to the sultans of Delhi who used it in defending their realm against the Mongols. But artillery warfare reached a new dimension when guns could be moved to the battlefield where they proved to be highly effective both against the cavalry and against war-elephants. Their deployment was, of course, a matter of great strategic skill. If the swift calvalry left the slow-moving guns behind, the battle was over before the guns were in position. The coordination of cavalry and field-artillery was the hallmark of a good general in this new age. Very often the use of the artillery degenerated into a mere display of firepower. Military showmanship was then more in evidence than strategic or even tactical skills. Generals had normally been trained as cavalrists and treated the artillery with disdain. They shared the feelings of the Syrians and Egyptians whom the Ottoman sultan, Selim I, had defeated with his field-artillery in 1517. They condemned artillery warfare as unchivalrous conduct. Selim, however, was victorious and emerged as the pioneer of this kind of warfare in Asia.

The Turks had learned this art from the Europeans. Charles the Bold of Burgundy had won several battles with his 'modern' field-artillery around 1470. His technicians had developed brass guns which could be adjusted with special mechanisms so as to aim at distant targets with great accuracy. This technology spread very fast and while Charles the Bold operated in a fairly small region, Selim extended his empire with his firepower very rapidly over long distances. Before he conquered Syria and Egypt in 1517 he had defeated the Safavid Shah Ismail of Persia in the battle of Chaldiran in 1514. (Chaldiran is located about 100 km southwest of Erivan, the present capital of Armenia.) Shah Ismail quickly recovered from this defeat and adopted artillery warfare too. Only twelve years after the battle of Chaldiran, Babur, the first Great Mughal, defeated the sultan of Delhi with the guns produced for him by Turkish experts.

Babur had been trained as an archer. Artillery warfare was new to him and yet he used it to such good effect that he conquered almost the whole of northern India with its help. His strategic design of the battle of Panipat near Delhi was admirable. He deployed his guns in a broad front, placing marksmen with muskets between them so as to prevent the enemy's cavalry from overwhelming the gunners. This was what Selim had done at Chaldiran, a battle plan which Babur obviously had studied in detail. But in addition Babur used the Uzbek tactics of archers on horseback to drive the huge army of the sultan towards the battery of guns.[20] The archers would dash along the flanks of the sultan's army, turn around their horses and shoot their arrows at the moment when the horse stood still. They repeated this manouevre again and again. Combining these tactics with artillery warfare was certainly a strategic feat. Presumably Babur was the first one to adopt this combination.

The field-artillery remained the mainstay of Mughal power throughout. It was an extremely expensive type of armament and its production required special skills. Even when the Rajputs had become trusted allies of the Mughals, the art of producing guns remained a secret which was not passed on to them. The Maharaja of Jaipur could start his own gunfoundry only much later when the power of the Great Mughal had declined.

The Mughals not only paid much attention to the gunfoundry, they also improved the gun carriages to make the guns more mobile and better suited for accurate firing. Babur's guns were only loosely mounted on carts and had to be taken down in order to be put in a proper firing position. In addition to the improvement of guns and carriages, the Mughals also produced better gunpowder than the Europeans, because they had access to excellent Indian saltpetre which was also exported at a handsome profit.[21]

The Great Mughal spent a great deal of his time on tour so as to display his power in all parts of his vast empire. His camp was huge and well equipped. The field-artillery always accompanied him. When the camp was shifted, the artillery was sent ahead two days earlier to the next location.[22] This was a rather leisurely procedure. But the artillery also accompanied the Mughal army to distant battlefields. Thus Prince Dara Shukoh on an expedition to Afghanistan managed to cross the Bolan Pass with his artillery in 1653.[23]

How did the introduction of field-artillery contribute to a new type of social stratification as the chariot, the elephant and cavalry warfare had done? Its impact was indirect rather than immediately obvious. First of all it remained a comparatively rare and highly centralized type of armament. Those who operated it were usually foreign specialists and their numbers were limited, they certainly did not constitute as new 'nobility'. But the indirect social consequences were important. The new Mughal imperial hierarchy of *mansabdars* created by Akbar could be conceived of only in an artillery-based empire with strong central authority. On the face of it, this was a hierarchy of cavalry officers defined to a large extent in terms of the number of horses and cavalrymen to be maintained by the respective *mansabdar*. But *mansab* meant 'rank' and though it was initially defined in terms of cavalry contingents, the system was also extended to all kinds of imperial officers and even to poets and musicians who were naturally not obliged to maintain cavalry troops. The regulation of *mansab* and the appointment of the officers remained an imperial privilege, and the emperor's superior position rested to a large extent on the power of his artillery.

In general a 'nobility' is constituted by birthright, officers appointed and removed at will by an emperor are usually not considered to be 'noblemen'. But detailed research has shown that the imperial hierarchy of the *mansabdars* under Mughal rule showed an amazing stability and continuity. Sons of *mansabdars* had a good chance to join the imperial service. They would not necessarily inherit the position which their father had attained at the end of his career, but they would often rise to a similar position during their lifetime. To that extent the *mansabdars* evolved into a quasi-nobility. Moreover, there was a peculiar mechanism which strengthened the position of this quasi-nobility, this was the pattern of succession to the throne of the Great Mughal. There was no primogeniture, any Mughal prince could aspire to the throne and sometimes the war of succession started even when the father was still alive. Such a war of succession would only be fatal for the princes who lost it. One could speak of a kind of dynastic Darwinism which actually strengthened the Mughal empire, because it would not be governed by a weakling who happened to succeed because it was his turn. The *mansabdars* would invariably take sides with one prince or the other in such a war of succession, but even if it turned out that they had been on the wrong side, this would in general not harm their career. On the contrary, the victor would do his best to reconcile them to his rule as he needed them in order to consolidate his control of the vast empire. The imperial 'quasi-nobility' thus held a fairly strong position for nearly two centuries.

This system collapsed in the eighteenth century, because the Mughal empire had so to speak lived beyond its means. The agrarian base could no longer bear the expensive superstructure. Local discontent of various types took a violent turn and challenged imperial authority. Such insurgency could not be easily suppressed by the mighty field-artillery. Guerrilla warfare eluded the Mughal army. The Great Mughal became a powerless figure in the eighteenth century who did not control more than his capital Delhi – and even that was sacked several times. A number of regional kingdoms emerged and there was a general commercialization of power. Tax farmers often controlled such regional states and had a greater say in the affairs of the state than the respective ruler. Artillery proliferated, its production was no more a closely guarded secret. All rulers had some guns, but as they still remained expensive, none of them had enough of them to build a new empire with their support. Moreover, the rulers of the eighteenth century rarely had the ability to use their artillery strategically as Babur had done. When there was another battle at Panipat in 1761, it took a course which was different from that of 1526. The Marathas met the Afghan ruler Ahmed Shah Durrani in this fateful battle. They had deployed an impressive field-artillery, but they had no means to drive the enemy's army towards their guns. The actual battle then took place beyond the reach of that mighty artillery. Ahmad Shah, however, used a very effective stratagem. He put light swivel guns on the back of camels and caused havoc among the Marathas in this way. Such swivel guns (*zamburak*) mounted on camels had earlier been used by Aurangzeb.[24] But it seems that only Ahmed Shah used it to good effect against an enemy who was not prepared for it. He won the battle but then retired to Afghanistan while the Marathas returned to their southern habitat. This left a power vacuum in northern India which was soon filled by the British. The secret of their success was based on a new type of warfare. They had drilled a native infantry which mowed down the Indian cavalry with merciless precision. The weapons used by those infantrists were freely available everywhere, they were also rather cheap. The superiority of the British-trained infantry was only a matter of military organisation, not of any technological advantage.

'STANDING ARMIES': THE RISE OF MODERN INFANTRY

Muskets and other such guns had been known in India since the days of Babur. But the typical Indian marksman was an individualist. He looked for his own specific aim and shot at it, often with remarkable precision. But the loading and cleaning of the type of guns available in those days took time. This could be only compensated for by carefully timed collective action. While one file of soldiers fired their shots the other would re-load their guns. With precise timing this kind of manoeuvre could produce the effect of a human 'machine gun'. This was a matter of drill and a few European drill sergeants were enough to introduce this new type of warfare in India.

Infantry warfare of this kind was a relatively new achievement even in Europe. Important advances in infantry warfare had been introduced in Europe even before infantrists were armed with guns. They were also based on well-timed collective action. Thus Swiss footsoldiers had been trained to form a tight column which could be driven like a wedge through the lines of the enemy. Once they were behind the lines, these infantrists would swarm out and attack the enemy from the back. This was not exactly chivalrous but very effective. In 1476 the Swiss were able to defeat Charles the Bold of Burgundy in this way at the battle of Murten.[25]

The Ottoman sultans had a well-trained infantry in the early sixteenth century, the janissaries, who were armed with muskets,[26] but the most prominent infantry of that century was the Spanish one. They impressed the enemy with huge formations which were called 'terzios'. A single *terzio* would often consist of 2,000 men, mostly armed with pikes, but with musketeers at the four corners. The imperial army of the Habsburg dynasty deployed such mighty *terzios* in the battles of the Thirty Years War. But they were confronted with a highly innovative enemy, the Swedish king Gustavus Adolphus, who perished in the battle of Lützen in Saxony in 1632 when he was only thirty-eight years old. He was the first to form small companies of musketeers who would take turns in firing their salvos and re-loading their guns. He also supplemented his cavalry with dragoons, musketeers on horseback, who could swiftly attack or encircle the enemy's lines.[27] His astute tactics and brilliant strategy were copied by others in later years. The common denominator of European infantry warfare was organized collective action and not individual marksmanship.

The rise of the new infantry warfare coincided with the recruitment of standing armies in Europe. The idea that one could defend oneself in a fortress and recapture one's territory after the enemy had disappeared was given up. The fate of states was now decided in the open battlefield where large numbers of troops were pitted against each other. These troops consisting of well-trained infantrists were housed in barracks and maintained on a permanent footing. In India troops were usually recruited *ad hoc* and there was always a floating population of soldiers looking for suitable employment.[28] Infantry drill, however, was like a strenous type of sport for which constant exercise was required.

Actually infantry warfare was not at all of the centralizing kind. It was cheap and it could easily proliferate. But in India, due to the prevailing cavalry mentality of its warriors who always looked down on the humble footsoldier, infantry warfare was simply beyond the comprehension of rulers and generals. The Mughals had never recruited a specialized infantry like the Ottoman janissaries.[29] At the most they relied on their marksmen (*toofangchis*) who aimed their shots individually but were not trained in collective action. This was of great advantage to the European East India companies. They did not attract much attention when they started to recruit native infantrists and trained them in their 'factories' as their trading posts were called. The French Governor Dupleix was the pioneer in this field. The British soon copied his methods and even imported British soldiers who could do double duty. As quite a few of them had been weavers before, they could give technical advice to Indian weavers so that they could produce exactly the kind of cloth which the East India Company needed – and they could also train native infantrists.[30]

By the early eighteenth century when this type of infantry warfare was introduced into India, the infantrists had not only mastered the method of rapid fire invented by Gustavus Adolphus, but also the additional skill of shifting to lethal attacks with the bayonet mounted on the gun which replaced the earlier pike in the late seventeenth century. When the pike was still in use it was wielded by infantrists without guns who usually outnumbered those carrying muskets. Combining the gun with the pike by means of the bayonet which could be fixed to the gun in no time made smaller contingents doubly effective. Moreover, the old musket had by now been replaced by improved guns with greater precision and more convenient ignition.

In addition to being masters of infantry warfare, the East India Company had also another great advantage. As it was in itself a product of the commercialization of power at home, it fitted quite well into the trend of commercialization of power in India in the eighteenth century. Moreover, its leading men were bookkeepers rather than daring military heroes. They always paid their soldiers regularly and never indulged in military adventures which were unprofitable. In this way they were far superior to Indian rulers and generals who often won a battle but lost the war, because they suddenly found out that they could not pay their soldiers any longer. This 'calculating' spirit of the British was accompanied by a rather reliable collective memory. All servants of the company, bookkeepers and heroes alike, were parts of an organization with a strong *esprit de corps*. Due to the need of reporting all essential events and decisions to the distant headquarters in London, the servants of the company kept records to which they could easily refer. Collective action backed up by collective memory was the secret of the power of the British in India.

THE MILITARY HERITAGE OF THE BRITISH INDIAN EMPIRE

While military organization was very important for the rise of British power in India, the consolidation of that power depended on the 'civil service'. Actually in the earlier years of British rule, many of the new 'civil servants' who formed the backbone of the territorial administration had a military background. But once they took up a 'civil' position, they became part of a bureaucratic hierarchy and the rank they had acquired as a military officer remained a purely honorific title. The military, on the other hand, retained its professional integrity and did not meddle with political affairs. There was never a military coup in the British-Indian empire. Of course, the large colonial army – first of the East India Company and then of the Crown – was an army of Indian soldiers commanded by British officers. The idea of a rebellious British officer leading his Indian soldiers against his own countrymen was simply inconceivable. The Mutiny of 1857 showed that it was not inconceivable that the soldiers got rid of their British officers and rebelled against British rule. But it also proved that without adequate military leadership such a mutiny was bound to fail. This confirmed the British resolve never to commission Indian officers. They had to break this rule only in the Second World War when two million Indian soldiers defended the empire and there were not enough British officers available at that time. This is how about 8,000 Indian officers were commissioned during the war who after independence formed the officer corps both of the Indian and of the Pakistan army.

The British success in controlling a large imperial army for about 150 years with a corps of expatriate officers and keeping the population unarmed by the rigorous application of an 'Arms Act' had no parallel in history. In addition, they managed to support this army entirely from the money paid by Indian taxpayers. When this army was serving abroad on imperial missions it was supposed to be financed from British sources, but even this was circumvented and the Indian taxpayer had to foot the bill for several of such ventures, too. For instance, when Indian troops were deployed in Egypt, the government in London argued that the Suez Canal was actually more important for India than for Great Britain so as to justify its refusal to pay for those troops.[31]

The British-Indian army was a big standing army. After the Mutiny it was considered to be necessary to station a substantial number of British soldiers in India (about 60,000) as a counterweight to the Indian soldiers (about 1,20,000). The cost of maintaining the British soldiers in India was much higher than the amount spent on the much larger Indian contingent. As imperial 'duties' such as the annexation of Upper Burma demanded more military power, the total strength of the army was augmented to 2,10,000. [32]

The infantry remained the mainstay of the British-Indian army. It was only at a very late stage that a new type of armament was introduced – the tank. This new military vehicle combined the mobility of a chariot with the ruggedness of a war-elephant and the firepower of the field artillery. Other services such as the navy and the airforce had no role in British-India. They emerged only in independent India and Pakistan.

The recruitment for the British-Indian army was highly skewed. As Sikhs and Punjabi Muslims had helped the British at the time of the Mutiny, they were praised as 'martial races' and were given preference in the British-Indian army. This meant that the Punjab benefited much more than any other British-Indian province from the remittances of the soldiers to their families at home. The lion's share of military emoluments was, however, claimed by the British officers who not only received a high pay while they were in service, but also very generous pensions after they retired and settled in Great Britain. These pensions were part of the notorious 'Home Charges', the substantial transfer of funds from India to Great Britain.

Indian nationalists had criticized this excessive expenditure and had asked for an 'Indianization' of the corps of officers. They could rejoice in the Indianization brought about by the Second World War. After the attainment of independence, the army was welcomed as a national asset and not treated as mercenaries of the British. The Indian National Army (INA) recruited from among Indian prisoners of war in Southeast Asia by the militant nationalist, Subhas Chandra Bose, was not re-integrated into the Indian army who regarded them as traitors. Some lip-service of national respect was accorded to the INA, but it simply faded away – as old soldiers are expected to do.

In Southeast Asia and even in Burma, which had been a part of British India until 1936, political armies emerged which had actively participated in freeing their nations from colonial rule. The officers of such political armies felt entitled to interfere with national politics. The INA could have easily emerged as such a force in India, but the course of events prevented this – and saved Indian democracy.

Strangely enough two very different armies emerged from the same stock of the British Indian army in India and Pakistan. The British tradition was that of a professional army loyal to civil authority. But preserving this tradition also required a strong civil authority. Such an authority emerged in India where Nehru as Prime Minister laid the foundations of a resilient parliamentary democracy. It did not emerge in Pakistan, where Jinnah opted for the post of Governor General and continued the viceregal tradition of running the state with the help of the bureaucracy. Moreover, Jinnah died very soon and his successors were not of his stature. Under such circumstances the army took over and ruled the country with the help of the bureaucracy.

Although the Indian and Pakistani armies were strongly influenced by British traditions, there soon emerged a fundamental difference of their social structure after independence. There was no conscription in British-India nor in independent India or Pakistan. As has been pointed out earlier, the British recruited their soldiers mostly from the 'martial races' of the Punjab. Of those 'martial races', India inherited the Sikhs and even today about 20 per cent of the officers of the Indian army are Sikhs. But as a democratic state, India had to balance its recruitment for the army so that all parts of India were adequately represented amongst its soldiers, the more so as service in the army is highly coveted. Soldiers are respected and comparatively well paid. The same is true in Pakistan, but there no compulsion was felt to deviate from the old practice of recruiting soldiers from among the 'martial race' of Punjabi Muslims. This produced a very cohesive army which is extremely proud of its valour and looks down upon every other army in South Asia. Unfortunately this has prompted the generals of that army to embark ever so often on risky ventures which invariably ended in defeat. Nevertheless they refused to learn from past experience, nor did any politician emerge who could put them in their place.

It so happened that this proud army again and again got a shot in the arm from the Americans who needed partners in first fighting communism, then the Soviets in Afghanistan and finally the Taliban who had been initially nurtured by Pakistan with American aid. All this contributed to the rise of the Pakistan army as a 'state within the state' claiming not only the attention of the Americans but also the lion's share of Pakistan's budget. This latter claim they could only sustain by constantly pointing to the Indian threat. In reacting to Pakistan, India obliged the Pakistan army in living up to such a threat perception. Sabre-rattling along the border thus became almost a standard ritual.

The most conspicuous defeat of the Pakistani army manifested itself in the loss of East Pakistan which then became Bangladesh. Actually the social composition of the Pakistani army which has been mentioned above contributed to this defeat and also helped it to shrug it off. When sent to East Pakistan to fight against secession, the Punjabi army behaved like a rather insensitive occupation force and thus precipitated this secession rather than preventing it. Faced with the loss of East Pakistan which had always remained a strange place to the Punjabis, they did not regret it very much. The 90,000 Pakistani soldiers who had been captured by the Indian army in what was now Bangladesh were promptly returned to Pakistan, thus the Punjabi army had lost very few men in that war and could return to business as usual.

President Bhutto who actually owed his rise to the presidency to the secession which he officially deplored but secretly enjoyed, tried to 'frame' his generals by holding them responsible for that defeat. He was finally executed by a general for this very reason. After having liquidated their most resourceful challenger, the Pakistani army could deal with lesser lights in due course.

Before meeting his fate, Bhutto had taken a major step in launching Pakistan on the path to nuclear power. As early as 1972 he was advocating the 'Islamic bomb' with which Pakistan hoped to gain parity with India. With the emergence of the atomic bomb, South Asia then parted with the British-Indian heritage and set up a completely new pattern. The contours of this pattern are not yet as clearly visible as the historical features which we have discussed so far. The last section of this paper is therefore conjectural rather than based on firm evidence.

THE CENTRALIZED POWER OF THE 'ATOM STATE'

In dealing with the 'atom state' in South Asia we are again primarily interested in the social and political consequences of the adoption of this new type of armament rather than in the technological and strategic aspects of nuclear warfare. Nevertheless, a short review of the emergence of the atom bomb in India and Pakistan is required in order to understand its consequences. Until the tests of 1998 all preparations were closely guarded secrets and 'nuclear ambiguity' was the policy of both India and Pakistan. Now, since the bombs are so to speak 'on display', the history of the respective preparations has been openly discussed. The review must also include a brief summary of the conflicts between India and Pakistan. These conflicts gave rise to the quest for the atom bomb and now shape the relations between the two atom states.

The quest for the bomb started in India in the late 1960s after China had joined the 'nuclear club' in 1964 and Prime Minister Shastri's idea of a 'nuclear umbrella' which another big power would be prepared to hold over India had failed for obvious reasons. In 1971 at the time of the secession of Bangladesh, President Nixon had sent an aircraft carrier armed with nuclear missiles into the Bay of Bengal. As he later on admitted, he would have used those missiles against India if the Soviet Union had joined the war. He would have probaby hesitated to do so if India would have had nuclear weapons, too. Indira Gandhi may have known about this, at any rate she ordered the explosion of a 'nuclear device' in 1974 and this spurred Bhutto to speed up his quest for an 'Islamic bomb'. He encouraged the activities of the Pakistani scientist, A.Q. Khan, who was later on praised as the 'father of the Islamic bomb', but he also got additional technological support from China. Writing about it in his death cell in 1977, Bhutto stated that his greatest claim to national fame could be based on his success of concluding a treaty on nuclear technology transfer with China in 1976. General Zia got Bhutto executed but continued his nuclear programme with equal vigour. In 1977 Morarji Desai had become Prime Minister of India. As an old Gandhian he did not like the idea of India having an atom bomb. He even deplored the explosion of a 'nuclear device' in 1974. Indira Gandhi then returned to power in 1980 and once more encouraged the quest for an Indian atom bomb. She actually wanted to conduct a test in 1983, but did not do it because of American pressure. By 1989 Indian scientists and engineers were already working on the actual production of such bombs.

By 1990 the Government of Pakistan was in a position to lower the veil of 'nuclear ambiguity' and actually dropped hints at its nuclear potential. When Prime Minister P.V. Narasimha Rao came to know that China had supplied Pakistan with M-11 rockets which could be fitted with nucelar warheads, he was about to order Indian nuclear tests in 1995 but then succumbed to American pressure. In 1996 Narasimha Rao lost the elections and Atal Behari Vajpayee failed to form a government, otherwise he could have fulfilled his party's programme of 'going nuclear' even at that time. The 'Third Force' of regional parties which then formed the government was neither willing nor able to 'go nuclear'. Moreover, Pakistan which was troubled by economic problems did not flaunt its nuclear potential at that time. When Vajpayee formed a coalition government in 1998, his first statement sounded as if he wished to continue the policy of 'nuclear ambiguity'. But soon thereafter Pakistan tested a missile called 'Ghauri', named after the Muslim conqueror who had overrun Northern India around AD 1200. The missile was of North-Korean origin and had only been renamed in Pakistan, but its new name was a message which Vajpayee could not ignore. He forthwith ordered the series of nuclear tests in May 1998 which were soon followed by Pakistan's. Both nations had now 'outed' themselves as atomic powers.

Vajpayee, who obviously believed that the theory of mutual deterrence would now also apply to India and Pakistan, started a 'peace initiative' by taking a bus to Lahore and embracing his Pakistani colleague, Prime Minister Nawaz Sharif. Sharif was embarrased by Vajapyee's hug, because he knew that General Musharraf, the chief of the Pakistan army, was preparing a 'proxy war' in Kashmir at that time. Musharraf, a specialist in mountain warfare, had made preparations for this venture for a long time. He firmly believed that such 'proxy wars' can be conducted without nuclear escalation. In fact, the threat of such escalation would give the aggressor a tactical advantage. In this particular instance his troops would cross the Line of Control in Kashmir and gain some advantages while the Indian defenders would be taken by surprise and not dare to cross the line for fear of nuclear retaliation.[33]

In the 'Kargil war' of summer 1999 which Musharraf had planned in this way, everything seemed to work according to his expectations – except for the swift Indian reaction. While the Pakistanis had crossed the Line of Control, the Indians did not do so but managed to defeat the Pakistanis nevertheless. By the end of June 1999 when Musharraf met the American Chief of Staff, General Anthony Zinni, who had come to Pakistan in order to put and end to this affair, Musharraf knew that his game was up and readily agreed to a withdrawal. But he also saw to it that President Clinton would receive Prime Minister Sharif in Washington on 4 July 1999. Sharif was not in Pakistan when Musharraf made this deal with his friend Zinni. When he returned Musharraf sent him off to Washington, assuring him of Clinton's personal interest and asserting that the Kashmir issue had been successfully 'internationalized' in this way.[34] Due to this clever arrangement, it was not Musharraf but Sharif who had to sign a capitulation in Washington, taking the blame for Musharraf's unsuccessful 'brinkmanship'.

Although the Kargil war ended with a defeat for Pakistan, it nevertheless established the fact that 'proxy wars' can be conducted under the roof of mutual deterrence. Of course, the USA and the Soviet Union had also conducted hot 'proxy wars' in the era of the Cold War, but these had not been fought across a Line of Control which was practically the border between the two nations. Actually it seems strange that Musharraf should speak of a proxy war in this context. But in order to understand this one must know that Pakistan maintained throughout that the troops that had crossed the Line of Control were 'Kashmiri freedomfighters' and not regular Pakistani soldiers. The Indian side could prove that they were fighting regular Pakistani troops and not 'freedomfighters', but the Pakistani side stuck to its pretense and even refused to accept the corpses of its soldiers.

The events of 11 September 2001 and the American 'alliance against terror' complicated the relations between the two South Asian atom states even further. Islamic terrorists now felt called upon to drive a wedge between the two new partners of this alliance. The first attempt was a suicide attack on the legislative assembly of the state of Jammu and Kashmir in Srinagar. Maulana Masood Azhar who planned this attack immediately thereafter released the names of four of those who had sacrificed their lives in Srinagar. They were all citizens of Pakistan. Obviously this was meant to embarass Musharraf whom the terrorists regarded as a traitor. India obviously saw this point and did not make much of this incident so as not to upset the American sponsors of the 'alliance against terror'. But the next attack which was probably also masterminded by Azhar could not be taken lightly. In December 2001 terrorists attacked the Indian Parliament. They were gunned down by Indian police at the last moment. They had used a police car and police uniforms to disguise themselves. The Government of India claims that they have firmly established the complicity of two Pakistani terrorist groups in this attack. The Pakistani side denies that, but has not offered an alternative explanation.

The Government of India had to react to this severe provocation and massed Indian troops at the border so as to force Musharraf to do something against the terrorists. He also had to respond to American pressure concerning this and got some terrorists arrested. He then made Prime Minister Vajpayee the target of all kinds of friendly gestures, but, of course, Vajpayee continued to see in him the man who had prepared the Kargil war while he was hugging Sharif in Lahore. For the time being the feud between the two atom states has been suspended due to massive American efforts at mediation. But the feud could easily flare up again due to some provocation. The special problem in South Asia is that this provocation may not come from a government but from freewheeling terrorists who have their own agenda.

When we turn to the centralizing aspects of the atom state which we want to highlight here, we may start with the issue of fighting terrorism, because terrorists pose a twofold challenge to the atom state, they may attack nuclear installations or steal nuclear weapons and they may cause a nuclear war between two atom states by hitting the centre (Parliament or government, etc) of one state while obviously representing the other. Therefore the atom state needs special methods and forces dedicated to counterinsurgency. India's National Security Guards ('Black Cats') are a special force of this kind. Nowadays they mostly serve as bodyguards of members of government. They are a small force of at the most 10,000 men. Their manpower and their equipment must be upgraded in order to meet the new requirements of the atom state.

'Black Cats' can only operate successfully if they are backed up by suitable intelligence. Very intensive surveillance will certainly be one of the undesirable but necessary consequences of maintaining an atom state. Citizens will have to acquiesce in it, because they otherwise face the alternative of perishing in a nuclear holocaust. The Inter-Service Intelligence (ISI) of Pakistan which has so far been mostly active in breeding terrorists may also be useful when it comes to controlling them.

But not only counterinsurgency requires new forces and new

methods, the armed forces in general have to face new tasks in an atom state. The hope that mutual deterrence may put an end to conventional warfare and help to reduce military expenditure is an illusion. Musharraf's Kargil war has demonstrated this very clearly. Moreover, there is the new type of auxiliary armament without which nuclear warheads would be useless. Rockets of various kinds are required, and there have to be rocket regiments to handle them. So far there are very few of such rocket regiments in South Asia, but they will certainly proliferate. Then there are military satellites which may be used for reconnaissance as well as for targeting. All this equipment is very expensive and will be a burden on the defence budget.

The central budget which in India has always been much larger than the sum of all state budgets will probably have to be upgraded for such purposes. This will be a further blow to Indian federalism. In fact, just as all other expensive instruments of warfare like elephants, good war-horses and field artillery which have been discussed above, the atom bomb privileges the central power. Moreover, decision making will have to be highly centralised in an atom state. In many ways the atom bomb serves as a symbol of centralised national power. India which has always been attuned to symbolism in politics has even managed to provide this with a personal equation. The new President of India, Abdul Kalam, has been hailed by the media as 'Father of the Indian Atom Bomb'. Actually he is not a nuclear physicist but a missile engineer. He has undoubtedly made a contribution to Indian defence efforts, but not to the production of the Indian atom bomb which has many fathers. But since a visible father of the bomb was required, the president was cast in this role.

NOTES

1. P.R.S. Moorey, 'The Emergence of the Light Horse-drawn Chariot in the Near East', in *World Archaeology*, 18 (1986), pp. 196-215.
2. A. Kuhrt, *The Ancient Near East c.3000-330 BC*, 2 vols, London, 1995, p. 190.
3. Kuhrt, *Ancient Near East*, p. 297.
4. W. Rau, *Staat und Gesellschaft im alten Indien nach den Brahmana-Texten dargestellt*, Wiesbaden, 1957, p. 68.
5. Rau, *Staat*, p.101.
6. Ibid.

7. Rau, *Staat,* p. 103
8. Ibid., p. 109.
9. M. Theunissen, *Pindar. Menschenlos und Wende der Zeit,* München, 2000, p. 888.
10. Rau, *Staat,* p. 112.
11. Ibid., p. 68.
12. Ibid., p. 128.
13. H.Kulke and D. Rothermund, A *History of India,* London, 1998, p. 117.
14. S. Digby, *War-horse and Elephant in the Delhi Sultanate,* Oxford, 1971, pp. 68.
15. Digby, *War-horse,* pp. 80 f.
16. J.J.L. Gommans, *The Rise of the Indo-Afghan Empire, c.1710-1780,* Delhi, 1999, pp. 91 f.
17. Gommans, *The Rise,* p. 80
18. Ibid., p. 89
19. Digby, *War-horse,* p. 37
20. S. Förster, 'Feuer gegen Elefanten, Panipat, 20 April 1526', in S. Förster et al. (eds.), *Schlachten der Weltgeschichte. Von Salamis bis Sinai,* München, 2001, pp. 123-37
21. J.J.L. Gommans, *Mughal Warfare: Frontiers and High Roads to Empire, 1500-1700,* London, 2002, pp. 148 f.
22. Gommans, *Mughal Warfare,* p. 107.
23. Ibid., p. 24.
24. Ibid., p. 128
25. G. Himmelsbach, 'Je l'ay emprins – ich habs versucht'. Murten, 22. Juni 1476', in Förster, *Schlachten,* p. 118.
26. G. Kronenbitter, 'Belagern und Entsetzen, Wien, 12. September 1683', in Förster, *Schlachten,* p. 155.
27. R. Weigley, 'Auf der Suche nach der Entscheidungsschlacht, Lützen, 16 November 1632', in Förster, *Schlachten,* pp. 142 f.
28. D. Kolff, *Naukar, Rajput and Sepoy: The Ethnohistory of the Military Labour Market in Hindustan, 1450-1850,* Cambridge, 1990.
29. Gommans, *Mughal Warfare,* p. 156.
30. S. Aiolfi, *Calicos und gedrucktes Zeug. Die Entwicklung der englischen Tuchveredelung und der Tuchhandel der East India Company, 1650-1750,* Wiesbaden, 1987, pp. 381 f.
31. W. Simon, *Die britische Militärpolitik in Indien und ihre Auswirkungen auf den britisch-indischen Finanzhaushalt, 1878-1919,* Wiesbaden, 1974, p. 229.
32. Simon, *Militärpolitik,* p. 277.
33. D. Rothermund, *Krisenherd Kaschmir. Der Konflikt der Atommächte Indien und Pakistan,* München, 2002, p. 99
34. Rothermund, *Krisenherd Kaschmir,* pp. 105 f.

BIBLIOGRAPHY

Aiolfi, Sergio (1987), *Calicos und gedrucktes Zeug. Die Entwicklung der englischen Tuchveredelung und der Tuchhhandel der East India Company, 1650-1750*, Wiesbaden.

Digby, Simon, *War-horse and Elephant in the Delhi Sultanate*, Oxford, 1971.

Förster, Stig, 'Feuer gegen Elefanten, Panipat, 20. April 1526', in Stig Förster et al. (eds.), *Schlachten der Weltgeschichte. Von Salamis bis Sinai*, München, 2001.

Gommans, Jos J.L., *The Rise of the Indo-Afghan Empire, c.1710-1780*, Delhi, 1994.

——, *Mughal Warfare*, London, 2002.

Himmelsbach, Gerrit, 'Je l'ay emprins – ich habs versucht'. Murten, 22. Juni 1476, in Stig Förster et al., eds., *Schlachten*, pp. 109-22

Kolff, Dirk H.A., *Naukar, Rajput and Sepoy: The Ethnohistory of the Military Labour Market in Hindustan, 1450-1850*, Cambridge, 1990.

Kronenbitter, Günther, 'Belagern und Entsetzen. Wien, 12.September 1683',in: Stig Förster et al. (eds.), *Schlachten*, 2001, pp. 154-68.

Kulke, Hermann and Dietmar Rothermund, *A History of India*, London, 1998.

Kuhrt, Amélie, *The Ancient Near East c.3000-330 BC*, 2 vols., London, 1995.

Moorey, P.R.S., 'The Emergence of the Light Horse-drawn Chariot in the Near East', in *World Archaeology*, vol. 18 (1986), no. 2, pp. 196-215.

Rau, Wilhelm, *Staat und Gesellschaft im Alten Indien nach den Brahmana-Texten dargestellt*, Wiesbaden, 1957.

Rothermund, Dietmar, *Krisenherd Kaschmir. Der Konflikt der Atommächte Indien und Pakistan*, München, 2002.

Simon, Werner, *Die britische Militärpolitik in Indien und ihre Auswirkungen auf den britisch-indischen Finanzhaushalt, 1878-1919*, Wiesbaden, 1974.

Theunissen, Michael, *Pindar. Menschenlos und Wende der Zeit*, München, 2000.

Weigley, Russell F., 'Auf der Suche nach der Entscheidungsschlacht. Lützen, 16. November 1632', in Stig Förster et al., eds., *Schlachten*, pp. 138-53.

CHAPTER 3

The State Society in India from Ancient Times to the Present

THE 'STATE-IN-SOCIETY' AND THE 'STATE SOCIETY'

In this paper I shall analyse the changing social context of state formation in India. State and society have usually been seen in terms of a juxtaposition. Moreover, the state has been studied as a rule-bound institution and subjected to a functional analysis of its elements. It is only in recent years that the American political scientist Joel Migdal has proposed a 'State-in-society approach'.[1] He argues that the state is embedded in its society and interacts with it. He also points out that 'the state continually morphs'.[2] The morphology of the state is conditioned by the society. Migdal asserts that the structure of society and the meanings which people generate in it affect the state and its chances of survival'.[3] The society which supports and transforms the state is not analysed in detail by Migdal. The concept of a 'state society' is an essential supplement to Migdal's 'state-in-society approach'. The concept of the 'state society' was introduced by B.D. Chattopadhyaya in his presidential address to the Ancient India Section of the Indian History Congress 1983.[4] Chattopadhyaya was mainly concerned with early medieval history in India and saw in the frequent references to dominant lineages in inscriptions from the seventh century to later periods the traces of a particular type of state society. The emphasis on genealogy is in keeping with this trend. The specific genealogy of lineages often included a mixture of mythology with historical evidence. Chattopadhyaya stressed the horizontal spread of this type of state society.[5] The states based on this kind of state society grew by means of an encapsulation of existing bases of power. In this process a proliferation of ranks among the leading members of the state society could also be noticed.[6]

While Chattopadhyaya was interested in finding a framework for the interpretations of medieval India, his concept of the "state society" could be applied to earlier as well as later periods of Indian history. State societies provide the foundations of political regimes, they survive regime changes and absorb their impact. But, of course, they also “morph” as the states do which are embedded in them. The state society does not necessarily encompass all people living within the territorial borders of a state. It can be restricted to a small ruling elite. But it can also spread in concentric circles encompassing different strata of the population. In a modern democratic state the state society would include all those who have the right to vote. In general, a more broad based state society would also be more stable. But fissures appearing in such a broad based state society may seriously affect the state embedded in it.

ANCIENT INDIA: JANAPADA AND SABHA

The ancient Indian term *janapada*, which refers to the people as well as to their territory describes an early state society. The meaning of this term shifted in the course of time. In early sources it refers to a people, later on it may also refer to a state.[7] The term *mahajanapada* then refers to a larger state with an elaborate state society. The linchpin of the state was the king. But he was by no means a despot. Political decisions were made by the members of the state society. These members often did not hold permanent ‘offices’ but congregated at certain times. In this context the evolution of the term *sabha* is of special interest. The lower house of the present Indian Parliament is called *Lok Sabha* (Assembly of the People). Originally the word *sabha* referred to an open ground as distinct from the house (*grha*), it could be used as a threshing floor or a place for playing games.[8] In due course it also meant an assembly in which decisions were made. *Sabha* thus refers to a public space which has its conventions of proper conduct. The term *sabheya* (fit for the *sabha*) indicated this type of conduct.[9] Thus from early times there was a notion of a public space and the right conduct in it. The old Sanskrit texts provide only glimpses of social life and since Sanskrit words have many meanings one must look carefully at their usage and this differs in various periods of history. The term *sabha* has some equivalents such as *samiti*, *samsad* or *parishad* which refer to meetings or councils.[10] There has been a tendency among nationalist Indian historians to take these terms as evidence for early Indian democracy. However, a participation of the people in general in such assemblies is not reported by the relevant texts. The society to which these texts refer was stratified. There was a higher nobility from which kings could emerge and a lower nobility which was debarred from kingship.[11] The texts provide an insight into the social structure of their time when they list the 'jewels' (*ratnin*) of the king whom he had to visit in the course of important royal rituals.[12] The foremost of the *ratnin* was the royal priest (*purohit*), being a Brahmin he was in a class of his own. Some of the *ratnins* who served the king in a military capacity may have been noblemen, e.g. the general of the army (*senani*), the herald (*suta)* who regularly accompanied the king and the charioteer (*samgrahitr*). But others such as the cook (*govikarta*), the carpenter (*taksan*) and the cartwright making chariots (*rathakara*) were probably commoners, though the latter was of great importance and seems to have been quite wealthy.[13]

Although the ancient Sanskrit texts highlight the role of the king, they also contain frequent references to deposed kings (*aparuddha*) who live in exile and try their utmost to regain their position. It is explicitly stated that such kings have been driven away by the people (*vish*).[14] The evidence for the existence of democracy in ancient India is not convincing, but the fact that the people did drive away kings shows, that the rulers had to be careful not to displease their subjects.

The Sanskrit texts composed by Brahmins also sometimes refer in a rather hostile tone to kingless states.[15] The hostility was due to the fact that kings patronized Brahmins who provided them with legitimacy, whereas in kingless states the Brahmins would not find such patrons. Buddhist sources contain more information about such states which were called *ganasanghas* (people's associations), because Buddhism emerged from this kind of state society. *Ganasanghas* were confederacies of warriors who maintained a kind of corporate government. They sometimes made decisions by taking a vote, however, they were not democracies but rather oligarchies of clan heads.[16] They did not follow Brahmin orthodoxy and were therefore suspect in the eyes of Brahmins. This type of political organization proved to be rather durable and survived for almost a millenium.[17] The *ganasanghas* could hold their own against neighbouring kingdoms because they followed the same methods of warfare. As they did not depend on the abilities of one king, they could throw up many more competent leaders when challenged in a war. In the *Arthashastra* of Kautilya it is stated that the *ganasanghas* were so closely knit that they were unassailable by enemies.[18] Being a Brahmin, Kautilya did not sympathize with them but rather provided detailed advice to the king who wanted to subdue a *ganasangha*. He suggested various methods of sowing dissensions among the members of a *ganasangha*. It seems that these methods did not work. These oligarchic states survived because their state societies were very cohesive. The Republic of India cites this tradition: its official name in Hindi is *Bharata ganarajya*.

NOBLE WARRIORS AND THEIR CHARIOTS

The types of warfare had an intimate connection with the rise of states and the characteristics of their state societies. In ancient India the chariot dominated the battlefield. It required professional archers and charioteers. The chariot had been fully developed in Western Asia by about 1800 BC.[19] The Hyksos used it when conquering Egypt and the Egyptians then adopted it. The Pharaos of the New Kingdom which replaced Hyksos rule over Egypt were depicted on chariots.[20] The Aryan tribes must have transferred chariot warfare to India in its fully developed style. Each chariot was manned by an archer and a charioteer. Both of them needed careful training in their specific skill. They usually did not change roles, though it is reported that in an emergency even kings volunteered to be charioteers. They observed strict rules of chivalrous conduct. The archer wore an armour of rhinoceros skin, but the charioteer was naked to the waist as the enemy would not shoot at him.[21]. The king himself would usually lead his group of chariots manned by his companions who were called *ugra* (the terrible ones). It seems that they belonged to the lower nobility.[22] The Mitanni empire of the Hittites in Northern Syria and Northern Iraq (around 1500 BC) also had groups of charioteers called *mariyannu*. They were an elite corps appointed by the king.[23] The *ugra* obviously played the same role in the ancient Indian states.

Chariot warfare was restricted to small areas with plane battlefields as chariots could not traverse the jungle and had to be carried on bullock carts so as not to harm their delicate structures. They were more suited to a kind of chivalrous tournament than for campaigns of large scale conquest. The ancient Indian states were often engaged in combat. The great epic poem *Mahabharata* portrays this type of internecine fighting.

EMPIRES AND ELEPHANTS

With the rise of great empires based on the use of war elephants the chariots and their noble drivers lost their significance. These empires arose in Eastern India which had fertile rice fields and large forests where elephants could be caught and tamed and pressed into service for the imperial armies. The elephants were guided by tribal people from their native forests. These *mahouts* were no nobles like the charioteers. On each elephant there were about a dozen archers, who were simple soldiers. Of course, the king would also lead his troops from the back of an elephant. The Nanda and the Maurya empires with their regional base in the area of Bihar and West Bengal could deploy thousands of elephants. When Chandragupta Maurya gave 500 war elephants to Seleukos Nikator, this was probably only a fraction of his elephant corps. Seleukos sent an ambassador, Megasthenes, to Chandragupta's court who left an account of the society which he encountered. It was a stratified society which he described in terms of seven estates without grouping them in a hierarchical order. He first mentioned the philosophers (brahmins) and then the peasantry[24] paying revenue to the king who was supposed to own the land. He added herdsmen and artisans and the warriors all of whom recived their wages from the king. War horses and elephants were also maintained at the expense of the king. As a sixth group Megasthenes mentioned the inspectors and spies who constantly provided the king with information. Last but not least there were the advisers and officers of the king in charge of administration, the law courts, etc.

The powerful, centrally administered state of the Mauryas must have generated enough surplus for the maintenance of a large army and the expensive elephant corps. The *Arthashastra* of Kautilya contains detailed instructions concerning the stables of elephants, their training, etc. Even the different temperaments of the elephants are described.[25] The attention which Kautilya pays to these animals shows that they were of great importance to the empire.

Elephant warfare had a centralizing effect. The maintenance of elephants was expensive, only rich rulers could afford them, less powerful kings could be easily subdued by thousands of well-trained war elephants. Moreover, the distance of intervention was greatly enhanced by the use of elephants which could cross jungles and rivers and live by foraging in the forests they passed. Chariots and horses were no match for them. The state society of the empires supported by elephants was rather different from that of the small states of noble charioteers. The new empires were based on large areas of settled agriculture administered by a corps of officers paid by the state. While the dynamics of conquest could help to consolidate such empires for some time, it was much more difficult to maintain them in periods of peace. Such a period was ushered in by Ashoka Maurya who wished to rule a pacific empire after the bloody conquest of Kalinga which he regretted – without withdrawing from Kalinga, however. Kautilya had not pronounced any political philosophy which could help to sustain an empire. Actually, he was quite cynical about such philosophies. When he mentioned the old rule that people must have kings who ward off chaos, he put this into the mouth of a secret agent talking to the people.[26] Kautilya seemed to indicate that such theories were good for public consumption but were otherwise not worth a detailed discussion. Ashoka found in Buddhism the essential message which helped him to proclaim a moral empire. He subjected himself to the exercises prescribed for a laybrother of the Buddhist *sangha* and could thus claim to have a say in the affairs of this religious order. He used Buddhist monks as ambassadors of peace, spreading his ideas far and wide.[27] Buddhism being a religion which teaches the extrication of man from the ties of this world, could not be easily converted into a state-supporting doctrine. But Ashoka managed to do this by interpreting the Buddhist *dhamma* as a message of universal peace. In the absence of a cohesive state society which would support his enormous empire, Ashoka obviously thought that Buddhism could help him to fill this gap. It was a bold venture, but it failed. Under his weak successors his empire soon dissolved and his message was forgotten.

Imperialism was revived by the Gupta dynasty (*c.* AD 300-500). Their home base was the same as that of the Mauryas and they also relied on war elephants. Their greatest conqueror, Samudragupta, traversed almost the whole of India at the head of his imperial army. He recorded this in a magnificent inscription on one of Ashoka's pillars. The Gupta empire also had a powerful central administration, but it had a very different state society. Trade and urban growth flourished under Gupta rule and the cities of Northern India were distinguished by a cultured urbanity. This fitted in well with the amazing achievements of classical Sanskrit literature. The great poet Kalidasa was patronized by the Chandragupta II and Kumaragupta.

They were very tolerant and supported Hindu temples as well as Buddhist monasteries. The sculptures adorning the Gupta temples were exquisite and served as models for the future development of Indian art.[28]

Whereas Ashoka had tried hard to build a state society around his *dhamma* message, the Gupta rulers resorted to the rich symbolism of the Hindu faith to propagate their imperial mission and reach out to a vibrant state society. Literature and the arts which they patronized provided a rich cultural context for this society. It seems that the Gupta dynasty could rely on a fairly cohesive state society. There was, however, a paradox in Gupta history. Chandragupta had married a Licchavi princess and his son Samudragupta proudly proclaimed that he was 'the son of the Licchavi'. The Licchavis belonged to one of the last great *ganasanghas* of northern India. In his conquest of many parts of India Samudragupta subdued such *ganasanghas*. They seem to have perished in his time.[29] Maybe the state society of the Gupta empire was strengthened by absorbing the *ganasanghas* and their traditions.

The Gupta empire was destroyed by the invasions of the Huns whose rule over northern India was shortlived. The imperial state society seems to have survived. This may have encouraged Harshavardhana of Kanauj to revive the empire in the first half of the seventh century. The four decades of his rule were once more a period of imperial splendour. He patronized Hinduism and Buddhism simultaneously and literature and the arts flourished in his reign.[30] Like Samudragupta, Harsha embarked on a tour of conquest, but he was defeated by the Chalukya king Pulakeshin II who marched with his army about 1,000 km to the north of his capital Badami to confront Harsha when he crossed the Vindhya mountains. This showed that by this time the rulers of southern India had gained the power of long distance intervention.

After Harsha's death his empire dissolved into numerous smaller successor states. Together with the kingdoms of southern India these states constituted the jigsaw puzzle of medieval regional kingdoms. The Gupta style of rule as well as of literature and the arts was replicated in all these states. Their state societies must have been rather similar. There was also a significant contribution of Indian philosophy to the cohesion of Indian society. Shankaracharya (*c.* 788-820) made a deep impact on Indian thought.[31] He adopted many ideas from Buddhist philosophy. Critics even called him 'Crypto-

Buddhist', but he greatly enriched Hindu philosophy in this way. By establishing spiritual centres (*math*) in all four corners of India he saw to it that his message of Advaita Vedanta was spread throughout the country.

MEDIEVAL INDIA: EPHEMERAL DYNASTIES AND STABLE STATE SOCIETIES

As B.D. Chattopadhyaya indicates, there were about 40 lineages which produced rulers of various Indian states in the eleventh century. These lineages had spread horizontally.[32] They migrated over long distances and could often be found far away from their places of origin. These lineages supplied personnel of various ranks which occupied different positions of rulership. Like the soil of a forest is penetrated by a mycelium from which mushrooms would sprout here and there, such lineages showed up everywhere in India and produced kings and tributary princelings. The term *samanta* assumed political importance in this context. Originally it just means a neighbour, but then it referred to a tributary prince subdued and reinstated by a more powerful king. This king then could boast of the glamour of the *samantachakra* surrounding him.[33] Usually the *samantas* had to attend the king's court at certain times. The king could then enjoy the glory cast upon him by the shining crowns of his *samantas*. The reference to their crowns shows that they were rulers in their own right though they were bound to serve the king. The *samantachakra* was the apex of the state society of medieval Indian states. Ranking was an essential element of the structure of this society. In due course *samantas* would also become high officials at the king's court and the term *mahasamanta* (literally 'great neighbour') referred to the king's chief minister.[34]

This type of 'feudal' ranking was also connected with the emergence of caste ranking in medieval India. In ancient Sanskrit texts there is little evidence of a 'caste-system' except for the distinction between Brahmins and Kshatriyas (warriors). The innumerable sub-castes (*jati*) which have often rather specific regional origins are mentioned only in medieval India. The stratification of the society was obviously a major concern of medieval states. It ensured the stability of regional state societies which supported royal dynasties. In fact, these dynasties were rather ephemeral. Powerful *samantas* often managed to overthrow their king and establish a new dynasty of their own. The style of kingship remained the same and the state society easily adjusted to the new regime.

The resilience of the state society was so great that it could also tolerate upstarts who did not belong to the 40 lineages mentioned earlier. Occasionally energetic chiefs of hill tribes conquered the adjacent plains and emerged as powerful kings. The Hoysala dynasty of Karnataka is a case in point. The Hoysalas were followers of Jainism and then converted to Hinduism. Some of the most exquisite Hindu temples of Southern India were built by them.[35] If they could not have relied on a pre-existing stable state society, this rapid cultural efflorescence would not have occurred.

The rise of regional kingdoms also encouraged the growth of regional languages and their literatures. Sanskrit was still widely used in medieval India by poets and religious teachers, but there were also writers who expressed themselves in Tamil, Telugu, Kannada, etc. This affected wider circles of the society which were not literate in Sanskrit. Those who were not literate at all could still admire the impressive temples with their beautiful sculptures. But the splendour of medieval India was erased in the twelfth century when Islamic invaders on their swift horses stormed into India.

THE SOCIAL IMPACT OF CAVALRY STATES

For more than a millenium elephants had dominated Indian warfare and horses had played only an auxiliary role. This changed very rapidly when the cavalry of West Asian Islamic rulers swept through India. Their cavalry warfare was based on a system of military slavery. Young boys were caught early and grew up riding horses and using their sabres to good effect. The cavalry officers and their troops were supported by land revenue grants (*iqta*). This system was suited to the rapid spread of a kind of military feudalism over vast areas. The man on horseback was a formidable revenue collector. In the early years of the eleventh century the Afghan conqueror Mahmud of Ghazni raided India 17 times with his swift cavalry and carried off the treasures of north Indian kings and temples. He did not intend to establish his rule over India and was satisfied with his plunder. The Indian rulers did not learn a lesson from this cavalry assault and were again taken by surprise when nearly two centuries later another Afghan ruler, Mohammed of Ghor, invaded India. His slave general Qutbuddin Aibak conquered large parts of northern India. When his master was murdered, he established an independent state which became the Sultanate of Delhi. It is telling that this state was known by the name of its capital and not by the name of a dynasty. Usurpation was the standard practice of capturing the throne of Delhi. Secession was less prevalent as the 'colleagues' would have easily vanquished a seceder. Ambitious military leaders had only one option: they had to capture Delhi and overthrow the sultan.

The state society in the days of the Delhi Sultanate consisted in its higher echelons only of cavalrists, mostly foreigners who subdued the indigenous population with their brutal power. This alien elite remained aloof from the Indians, even from those converted to Islam.[36] The linchpin of the sultanate's administration was the local cavalry commander who was in charge of the garrison but also of civil administration. The town which served as market centre as well as local military headquarters was called *qasba*. These *qasbas* were the pillars which supported a platform state covering a large territory with only limited contacts with the indigenous people. It was not a 'state-in-society' but a state above society.

Hindu rulers had to adopt the same style of cavalry warfare in order to survive. Their cavalry captains (*nayaks*) became the local linchpins of a new type of state society. These captains were usually strangers appointed to their posts by a distant ruler.[37] But since Hinduism prevailed in those states, there were closer connections between the state and the people. The Vijayanagar empire in Southern India was a typical cavalry state. It was founded by two *nayaks,* Harihar and Bukka, who were in the service of the last Hoysala king.[38] Just like the Delhi Sultanate, the Vijayanagar empire was named after its capital and not after a dynasty. Usurpation was also practised here. Unlike the Delhi sultans, the rulers of Vijayanagar could serve as umpires in religious conflict arising among the sects of their realm. An edict of Bukka dated 1368 provides an interesting example, the Jains and Srivaisnavas had a dispute and petitioned the king to settle it. Bukka summoned the parties, declared that their doctrines were both good and that they should live in peace with each other. The edict was reproduced in an inscription at Penugonda Fort, one of the strongholds of the Vijayanagar empire.[39] The greatest ruler of Vijayanagar, Krishnadevaraya, once referred to himself as a 'Hindu Sultan' because his state was based on the same ground rules as the sultanates of the north. But he was also a great templebuilder and used Hinduism as an important element for consolidating his 'state society'. He concentrated his temple-building activities in Tamilnadu which he had conquered and which he wanted to reconcile to his rule.[40] The Vijayanagar empire was dominated by Telugu warriors, but its rulers tried to establish good relations with the local people in the many provinces of their realm. Hinduism provided a common denominator for the social cohesion of the people. In using this term, I am aware of the fact that Hinduism is a 'shorthand' designation for a variety of religious beliefs and practices. There is no single *marga* in Indian religious life but there is a family resemblance among all Hindu beliefs. Moreover, Hindu religious life projected a panorama of images and rituals which could also reflect political relationships. The narrative of rituals supported royal hegemony and influenced the state society.

THE STATE OF THE GREAT MUGHALS

In 1526 a new type of warfare was introduced into India when the Great Mughal Babur vanquished the much larger army of the Sultan of Delhi by using field artillery on the battlefield of Panipat. This was a powerful anti-elephant weapon. It also served as a permanent support of the central power of the Mughal dynasty as the Great Mughals kept the manufacture of canons as a closely guarded secret which they did not even share with their allies, the Rajputs. The Great Mughals toured their expanding empire incessantly and spent much of their time in camps. The field artillery accompanied them on these tours and demonstrated their superior power.[41]

Although the Mughal empire was a 'gunpowder empire' like the contemporary Ottoman and Safavid empires, it also remained a cavalry state like the Delhi Sultanate. Akbar, the greatest of the Mughals, even constructed an ingenious system of matching an imperial ranking order (*mansab*) with revenue grants (*jagir*) to cavalry officers who had to maintain a number of horses equivalent to their rank.[42] The system was flexible; artists, poets and scholars could also be included it it. They would not need to maintain troops. The Great Mughal appointed all *mansabdars* himself and also controlled their promotions, etc. The military *mansabdars* were co-sharers of his realm as they were subcontractors in the huge military labour market. It is said that there were about four million soldiers available in this market and a substantial share had to be absorbed by the Mughal army. With such an abundant supply of military manpower, military slavery was no longer required in the Mughal empire.

The *mansabdars* constituted the inner circle of the Mughal state society. The military *mansabdars* holding ranks from 500 to 7000 amounted altogether to about 100 under Akbar, Jahangir and Shah Jahan. Aurangzeb doubled this number so as to accommodate the elites of the territories conquered by him. Akbar had seen to it that the various ethnic elites supporting his realm were proportionately represented in the top echelon of his *mansabdars.* The Turanis from Central Asia made up about one third of this group, Iranis and Hindu Rajputs nearly a quarter each, Indian Muslims contributed less than one seventh. Under Jahangir and Shah Jahan, the Iranis claimed one third, while Turanis and Rajputs contributed about a quarter each.[43] Under Aurangzeb there were 200 *mansabdars.* The Iranis retained one third of this larger group, there were some more Afghans and Indian Muslims. The Hindu Marathas claimed 7 per cent under Aurangzeb who was eager to please them. Since the Mughals did not follow the rule of primogeniture, all Mughal princes could claim the throne. Thus there were usually internecine wars of succession in which the *mansabdars* joined different princes. The princes who did not win died on the battle field or were executed. This amounted to a kind of dynastic Darwinism. The most competent or most ruthless prince became the Great Mughal. He pardoned the *mansabdars* who had been on the side of the losers, because he needed them for the consolidation of his power. This contributed to an amazing stability of this inner circle of the political elite. The Great Mughals practically created a kind of hereditary nobility.[44] But these 'nobles' – except for the Rajputs – were never attached to a permanent territorial base as the Great Mughal appointed them to various assignments in different parts of the empire.

In addition to the *mansabdars* there were the *zamindars* (landlords) who constituted an outer circle of the state society. In the Mughal empire *zamindar* was a legal category which could encompass subdued tribal chieftains or Hindu princes as well as substantial landholders of any kind. Mughal revenue administration was generally based on an accurate measurement (*zabt*) of the land and a proper assessment of the revenue demand (*jama*). But there were many areas which were subjected to a summary settlement (*nasaq*). This meant that a kind of 'tribute' was fixed which was to be paid by the 'zamindar'. In general Mughal administration was organized on rational and universally applicable principles, but local adjustments were made wherever the enforcement of the principles proved to be difficult.[45] In this way the Great Mughal managed to rule a far-flung empire and extract enough revenue for the support of an enormous army and an elaborate imperial establisment. It was only under Aurangzeb that 'imperial overstretch' caught up with Mughal rule. Moreover, Aurangzeb lived too long and thus upset the mechanism of dynastic Darwinism. Some of his sons died before Aurangezeb and the one who finally succeeded him was an old man of no superior quality as a ruler.

The Mughal empire dissolved in the eighteenth century although the Great Mughal continued to exist as a figurehead. Earlier Mughal governors and other high officials of the realm established states of their own. The Mughal state society was fissured, but its parts retained much of the earlier tradition. The Persian terminology introduced by the Great Mughals prevailed in most departments of government. The fact that the Mughals had managed to monetize the land revenue enabled the new governments which emerged in the eighteenth century as well as the East India Company when it transformed itself into a territorial ruler to 'cash in' on their conquests.

There was a growing commercialization of power in the eighteenth century. There were instances when a local ruler mortgaged his state to a moneylender who then took over the fiscal administration of that state. The East India Company which was a product of a similar trend of the commercialization of power in contemporary England fitted in very well with this development in India. It was superior to the powers it had to contend with in terms of its better management of military finance. Moreover, it relied on an inexpensive and yet highly effective infantry. It recruited Indian soldiers and subjected them to modern European drill. Such infantry units shot off their rounds like a human machine gun and devastated the cavalry of Indian rulers. Foot soldiers had always played a very inferior role in Indian armies, now they dominated the battlefield.[46]

CONQUEST BY INFILTRATION: BRITISH RULE IN INDIA

The conquest of India by a British trading company once more changed the ground rules for the constitution of a state society. The British established a state by infiltration. They never really 'occupied' India. The famous Indian Civil Service consisted of about 1,200 superior officers who manned the essential posts of government. This was a paper-thin strata of bourgeous civil servants who obeyed the dictates of a distant centre. They used the levers of power which they had inherited from the Mughal empire. But whereas that empire had been supported by a military elite, the new civil service had a very different life style and mode of operation. For the most part, the new ruling elite kept aloof of the Indian people and cultivated the idea that they belonged to a superior race. Therefore it was most embarrassing to these colonial rulers when 'low and licentious Europeans'[47] such as sailors, loafers and prostitutes appeared in India who did not at all conform to the image of a superior race. But the total number of Europeans in India was so small that millions of Indians never saw a European in their lifetime.

The acme of British remote control of Indian society was the system of indirect rule practised in the Indian princely states. In the course of the conquest of India, more and more Indian princes had surrended and signed contracts of subsidiary alliance with the East India Company. These princely states whose combined territory constituted almost one third of the Indian territory were engulfed by British India like insects in amber. They retained their internal autonomy, but the British residents stationed at the court of the respective Indian prince told him what to do and what not to do.

The Indian state society of the Mughal type had more or less survived, but the British disarmed and paralysed this society and subjected it to the control of a modern bureaucracy. They also introduced their laws and their jurisdiction. Colonial law courts proliferated throughout the country and Indian litigants flocked to them. The court fees which the British collected not only paid for the judicial establishment but yielded a handsome revenue to the colonial state. This system also provided employment for Indian lawyers and judges.[48] They became important members of the colonial state society. The British also needed thousands of clerks and accountants to run their colonial administration. Those who wished to qualify for such appointments had to attend the schools and colleges which offered a curriculum dictated by the British.[49] All this contributed to the growth of a state society which was, however, completely under the guardianship of its foreign rulers. It took a long time before the desire for political emancipation could arise in this stunted state society.

INDIAN NATIONALISM, THE PEASANTRY AND THE REPUBLIC OF INDIA

For a long time Indian nationalism was confined to urban educated people. They shared the ambivalent experience of being part of an 'imperial social formation'.[50] Many of them were deeply influenced by British political thought and felt that British institutions were required for the growth of a modern Indian nation. But some of them who may be called 'national revolutionaries' insisted that India had always been a nation and only needed to break the shackles of foreign rule.[51] Some of the younger revolutionaries resorted to terrorism in order to reach this aim. After the first world war Mahatma Gandhi assumed the leadership of a non-violent freedom movement. He had much in common with the national revolutionaries as he did not believe in the need of British institutions for the growth of an Indian nation, but he rejected terrorism. His campaigns of non-cooperation and then of civil disobedience greatly widened the circle of those who worked for India's political emancipation.[52] It could be said that within the colonial state he created an anti-state society which could then become the state society of independent India.

Jawaharlal Nehru who participated in Gandhi's campaigns and remained with him despite some fundamental political disagreements shared with him a deep interest in the mobilization of the peasantry. Unless the peasantry joined the national movement the colonial rulers could belittle that movement as it was backed only by the small minority of the urban educated people. The British had passed many laws protecting the rights of the substantial peasants and had hoped to encompass them in a colonial state society which would support their rule.[53] They had been successful in this endeavour until the Great Depression turned the peasants against them. The fall in agrarian prices cut the incomes of the peasants by half while they were still faced with the same revenue demand and the old burden of debt service.[54] Nehru organized peasant campaigns in 1930. The Indian National Congress led by Gandhi and Nehru became a peasants party. When provincial elections were held in 1935/7 Congress attained a majority in seven of the nine provinces of British India. The colonial rulers had only enfranchised about 10 per cent of the Indian population and the franchise was based on qualifications in terms of property or the amount of rent paid. In Bengal everybody who lived in a stone house and not in a mud hut was entitled to vote. This described the limits of the state society on which the colonial rulers wished to rely.[55] They were disappointed when the peasants turned against them.

After the Second World War when new elections were held, the Congress could repeat its earlier performance. It remained a peasants party for a long time. After independence Nehru as Prime Minister introduced the conventions of parliamentary democracy in which he firmly believed. He also made a bold move when he held elections based on adult suffrage which he had advocated for a long time. India still had a high rate of illiteracy at that time, but Nehru trusted that even the illiterate voter was mature enough to express his political preferences. He thus established a broad state society in which the new Republic of India was firmly embedded.[56]

For the first two decades of the new republic, the old leadership of the freedom movement was still alive and could man all important political posts. They backed Nehru's socialist economic policies at home and his non-aligned policy abroad. Later generations have criticized Nehru for imposing a low rate of growth on India which a witty Indian economist called the 'Hindu rate of growth' (at 3.5 per cent per year).[57] But this slow growth also helped the new republic consolidate its independent existence without being exposed to the vagaries of the world market and internal social tensions which could have disrupted the state society.

ECONOMIC GROWTH AND ITS SOCIAL AND POLITICAL CONSEQUENCES

Inspite of his restrictive socialist policy, Nehru did manage to triple India's industrial production before he died in 1964. He had done less for agriculture as he had kept the grain prices low so as to keep industrial wages at low levels in order to encourage industrial growth.[58] His appeals to the peasants to embark on joint collective farming had met with their resistance and he relented as he depended on their votes. Agricultural production nevertheless increased, but this was due to the increased cultivation of marginal soils. When the monsoons failed soon after Nehru's death, this led to an agrarian crisis. After this prices rose and the Green Revolution took its course.[59] This benefited mostly the richer peasants. Irrigation spread and marginal soils were no longer cultivated. Population growth increased the ranks of landless labourers who could be exploited by rich landholders. Social discrepancies increased not only between the rich and the poor in general but between different regions of India.[60] This affected the cohesion of the state society. Political conflicts became more acute and left their mark on the party system. For a long time the Congress party had practically 'possessed' the state society. It had always steered a middle course so as to maintain a national consensus. The Congress avoided coalition politics, because this would compromise its 'centrist' position. When it lost the elections of 1989 it still remained the largest party and could have headed a coalition. Instead of this it left the field to minority governments and finally to the right-wing Bharatiya Janata Party which did not mind entering into a coalition with all willing parties. Finally the Congress party learned its lesson and adopted coalition politics to good effect in 2004 and 2009.[61]

In the meantime India had experienced rapid economic development after a balance of payment crisis had forced the government to introduce economic reforms in 1991. Structural adjustment did cause a short downturn in 1992, but by 1996 Dr. Manmohan Singh, the finance minister who had introduced the reforms, could proudly point to the the amazing upswing of the mid-1990s.[62] In subsequent years the Indian economy forged ahead at growth rates of up to 9 per cent per year, this was not just due to export-led growth. The home market expanded as well, but Indian exports for the first time made a mark after India's share in world trade had dwindled to insignificance in earlier decades. Computer software, polished diamonds and readymade garments proved to be in the vanguard of India's new export economy.[63]

Economic growth has led to the rise of a new middle class. Actually 'middle class' is a misnomer, bccause these people belong to the upper quintile of the Indian population. But this means nevertheless that this class consists of about 200 million people. Their relative affluence is in stark contrast to the two lowest quintiles which remain trapped in dire poverty.[64] Most of the poor live in the rural areas. Remedial measures of the government have guaranteed employment to those rural workers who have to cope with long periods of seasonal unemployment. But this does not solve the problem that Indian agriculture had to absorb a growing population whose productivity is extremely low.

India's 'population explosion', which assumed alarming dimensions in earlier decades when death rates fell but birth rates continued to be high, has subsided in recent years. In southern India fertility rates have dropped so rapidly that in some regions they are already below the reproduction rate of 2.1. India can now enjoy the benefits of a 'demographic dividend' which accrues to societies in which there are fewer dependents than working members of the family.[65] However, there will be no dividend unless enough employment will be found by those who look for it. Young people who are unemployed are potentially dangerous, the more so if they are mobilized by agitators. Kashmir is a case in point, it harbours a frustrated young population. Investors avoid this state because of its political instability. This creates a vicious circle of unemployment and increasing tension. The areas of eastern India which are now infested by Maoists show a similar pattern. Economic development in this part of the country is limited to some enclaves. Investors are eager to tap the natural resources of these areas, but mining operations, etc., only lead to the displacement of people and offer few jobs. The Maoists have definitely opted out of the state society and want to subvert it by violent means. They are like the 'social bandits' studied by Eric Hobsbawm who 'champion the cause of the peasants'.[66]

Hobsbawm argues that such bandits usually appear when the 'traditional equilibrium is upset . . . or the jaws of the dynamic modern world seize the static communities in order to destroy and transform them.'[67] The fact that the Maoist menace has increased in recent years may indicate that the bite of those jaws has been felt more intensely with the rapid progress of India's economic growth.

Social tensions have also affected the relations between Hindus and Muslims in India. Many politicians have tried to integrate the Muslims into the Indian state society. But some Hindu politicians have also made them a target of hostile confrontation. The Muslim pogrom in Gujarat in 2002 has been a gruesome incident which revealed social fractures that could disrupt the Indian state society. Gujarat is India's most developed industrial state with an affluent middle class. Unlike other regions of India where Muslims are mostly poor artisans and labourers, Gujarat has a prosperous Muslim middle class which seemed to be socially well integrated. It was an alarming feature of the pogrom that elements of the Hindu middle class turned against the Muslim middle class. Since this particular social cleavage had no parallels elsewhere in India, there were no pogroms in other parts of the country. The fact that India is a federal republic also helped to prevent a spillover of events in Gujarat to other states.

Federalism had been introduced in India by the colonial rulers as a device of a devolution of power to 'autonomous' provinces of British India while remaining in firm control at the centre. This heritage is still reflected in contemporary centre-state relations. The Indian nationalists were originally anti-federalists as they were well aware of the intentions of the colonial rulers.[68] But after the 'transfer of power' in 1947, the new government of India preserved the federal structure. This structure has served India well, because it has helped to encourage regional identities but also to isolate regional problems. A basic feature of regional identity is the prevalence of different languages. Mahatma Gandhi has recognized this when he reorganized the provincial committees of the Indian National Congress along lingustic lines.[69] He felt that people should articulate their political aims and ideas in their mother-tongue rather than in English, because English was only the language of a small Indian elite. In independent India movements emerged which demanded the establishment of linguistic states along those lines. Nehru was against this as he feared that it would destroy national unity. But he then relented and Indian federalism assumed its present form.[70] The renaissance of regional traditions could draw upon a medieval heritage which has been discussed above. The Indian state society thus became a federation of regional state societies. This was also reflected in the development of the party system. Regional parties which are often restricted to one state have consolidated their position.[71] In parliamentary elections they were earlier disadvantaged due to the working of the majority election law. In recent years regional parties have captured about 50 per cent of the seats in the central parliament. Results which are normally expected from a proportional system of elections have emerged inspite the retention of the majority election law which usually produces a two party system. Coalition politics in India therefore has to be based on a careful balancing of regional interests. This has actually strengthened the composite state society of India. Economic growth has led to the rise of new regional elites which must be accommodated.

Cutting across this trend of regionalism, there are also other tendencies of social development in India. Most Indian middle class families now have some relatives in America who are doing very well there.[72] In analogy to the imperial social formation mentioned earlier one now finds a global social formation in which Indians hold an increasing share. The NRI (non-resident Indian) plays an important role in Indian society. Though he obviously does not belong to the Indian state society he influences it in many ways and thus also the state which is embedded in it.

Joel Migdal has stated that 'the state has become the grand arena of accommodation'.[73] In order to support the state in this endeavour, the state society has to be attuned to a spirit of accommodation. The working of the democratic process in India has so far fostered this spirit. But the state is not only an arena of internal accommodation, it also has to cope with global forces. Jawaharlal Nehru was aware of this and constantly tried to widen the horizon of the Indian state society. This endeavour is even more important today, when globalization proceeds at a much faster pace.

NOTES

1. J.S. Migdal, *State in Society: Studying How States and Societies Transform and Constitute One Another*, Cambridge: Cambridge University Press, 2001
2. Ibid., p. 23
3. Ibid., p. 150
4. For the reprinted text of this address see H. Kulke, ed., *The State in India, 1000-1700*, Delhi: Oxford University Press, 1995, pp. 195-232.
5. Ibid., p. 228
6. Ibid., p. 229
7. W. Rau, *Staat und Gesellschaft im Alten Indien*, Wiesbaden: Harrassowitz, 1957, p. 65
8. Ibid., p. 76.
9. Ibid., pp. 77 f.
10. Ibid., pp. 70 f.
11. Ibid., p. 107.
12. Ibid., pp. 108 f.
13. Ibid., p. 112.
14. Ibid., p. 129.
15. Ibid., p. 82.
16. R. Thapar, *Early India: From the Origins to AD 1300*, London: Allen Lane, 2002, pp. 146 f.
17. Thapar, *Early India*, p. 284.
18. R.P. Kangle, *The Kautilya Arthasastra*, part II, Bombay: University of Bombay, 1963, pp. 256 f.
19. P.R.S. Moorey, 'The Emergence of the Light Horse-drawn Chariot in the Near East', in *World Archaeology* 18 (1986), pp. 196-215.
20. A. Kuhrt, *The Ancient Near East, c. 3000-330 BC*, London: Routledge, 1995, p. 211.
21. Rau, *Staat*, p. 101
22. Ibid., p. 114.
23. Kuhrt, *Ancient Near East*, p. 297.
24. H. Kulke and D. Rothermund, *A History of India*, 5th edn., London: Routledge, 2010, p. 35
25. Kangle, *Arthasastra*, part II, pp. 201 f.
26. Ibid., part II, p. 31

27. Kulke and Rothermund, *A History of India*, pp. 38 f.
28. Ibid., pp. 59 f.
29. Thapar, *Early India*, p. 284.
30. Ibid., pp. 287 f.
31. Ibid., pp. 349 f.
32. Chattopadhyaya, Presidential Address, p. 217.
33. H. Kulke, 'The Early and the Imperial Kingdom', in Kulke, ed., *The State in India*, p. 247.
34. Ibid. p. 249.
35. J. Duncan M. Derrett, *The Hoysalas: A Medieval Indian Royal Family*, Madras: Oxford University Press, 1957.
36. Kulke and Rothermund, *A History of India*, p. 126
37. Ibid., p. 132.
38. Ibid., p. 133.
39. R. Vasantha, *Penungonda Fort: A Defence Capital of Vijayanagara Empire*, Delhi: Sharada, 2000, pp. 40, 131 f.
40. Kulke and Rothermund, *A History of India*, p. 135.
41. D. Rothermund, 'From Chariot to Atom Bomb: Armament and Military Organization in South Asian History', in J. Gommans and Om Prakash, eds., *Circumambulations in South Asian History: Essays in Honour of Dirk H. A. Kolff*, Leiden: Brill, 2003, pp. 336 f.
42. Kulke and Rothermund, *A History of India*, p. 145.
43. M. Athar Ali, 'Towards an Interpretation of the Mughal Empire', in H. Kulke, ed., *The State in India*, p. 273.
44. Ibid., p. 272.
45. Kulke and Rothermund, *A History of India*., p. 154.
46. Rothermund, 'From Chariot to Atom Bomb', pp. 340 f.
47. H. Fischer-Tiné, *Low and Licentious Europeans: Race, Class and 'White Subalternity' in Colonial India*, Hyderabad: Orient Black Swan, 2009.
48. Kulke and Rothermund, *A History of India*, p. 180.
49. Ibid., pp. 186 f.
50. This is a term used by Mrinalini Sinha, see M. Sinha, 'Teaching Imperialism as a Social Formation', in *Radical History Review*, 67 (1997), pp. 175-86.
51. Kulke and Rothermund, *A History of India*, pp. 211 f.
52. Ibid., pp. 217 f.
53. D. Rothermund, *Government, Landlord and Peasant in India: Agrarian Relations under British Rule, 1865-1935*, Wiesbaden: Steiner 1978, pp. 86 f.
54. D. Rothermund, *India in the Great Depression, 1929-1939*, Delhi: Manohar, 1992, pp. 79 f.
55. Ibid., 222 f.
56. Kulke and Rothermund, *A History of India*, pp. 243 f.
57. V. Krishna, 'Raj Krishna', in K. Basu, ed., *The Oxford Companion to*

Economics in India, New Delhi: Oxford University Press, 2007, p. 325.

58. Kulke and Rothermund, *A History of India*, pp. 246 f.
59. Y.K. Alagh, 'Green Revolution', in Basu, ed., *Oxford Companion*, pp. 229 f.
60. D. Rothermund, 'Economic and Social Indicators of Regional Disparities in India', in D. Rothermund and S.K. Saha, eds., *Regional Disparities in India: Rural and Industrial Dimensions,* Delhi: Manohar, 1990, pp. 1 f.
61. D. Rothermund, 'Congress Comeback in the Indian Elections of 2009', in *ASIEN: The German Journal on Contemporary Asia,* nos. 112-13 (October 2009), pp. 123 f.
62. Manmohan Singh, 'Inaugural Address', in D. Rothermund, ed., *Liberalising India: Progress and Problems*, Delhi: Manohar, 1996, pp. 21 f.
63. D. Rothermund, *India: The Rise of an Asian Giant*, New Haven and London: Yale University Press, 2008, pp. 96 f.
64. Ibid., pp. 196 f.
65. Ibid., pp. 176 f.
66. E.J. Hobsbawm, *Primitive Rebels*, Manchester: Manchester University Press, 3rd edn., 1971, p. 21.
67. Ibid. p. 24.
68. Kulke and Rothermund, *A History of India*, p. 227.
69. Ibid., p. 219.
70. Ibid., p. 248.
71. Ibid., pp. 260 f.
72. Rothermund, *India: The Rise of an Asian Giant*, pp. 236 f.
73. Migdal, *State in Society*, p. 92.

CHAPTER 4

Akbar and Philip II of Spain: Contrasting Strategies of Imperial Consolidation

Global historiography benefits from contrasting comparison. Rulers who faced similar problems in different contexts at about the same time are suitable subjects for such a study in contrast. Akbar and Philip both began their reign in 1556 and continued it for more than four decades. They had inherited large realms and expanded and consolidated them with great determination. Since their realms were far apart, they interacted only indirectly. Philip spent the silver mined in his American colonies in his continuous wars and much of it found its way to India where it helped to monetize the land revenue which was the mainstay of Akbar's power. After taking over Portugal whose throne he had inherited in 1580, Philip also became the head of the Portuguese *Estado da India*. Akbar was obviously interested in being on good terms with him. In 1582 he dispatched a letter to Philip in which he described his interest in different religions and also asked for copies of the Christian scriptures in Persian and Arabic. He sent the letter with a learned noblemen, Sayyid Muzaffar, who was supposed to explain Akbar's views to Philip personally.[1] But Sayyid Muzaffar did not agree with Akbar's syncretistic views and fled to the Deccan before he could embark for Spain.[2] If Philip had received the letter, he would probably have sent a diplomatic reply so as to please Akbar who welcomed the Portuguese as traders. They brought silver to India and also protected Mughal ships taking Muslim pilgrims to Arabia. However, this study of Akbar and Philip is not concerned with their interactions or their awareness of each other, but with their respective strategies of imperial consolidation. The most obvious contrast in these strategies was in their approach to religion. Akbar's religious tolerance was in striking contrast with Philip's reliance on the Spanish Inquisition which became proverbial for the worst type of intolerance and persecution.

TOLERANCE VERSUS INTOLERANCE: *SULH KUL* AND THE SPANISH INQUISITION

Both Akbar and Philip were faced with the enormous heterogeneity of their subjects. Akbar accepted that the majority of his subjects were Hindus who could not be easily converted. He respected the valour of his chief Hindu adversaries, the Rajputs, and decided to befriend them. He married a Rajput princess and did not force her to embrace Islam and he abolished the poll tax which Muslim rulers imposed on 'infidels'. His own religious feelings, influenced by Sufi mysticism, led him to a policy of tolerance, but this also made good sense as far as imperial consolidation was concerned. *Sulh kul* (universal peace) was his formula for tolerance and it also served as an appropriate ideology for keeping peace within his realm.[3] While Akbar's Hindu subjects appreciated his tolerance very much, the orthodox Muslim *ulema* criticized him for deviating from the principles of Islam. He certainly did not relish this criticism, but tolerated it.

Philip had inherited an even more heterogeneous realm from his father, Emperor Charles V, who had waged four wars against France to defend his scattered dominions. Charles was born in Ghent in what is now Belgium and was imbued with his Burgundian heritage. Burgundy had been one of the wealthiest states of Europe. Charles' inheritance also included the Dutch Netherlands whose population was the most urbanized in Europe. The Netherlands were studded with many rich and well fortified towns with proud citizens.[4] As emperor, Charles controlled most of Germany and Austria as well as parts of Italy (Milano and Naples). His father had married a Spanish princess and thus Charles inherited the kingdom of Castile. He had faced the armed resistance of many strong Spanish municipalities.[5] After this resistance was crushed, his son Philip who was born and brought up in Spain inherited the Spanish throne. When he was still a young prince, he ruled this big country and its overseas colonies as a regent whenever his father was absent. Charles abdicated in 1555 and withdrew to a Spanish monastery. It served Philip well, that Charles bequeathed the empire (Germany and Austria) to his brother Ferdinand, Philip's uncle, leaving Spain, the Netherlands and the Italian possessions to Philip. Actually at the beginning of his reign, Philip also had strong links with England as he had married Mary Tudor, 'the Catholic', in 1554.[6] The marriage contract stipulated that he had no right to rule England. But nevertheless this marriage alliance could have been of great importance for the future course of European history. However, Mary's death in 1558 deprived Philip of this alliance.

Philip was not an aggressive conqueror like Akbar. In fact, he only once participated in a battle – once more against the French – at St. Quentin in the Netherlands in 1557. Otherwise all his wars were conducted by his generals. He was a cautious diplomat, but the defence of his vast realm forced him to wage wars almost incessantly. Throughout his long reign which ended with his death in 1598 he only experienced six months of peace in 1577.[7] His chief enemies were the Ottomans in the Mediterranean, the Protestants in the Netherlands and – in league with them – England under Queen Elizabeth.

Philip was a devout Catholic and being faced with Muslims and Protestants as his chief enemies, he stressed Catholicism as the leading principle of his realm with a vengeance. Organizing the inquisition not only in Spain, but also in the Netherlands and in Latin America was not just matter of faith, it also served as an instrument of political consolidation. The Catholic clergy thus became an arm of Philip's state – and a very strong arm at that. But his reliance on the clergy and the inquisition caused problems even in Spain. This was shown by the rebellion of the Moriscos in 1568. These people were the offspring of the subjects of the Sultan of Granada whose realm had been conquered by the Spanish in 1492. Those who had stayed on in Spain had been assured of the toleration of their faith. But this was changed in 1508 when many of them were compulsorily converted. They remained nominal Christians and continued speaking Arabic and wearing their traditional gowns. The local Spanish lord tolerated this as they were good taxpayers. 'Moorish silk' was their most important product and this industry continued to flourish. Fighting the Ottomans in the Mediterranean, Philip suspected the Moriscos of being a fifth column of his enemies. In 1561 a very harsh new tax was imposed on Moorish silk. A new Archbishop of Granada was appointed who tightened the discipline of the church. In 1568 the government introduced 'reforms', i.e. the enforcement of the ban of Arabic, etc. The local lord who had tolerated the practices of the Moriscos was superseded when a zealous clergyman was made the chief of the civil administration of Granada. This man was an old rival of the local lord. He tried to make a mark with his stern measures and thus triggered off the rebellion. The Moriscos swept down on

Granada and destroyed Christian churches. A cruel war ensued which took about two years and was conducted by Philip's young half-brother, Don Juan de Austria. The Moriscos were crushed and Philip forcibly resettled 80,000 survivors in other provinces of Spain.[8] Their silk industry was obliterated in this way. The last remnants of Arabic scholarship for which Spain had once been famous were also destroyed at that time.

With all this emphasis on Catholicism, one should have expected that Philip was an obedient servant of the pope, but this was not so. With most popes who held office during his long reign he had serious political conflicts.[9] But these conflicts concerned only temporal affairs, not the dogma of the church. In matters of faith, he was very dogmatic. He also spent hours in intense prayer. His Catholic subjects worshipped him. They called him 'the prudent king' and compared him to King Solomon, a comparison which Philip cherished.[10] In this respect he was not unlike Akbar who also had a high opinion of himself. However, while Akbar did not interfere with the belief of others, Philip felt called upon to fight heretics. When his Dutch subjects converted to Protestantism, he sent his army against them. To some extent he was successful in purely military terms, but in the long run he could not crush their resistance which flared up again and again.[11]

The intolerant king then directed his wrath against Protestant England which supported the Dutch rebels. When English ships also boldly attacked Spanish ports, he resolved to invade England and to reclaim it for Catholicism. Philip then equipped a mighty Armada which carried troops for the invasion. Additional troops stationed in the Netherlands were supposed to join them in this venture. Philip had carefully planned this, but it did not work. The English ships were better armed and were designed so as to outmanoeuvre the cumbersome Spanish ships. They badly mauled the Armada in 1588.[12] The failure of this risky venture was a blow to Philip from which he never recovered. He restored the Armada which later on won some maritime battles against the English navy, but all this at an enormous cost. Even his Spanish subjects then lost faith in their 'prudent king'.

ORGANIZING THE EARLY MODERN STATE

Both Akbar and Philipp had to solve the problem of organizing an early modern state, depending on expensive armament like the artillery and a large standing army. For this there had to be a reliable tax base and an efficient territorial administration. In this Akbar was also more successful than Philip although the 'prudent king' was a hardworking bureaucrat, devoting attention to every detail of his administration. Akbar was saved from getting bogged down in bureaucratic detail by being an analphabet. He got to the heart of the matter by discussing it with his ministers and taking bold decisions. One of these bold decisions resulted in the compilation of the *Dassalnama*, a land revenue survey of his realm conducted for a period of ten years in which all emoluments paid from revenue assignments were paid directly through his treasury. The survey permitted the calculation of an average *jama* (revenue assessment) on which subsequent assignments could be based. It also absolved Akbar from making an annual decision on the revenue rate, taking into consideration the vagaries of the monsoon. Traditionally this decision had been left to the ruler, because it was bound to be arbitrary and only the ruler could bear the responsibility for it. Akbar's realm was too large for this type of decision which could not reflect regional variations. Akbar's method of revenue assessment fitted in very well with his system of granting *mansabs* (i.e. graded revenue assignments) according to the rank of the respective officer in his army or at his court. Each *mansabdar* was graded in terms of two amounts, one referring to the number of troops which he had to maintain and one stipulating his personal salary. In this way both military officers and 'civil servants' could be included in this scale. The *mansab*-system established a rational hierarchy.[13] Appointments and supervision were left to Akbar, but he did not interfere with the normal work of his *mansabdars*. While the *mansab* was a hierarchically ordered rank, it did not necessarily reflect the hierarchy of command in a military campaign. Akbar could nominate the commander as he pleased, he could also select the governor of a province according to his judgement and even appoint a commander of a fortress in that province who was equal in rank to the governor as a *mansabdar*. With this flexible system Akbar could organize his state very well, reserving only essential decision for himself and refraining from 'micromanagement'.

Philip, by contrast, was a compulsive 'micromanager' who drafted and signed hundreds of documents every day. He hardly attended meetings which he considered to be a waste of time. He was the first king to create a modern bureaucratic machine and also built an impressive archive at Simancas in order to preserve the government papers. Although he could not read, Akbar was also conscious of the need for preserving state papers and instructed his officers to keep them in archives. Philip not only preserved state papers, he also generated them very assiduously. A visitor once described the bureaucratic cottage industry of the royal household: Philip signed the documents, the queen sprinkled sand over them so as to dry the ink, the princesses took the finished documents to the desk of the private secretary who put them together for dispatch to the government departments, etc.[14] There were councils for each of the major territorial divisions, e.g. Castille, Aragon et al. in Spain, Italy, the Netherlands, etc. There were also councils for finance, the inquisition, etc.[15] These councils were run by experienced civil servants and Philip hardly ever attended their meetings. Philip also prided himself on having an network of ambassadors and spies which made him the best informed ruler in Europe. He wanted to rule the whole world by remote control and when he had annexed Portugal, medals were struck with the motto *Non sufficit orbis* (The world is not enough).[16] Even Akbar would have refrained from such hubris.

In one respect, however, Philip confessed his shortcomings: he did not know how to examine budgets and control his financial affairs.[17] This was a major drawback in view of his constant military campaigns. Four times in his reign he had to declare the bankruptcy of his state. As states cannot really go bankrupt, this just amounted to a suspension of debt service which was resumed once his creditors had agreed to a rescheduling of the debt. Spain was thus constantly burdened by a mountain of debt which was only occasionally diminished by windfall gains from the colonies. In the meantime the Spanish troops in the Netherlands mutinied whenever they did not receive their pay.[18] Philip was also besieged by military contractors who had recruited troops for him at their own expense and had to wait for refunds.[19] The taxbase of Philip's state was not as solid as that of Akbar's realm. Spanish taxation mostly relied on the sales tax. There were also peculiar taxes like those on the sheep.[20] There were about 7 million people in Spain at that time and 4 million sheep. The *Mesta,* a national corporation of the shepherds which organized the seasonal transhumance from north to south and back again, enjoyed the special protection of the Spanish crown which could rely on the tax derived from this source. The settled agriculturists were often aggrieved by this custom as they had to tolerate the grazing sheep. The export of wool was very profitable for Spain. Philip also tried to increase the taxation of the Netherlands which was resented by the people and inflamed the spirit of rebellion. The introduction of the Spanish sales tax (*alcabala*) at 10 per cent in 1572 triggered off a strike of the merchants. It had to be enforced with the aid of the military.[21]

Akbar did not face such troubles. He left a full treasury to his successor. This was due to his wise restraint in military matters. Unlike his successors he hardly ever conducted campaigns which did not yield handsome dividends. Achieving control over Gujarat and Bengal gave him access to the Arabian Sea and the Gulf of Bengal. Although he would have loved to retrieve the ancestral lands of his dynasty in Central Asia, he never embarked on a campaign like that launched by Shah Jahan later on. For Akbar the control of Kabul and Kandahar was sufficient for guarding the Western border of his empire. He did conquer Kashmir, but the Pashtoons of what is now the Northwestern Frontier Province could not be subdued by him. His famous Hindu general, Maharaja Jai Singh, tried twice to penetrate this area. Akbar's witty companion, Raja Birbal, lost his life in one of these campaigns. Finally Akbar did not pursue this line of conquest any longer, the more so as it would not have been very profitable. He also refrained from conquering the distant southern highlands which would not yield as much revenue as the fertile Gangetic plains which provided the main financial support of Akbar's empire. The epithet 'prudent king' would have been better applied to Akbar than to Philip.

THE METHODS OF INCORPORATION AND NETWORKING

Unlike the later modern state which depends largely on impersonal institutions, the early modern state had to rely on personal ties of the monarch with the ruling elite of his realm. These were no longer the ties of feudal vassalage and homage. Whereas the feudal lord based his strength on the control of his hereditary territory, the new ruling elites owed their position to the monarch who appointed them. In the Islamic realms, military slavery had often served as a recruiting ground for the ruling elite. The Mughal empire no longer depended on such slaves as competent warriors from Western and Central Asia made a beeline for India in order to serve the Mughal.[22] In Akbar's time this attraction was so great that he could select the best candidates for his *mansabdar*-system. The *mansabdars* were the shareholders of his realm. They had to control the enormous military labour market. There were about four million warriors available for recruitment in Akbar's realm.[23] It would have been dangerous to leave the majority of them unemployed. For the incorporation of the *mansabdars* in his court, Akbar practiced a highly elaborate court etiquette. Although Akbar could be quite informal when he was so to speak 'off-duty', he was a stern disciplinarian when enforcing court etiquette. Even the distance from his throne which a courtier had to observe when attending his court was minutely determined by the emperor's protocol.[24] As a special sign of incorporation the members of the ruling elite would be presented with honorific garments (*khilat*)which had been touched by the emperor. These honours were distributed quite generously. Akbar had a workshop near his palace for the manufacture of such garments.[25] But there was an even more intimate method of incorporation: the admittance to the order of *Din-i-Illahi* (Faith in God) founded by Akbar. It has often been assumed that Akbar wanted to establish a new syncretistic religion under this name. His Muslim critics attacked him for this. But actually he imitated the pattern of the Sufi orders. He was the *pir* (spiritual master) and those admitted by him were his *murids* (disciples). Their devotion to the master was absolute. Prostration was the adequate form of greeting the master in the assembly of this order whose membership was restricted.[26] This was certainly one of the most intense forms of incorporation practiced by a ruler.

Philip had a similar instrument of incorporation in the form of the Order of the Golden Fleece of which he became the head in 1555 as successor to his father, Emperor Charles V. The order had been founded by Duke Philip of Burgundy in 1430. The rulers of Burgundy had also established the most elaborate form of court etiquette in Europe which was in due course adopted by all other European courts. Just as Mughal court etiquette, this was a powerful form of hierarchical incorporation. Becoming a member of the Order of the Golden Fleece was the highest mark of distinction. The members of the order were considered to be of equal status and addressed each other as 'Cousin'. This included the emperor or king as head of the order. Fictitious kinship had always been a potent instrument of incorporation. Philip was very proud of being head of this distinguished order. His dress was always an austere black with no decorations. But he always wore the emblem of the Order of the Golden Fleece. Initially the order had only 21 members, but in due course it had been substantially enlarged. In 1556 Philip nominated a whole batch of new members and it is interesting to note whom he included in it at that time.[27] First of all he included his son Don Carlos and among Spanish noblemen, the Almirante de Castilla and the Duque de Cardona. He also took care to nominate eminent German and Austrian princes such as Duke Heinrich of Braunschweig and the Archduke Ferdinand of Tyrolia as well as a young Moravian nobleman, Vratislav von Pernstein, who later on became chancellor of Bohemia. Italy was also well represented by members of distinguished families: The young Ferrante Francesco, Marchese de Pescara, the Conte de Santa Fiore and Antonio Doria of the famous Genuese family who had served Charles V as a military officer. Philip also incorporated three leading members of the aristocracy of the Netherlands: William of Orange, Count Philip Hoorne and Philip Croy, Duc d'Arschot. This sample shows that he tried to include representatives of several parts of the empire and not only leading members of the Spanish aristocracy. In addition to admitting influential men to the Order of the Golden Fleece he also paid substantial 'pensions' (annual gratifications) to key members of the imperial bureaucracy and conducted a lively correspondence ('*buena correspondencia*') with them which kept him well informed. Some pensions were also granted to noblemen such as the Austrian Count Hohenems or the German Duke Ernst of Braunschweig who conducted military campaigns and recruited troops for him.[28] Philip's 'networking' was amazing and it served him well.

MIRRORS OF THE MIND: FATEHPUR SIKRI AND THE ESCORIAL

The building of Akbar's new capital Fatehpur Sikri and of Philip's monumental palace, the Escorial, were planned by the two rulers almost at the same time. Both rulers devoted much attention to the design and execution of these buildings which reflected their personalities. Akbar was attracted to Sikri by the Sufi saint, Salim Chishti, who lived there. The saint had predicted the birth of Akbar's son who was then named after him. Akbar regarded Salim Chishti as his spiritual father. The saint died in 1571 and his tomb is located in the middle of Akbar's capital. It is a place of pilgrimage even today. Philip conceived of a plan for a church, monastery and palace which should house his father's tomb. For Akbar the site of his new capital was predetermined by Salim Chishti's place of residence.[29] Unfortunately this place lacked a sufficient supply of water and so Akbar had to abandon it in 1586. The site of the Escorial, however, was not predetermined. It was finally located at the foot of a mountain range, the Sierra Guadarama, because of the ample supply of water available there.[30] Both Fatehpur Sikri and the Escorial were not fortified so as to withstand the attack of an enemy. They were abodes of rulers who relied on their standing armies. The Escorial was not shielded by any defences and Fatehpur Sikri was surrounded by a thin wall which was a symbol rather than a fortification.

The contrast between these two monuments of imperial glory would immediately strike even a casual visitor. Fatehpur Sikri harbours a beautiful ensemble of buildings of warm red sandstone, the Escorial is a huge block of grey granite of austere simplicity. In both these buildings their creators celebrated themselves. Akbar might have acknowleged it; Philip would have rejected this thought although this is what he actually did. Both rulers were great patrons of the arts and obviously did not only wish to collect and admire works of art but also to commission such works according to their own taste. Akbar showed amazing originality in guiding those who built Fatehpur Sikri and Philip transferred the art of the Italian Renaissance to Spain whose art was rather provincial before his time.

The most impressive Mughal building which was erected almost immediately preceding Fatehpur Sikri was Humayun's tomb in Delhi which was completed in 1565 and was influenced by contemporary Persian architecture.[31] In Fatehpur Sikri the further development of this style is in evidence in the mighty gate, the Buland Darwaza, and the adjacent great mosque. But even these buildings are loftier and lighter than Humayun's tomb. The palace complex probably shows Akbar's influence most directly. Instead of one imposing structure there is a rhythmic sequence of courtyards and pillar halls.[32] These halls and their ornaments reflect the Hindu style of wooden buildings whose delicate carvings are here transferred to stone – presumably according to Akbar's wishes. Historians of architecture have also pointed out that the grouping of the buildings to some extent reflects the structure of Mughal camps with their many tents.[33] Akbar had to spend several months in camp every year so as to inspect all parts of his empire. This may have inspired him to design his new capital as an encampment chiselled in stone. There are, however, some buildings which would not be found in a camp and are unique in their design. Among them is the Diwan-i-Khass, a small audience hall. It is a square building with a central pillar on which Akbar's throne was placed. The throne was accessible by passages which traversed the building diagonally. There is a balcony along the walls which connects these passages. Under this elevated structure there is a hall which could accommodate those who would only listen to the discussion going on literaliy over their heads. The structure clearly indicates the nature of the transactions. Akbar occupied a central and exalted position but was accessible from all sides to those whom he had invited to discuss matters of state or philosophical problems with him. Since the building had a dimension of about 12 by 12 metres, its internal space was limited and encouraged an exchange of views at close quarters. The entire design of Fatehpur Sikri signalled openness and accessibility, the very opposite of the forbidding structure of the Escorial.

Philip was a Catholic Puritan who preferred an austere style. This style had its precedent in the Portuguese 'plain style' which was a reaction against the ornate style favoured by the Portuguese king Manuel I, Philip's maternal grandfather.[34] As a young prince, Philip had toured Europe. In his company was a courtier, Juan de Herrera, who was three years junior to him. Herrera was a man of technical ingenuity and artistic sensibility. He probably had an influence on Philip's growing interest in art and architecture even at that time. Later on Herrera became the main architect working on the completion of the Escorial.[35] But after the European tour he first spent some years as a military officer in Italy. When he returned to Philip's court he was still too young and inexperienced to work as a royal architect. It was probably at his recommendation that Philip invited Juan Bautista de Toledo to take up this position. Toledo was born in Spain but had spent most of his life in Italy.[36] He had worked as Michelangelo's assistant for some time and had then settled down in Naples as royal engineer and architect. He arrived in Madrid in 1559 and his wife and daughters were to follow him later. They perished at sea and Toledo obviously never recovered from this shock. He designed the plans for the Escorial but then annoyed the king by his irregular habits. Toledo died in 1567 before the building of the Escorial could begin. His task had been a very difficult one. The Escorial was to contain a monastery of the Hieronymite order, a huge church with the tomb of Charles V. and other members of the Habsburg dynasty and the palace of the king – all in one large building with a facade 200 m long and 20 m high. The building enveloped the church whose big cupola attained a height of 90 m. Philip's bedroom was placed in such a way that he could have a look at the altar when he woke up in the morning. The Escorial was raised on a vast platform of slabs of granite. A perceptive author has called this product of Philip's imagination a 'stonescape'.[37]

The hundred monks housed in the Escorial had an important task. They were to read masses in the church almost incessantly in memory of the illustrious dead buried there. While the Escorial was being built the prior of the monastery also served as the 'landlord' in charge of the construction work.[38] Philip often inspected the work and even the nearby quarry where the stones for the Escorial were cut. He also took great interest in the work of his court painters whom he often visited unannounced. In general he did not interfere with their work, but sometimes he did ask for corrections, e.g. Mary had to look demure and submissive and not too bold.[39] He also changed Toledo's design of the church after a leading Italian architect had criticized it. The final design was square without an apse.[40] It was only when Herrera was finally appointed as his royal architect that further work proceeded smoothly. Herrera and the king were working on the same wavelength. Herrera simplified Toledo's design even further. He restricted the number of towers to four at the corners and eliminated those at the entrance. Instead he stressed the importrance of the entrance by adding a storey above it which housed the library.[41] With 40,000 volumes this was about the biggest library in Europe at that time. Its ceilings were decorated by the Italian painter, Pellegrino Tibaldi, who also contributed many more pictures to Philip's great edifice. Tibaldi whose style echoed that of Michelangelo was obviously the painter whose work appealed most to Philip.[42] He had earlier appreciated the work of the Spanish painter Juan Fernandez de Navarrete. This mute genius had been sent by his parents to study in Italy and when he returned to Spain, Philip had recognized the great talent of this 'Spanish Titian' and had asked him to do the most important paintings for the Escorial, including those for the main altar. Unfortunately Navarrete died in 1579 before he could complete his work.[43] Philip knew Titian well and had commissioned him to paint several mythological pictures for him in the 1550s. Later on Titian would have loved to work in the Escorial but his old age prevented him from doing so.[44]

Philip was not only a patron of painters, he also commissioned a series of impressive sculptures for the Escorial. They were mostly produced in the workshop of Pompeo Leoni in Milano.[45] Among these sculptures are several statues of saints and the more than lifesize statues of Philip and his family in prayer and similar statues of Charles V and his family. The goldplated bronze of these statues radiates in this sombre church. As a connoisseur and munificient patron of the arts Philip was outstanding in the Europe of his time. He should have been praised by subsequent generations as a great man, but instead he is only remembered for his fervent intolerance.

CONCLUSION: CONSOLIDATING EMPIRES

Akbar was obviously more adept at consolidating an empire than Philip. Cultivating his personal charisma rather than strictly adhering to Islam, he alienated a small orthodox Islamic elite but attracted the majority of his Hindu subjects. But, of course, charisma alone would not suffice. Akbar was also good as an administrator and as an expert in military technology. He devoted special attention to the artillery which provided the backbone of the central power of his empire. Akbar improved the gun carriages so as to make the field artillery more mobile. The technical secrets of gun production were guarded by him. They were not even passed on to his faithful Rajputs. Akbar also personally designed a new type of barrel for muskets.[46] His muskets helped marksmen to hit their target with precision. These barrels did not explode as others had often done. However, the very stability of the empire which Akbar left to his successors tempted them to indulge in 'imperial overstretch'.

Philip experienced the dangers of imperial overstretch even before his reign came to an end. He was a recluse with no personal charisma, but he was highly intelligent and played his diplomatic game very adroitly. He managed to form an alliance with the tricky Venetians and with their help his navy vanquished the Ottoman fleet in the battle of Lepanto in 1571.[47] Annexing Portugal, his grandfather's realm, in 1580 was a masterstroke. He thus combined the Spanish transatlantic empire with the Portuguese seaborne empire with its many bases in Asia. Philip devoted great attention to his Latin-American possessions. The Viceroy Don Pedro de Toledo whom he sent to Peru in 1568 and who served there until 1580 proved to be a very efficient administrator who set the style for the government of the Latin-American provinces and assured the flow of silver from the mines of Potosi.[48] By 1585 when Philip finally took up his residence in the Escorial his empire was at its zenith. But with his new motto *Non sufficit orbis* he unwittingly characterized the very essence of 'imperial overstretch'. Nevertheless, he could have preserved his empire without a setback if he had not embarked on the ill-fated project to invade England. He was fully aware of his other options of defending himself against the English ships at sea and that the invasion of England was not necessary. He stressed this when asking the pope for financial support of the invasion, because the pope seemed to feel that Philip would have to invade England anyhow. Philip argued that he could very well secure the Atlantic convoys and the Americas with his navy without embarking on a difficult enterprise as the invasion of England was bound to be. He would do it only to serve God.[49] The venture failed miserably in 1588. Philip dispatched another armada a few years later; this second attempt was also in vain. In 1596 a British fleet attacked Cadiz, the major southern port of Spain. The city was devastated and about 200 Spanish ships were burnt by the British. Philip was humiliated, the more so as he was no longer in a position to take revenge for this attack.[50] He died two years later. Defeated and humiliated he felt that God had forsaken him. Akbar would have never been tormented by such doubts, because he thought of himself as a god on earth.

NOTES

1. Jorge Flores and Antonio Vasconcelos de Saldanha, *Os Firangis na Chancelaria Mogol/ The Firangis in the Mughal Chancellery: Portuguese Copies of Akbar's Documents*, Delhi: Portuguese Embassy, 2003, p. 86 ff.
2. Ibid., p. 47.
3. Harbans Mukhia, *The Mughals of India*, Oxford: Blackwell, 2004, pp. 43 f.
4. Geoffrey Parker, *The Grand Strategy of Philip II*, New Haven and London: Yale University Press, 2000, pp. 115 ff.
5. Walther L. Bernecker and Horst Pietschmann, *Geschichte Spaniens*, Stuttgart: Kohlhammer, 1993, pp. 81 f.
6. Parker, *Grand Strategy*, p. 147.
7. Ibid., p. 2.
8. Bernecker/Pietschmann, *Geschichte Spaniens*, p. 101.
9. Ibid., pp. 80 f.
10. Ibid., p. 97.
11. Ibid., pp. 117 ff.
12. Ibid., pp. 251 ff.

13. Jos Gommans, *Mughal Warfare*, London: Routledge, 2002, p. 85.
14. Rosemarie Mulcahy, *Philip II of Spain: Patron of the Arts*, Dublin: Four Courts, 2004, p. 79.
15. Parker, *Grand Strategy*, p. 22.
16. Ibid., pp. 4 f.
17. Ibid., p. 41.
18. Ibid., p. 133.
19. Friedrich Edelmayer, *Söldner und Pensionäre. Das Netzwerk Philipp II. im Heiligen Römischen Reich*, München: Oldenbourg, 2002, pp. 197 f.
20. Bernecker and Pietschmann, *Geschichte Spaniens*, p. 52
21. Parker, *Grand Strategy*, p. 123.
22. Gommans, Mughal Warfare, pp. 41, 83.
23. Ibid., p. 74.
24. Mukhia, *Mughals*, p. 83.
25. Ibid., pp. 104, 164.
26. Ibid., p. 91.
27. Edelmayer, Söldner, p. 169.
28. Ibid., pp. 177 ff., 187 ff.
29. Attilio Petruccioli, *Fatehpur Sikri*, Berlin: Ernst & Sohn, 1992, p. 8.
30. George Kubler, *Building the Escorial*, Princeton: Princeton University Press, 1982, p. 61.
31. Heimo Rau, *Stilgeschichte der indischen Kunst*, Graz: Akademische Verlagsanstalt, 1987, p. 365
32. Petruccioli, *Fatehpur Sikri*, pp. 9 f.
33. Ibid., p. 13.
34. Kubler, *Escorial*, p. 127
35. Ibid., pp. 20 ff.
36. Ibid., pp. 22 ff.
37. Ibid., pp. 98 ff.
38. Ibid., pp. 30 ff.
39. Mulcahy, *Philip II*, pp. 245 f.
40. Kubler, *Escorial*, p. 48.
41. Ibid., p. 95.
42. Mulcahy, *Philip II*, p. 44.
43. Ibid., pp.117 ff
44. Ibid. pp. 6 ff.
45. Ibid., pp. 215 ff.
46. Gommans, *Mughal Warfare*, p. 154.
47. Parker, *Grand Strategy*, pp. 100 f.
48. Ibid., p. 39.
49. Ibid., p. 286.
50. Henry Kamen, *Philip of Spain*, New Haven and London: Yale University Press, 1997, pp. 306 f.

CHAPTER 5

Gandhi and Nehru: Two Visions of India

THE MAHATMA AND THE PANDIT

Mahatma (Great Soul) is an honorific title. It cannot be 'earned' and it is not bestowed by any institution. Hindus believe that the divine manifests itself in some great individual souls. Even a look (*darshan*) at such individuals is of spiritual benefit. This is why Gandhi was often surrounded by crowds of people who just wanted to see him. It is said that the great poet, Rabindranath Tagore, was the first who called Gandhi a Mahatma. Gandhi himself initially rejected this honorific title, he got used to it only in the course of time. But even in the last year of his life he had doubts whether he really deserved to be called Mahatma. He set a test for really deserving this title: if he could face his murderer without running away, he would be rightly called a Mahatma. At the time of his death, he passed this test.

When Gandhi was a young barrister he was well dressed in the British fashion and looked like any other Indian who had made a career in the colonial society. Later on he shocked the British by being scantily dressed. Churchill called him a 'half-naked faqir'. He may have thought that Gandhi had deliberately adopted this style so as to impress the Indian people – and to shock the British. But he wore his loincloth since an encounter with Indian workers who had argued with him about recommending handwoven Indian cloth instead of cheap imported British cloth. They said his cloth was much too expensive for them. Gandhi replied that in this case the cloth had to be cut down to affordable size and then set an example himself. His new style of dress was not a symbol of renouncing the world, it was simply an argument in his debate with the workers who had challenged him. But, of course, for those who saw Gandhi in his new attire it appeared to be a signal of his solidarity with poor peasants. It remained his unique personal style. None of his followers adopted it. They wore handwoven cloth and the cotton cap which he had worn for some time, but they did not wear the loincloth.

Jawaharlal Nehru, who joined Gandhi in 1920, appeared in every respect to be in striking contrast with the Mahatma. He was a distinguished gentleman, impeccably dressed and not at all a rustic type. His honorific title 'Pandit' was inherited by him as every Kashmiri Brahmin was addressed in this way. Originally, a pandit was a traditional scholar well versed in the Sanskrit scriptures. Nehru was not at all a pandit of this kind, but he was erudite in the modern arts and sciences. After he had discarded his British clothes, he had adopted the North Indian aristocratic dress: the long coat and tight trousers. He remained a distinguished gentleman also in this new attire.

To the Indian people Gandhi and Nehru in the way they presented themselves to them appeared to be familiar figures to which they could relate in their respective ways. They worshipped Gandhi, the renouncer, and they adored Nehru, the gentleman, who took a sympathetic interest in their lives. In this way, the Mahatma and the Pandit became a great team as leaders of India's freedom struggle.

GANDHI'S ENGLAND, NEHRU'S ENGLAND

Both Gandhi and Nehru owed much to the formative years which they spent as students in England. Gandhi arrived in London in 1888, when he was eighteen years old. Nehru reached England in 1905 at the age of fifteen years. Although only seventeen years had passed between the dates of their arrival, they experienced a very different country. During Gandhi's days in London, Great Britain was ruled by the Conservative Premier, Lord Salisbury, who embodied the reaction against the earlier Liberal regime of William Gladstone. Soon after Nehru's arrival in England, the Liberals had a great comeback in the elections of 1906. They ruled the country during all the years which Nehru spent in England. His particular hero was David Lloyd George who initiated important social legislation and curbed the power of the House of Lords in 1911 as it had blocked this legislation.

Gandhi's father had been prime minister of a small princely state in Gujarat. His family hoped that Gandhi would also attain such a position, but they knew that now this would require a British law degree and they pooled their resources in order to send him to London. Gandhi did manage to get the coveted law degree of barrister within three years. In this limited time he also passed the British school leaving exam and learned French and Latin. In his autobiography, Gandhi ridiculed his youthful exploits in London. From hindsight they appeared to him as silly adventures, but they all showed his eagerness to be an English gentleman. London society was both very open and very exclusive in those days. Anybody who had proper manners and adopted the right lifestyle was welcome in this society. Gandhi soon gave up his 'gentlemanly' aspirations and led a frugal life. He took a particular interest in vegetarianism and became secretary of the Vegetarian Society, editing its journal which was his first experience in journalism. Gandhi had grown up as a vegetarian but was not a vegetarian by convicition. He became convinced of the virtue of vegetarianism only after reading the writings of Henry Salt who became his lifelong friend. Henry Salt (1851-1939) was a reformer and socialist who had taught classics at Eton. He had left his academic position and he and his wife moved to a village and led a simple life. He was a prolific writer. In addition to his *Plea for Vegetarianism*, he had published a biography of the American writer Henry Thoreau. Gandhi encountered the idea of Civil Disobedience for the first time when he read this book.

During his London years, Gandhi was a regular reader of British newspapers. His favourite paper was the *Pall Mall Gazette*, edited by William Stead at that time. Stead was an innovative journalist who introduced investigative journalism and championed social causes. His writing was always clear and to the point and it seems that he greatly influenced Gandhi's style. Another important influence on Gandhi was that of the theosophists who were very prominent in London in those days. Two theosophist friends asked Gandhi to explain Hinduism to them. They read the *Bhagavadgita* together. Although Gandhi was a pious Hindu, his mother's Gujarati folk religion was all he knew about Hinduism. Thus the questions asked by the theosophists were a real challenge to him. Later on he once stated that he owed his knowledge of Hinduism to Max Müller. This is a strange statement for a pious Hindu, but it may very well be that Gandhi had read Max Müller's writings in order to answer the questions of the theosophists. Müller was at the height of his fame in London in those days.

The great strike of the dockworkers of 1889 was an event which impressed Gandhi very much. The dockworkers were exploited by their employers. They staged peaceful demonstrations in London and the policemen did not take action against them because they sympathized with their cause. Finally Cardinal Manning was asked to mediate in this case and he was successful in doing this. Gandhi greatly admired the cardinal and met him personally. Mediation rather than winning law suits remained Gandhi's ideal in his work as a lawyer in subsequent years.

During his stay in London, Gandhi enjoyed the company of his Gujarati countryman Dr. Pranjivan Mehta (1864-1932). Mehta was a medical doctor and a lawyer and – as Gandhi once wrote – 'an intellectual giant' . Mehta later on earned much money as a diamond merchant. He was to be Gandhi's lifelong friend and supported him and his activities financially. They had first met immediately after Gandhi's arrival in London and Mehta had helped him to get settled there. Mehta moved to Burma in 1899, but he was back in London in 1909 when Gandhi was there for negotations on behalf of the Indians of South Africa. They had very intensive discussions at that time which were recorded in Gandhi's manifesto *Hind Swaraj*.

Gandhi revealed only after Mehta's death, that the 'Reader' who engages in a dialogue with the 'Editor' (Gandhi) in *Hind Swaraj* was Mehta.

Nehru was a school boy when his father enrolled him in the famous elite school Harrow where he spent two years before he could join Trinity College, Cambridge, where he studied natural sciences. The 'scientific temper' which he stressed so often in later years must have been acquired by him during those college years. After completing his studies in Cambridge, he studied law in London as his father wanted him to do that. In 1912 he returned to India and joined his father as a junior lawyer. His seven years in England were an important stage in his life. In his autobiography he played this down. But he had travelled widely in Europe and had read a good deal. Among the authors who inspired him was Meredith Townsend (1831-1911) whose book *Asia and Europe* was an eyeopener for Nehru. Townsend was a Conservative who had worked in India as a journalist from 1848 to 1860. He was pessimistic about the empire and felt that Europeans could not dominate Asia for a long time. The impact of the British on India was superficial and they would be lost in India without the help of the Indians. He thus anticipated Gandhi's analysis which led to non-cooperation. Townsend's pessimistic message was a ray of hope for Indian nationalists and Nehru must have seen it in this light. Another author whom he read in those years was William Morris (1834-96), an artist and socialist, who had published his utopian novel *News from Nowhere* in 1890. In this novel Morris had described a socialist revolution which was combatted by a group which called itself 'Friends of Order'. These people were proto-fascists. Nehru's later encounter with fascism may have been conditioned by what he had learned from Morris.

Back in India both Gandhi and Nehru experienced that their formative years in England did not help them when dealing with the British colonial rulers. In England they had got used to meeting the people on equal terms, back at home they once more felt the distance between the rulers and the ruled. If they had never left India, they would have taken this distance for granted, but now they were no longer prepared to accept it like a law of nature.

AN UNEASY PARTNERSHIP

Nehru met Gandhi first in 1916, but this initial meeting had no immediate consequences. Gandhi had still to get used to India after decades in South Africa. Nehru was newly married, his daughter Indira was born in 1917. He was busy in his father's chambers as a budding lawyer. It was the shocking experience of the massacre at Jallianwala Bagh in 1919 which made Nehru join Gandhi when Gandhi was asked by the Indian National Congress to write the report on this terrible event. Nehru worked as Gandhi's assistant and had no major role in drafting the report, but he could witness how Gandhi handled this task. Some ardent nationalists who worked with Gandhi on this report would have liked to make it a passionate indictment of British rule, but Gandhi restricted it to a factual account based on documented evidence. Finally, this had a more devastating effect than an impassioned statement of nationalist fervour would have had. Nehru then joined Gandhi's Non-cooperation campaign of 1920 and saw to it that his father, Motilal Nehru, would also join it. Motilal had earlier been a moderate constitutionalist but now he turned into an ardent follower of Gandhi.

For Gandhi this new partnership with the Nehrus was an uneasy relationship. They were not uncritical acolytes and had their own views. They wholeheartedly participated in Gandhi's campaign but when he terminated it in 1922 after a frenzied mob had burned policemen in their station at Chauri Chaura in northern India, the Nehrus were perplexed. Why should an isolated outrage put an end to a national campaign? Gandhi felt that his non-violent campaign was about to disintegrate into a chaos of such individual outrages. He knew that the British were well prepared to deal with such violence.

He wanted to save his campaign from such an end. Jawaharlal Nehru could not see it that way and remained a 'no-changer' as those Congressmen were called who would have liked to resume the campaign. Motilal Nehru, on the other hand, returned to the 'parliamentary path' and founded the Swaraj Party which turned agitational fame into success at the subsequent elections.

Gandhi had been sentenced to six years rigorous imprisonment in 1922 but was released in 1924 as he had to undergo an operation. The Government of India was glad to be able to release him for this reason. The Labour Party had come to power at that time and it was expected that the new government would order the release of Gandhi which would have meant a loss of prestige for the Government of India. Gandhi was elected Congress President in that year and gave his blessings to the Swaraj Party. Motilal Nehru was then at the zenith of his fame, but Jawaharlal was dejected. He felt that Gandhi had lost his charisma and that the freedom movement was at a standstill. Therefore he was glad that he could leave India in 1926. His wife, Kamala, was suffering from tuberculosis and he accompanied her to a hospital in Geneva.

NEHRU AND THE MAGIC OF MARXISM

The most exciting event of Jawaharlal Nehru's time in Europe was the Congress of the Oppressed Nations in Brussels in 1927 which he attended as the only Indian delegate. This congress was convened by Willi Münzenberg (1889-1940), a German Communist and associate of Lenin. Münzenberg was a media czar, running newspapers which had a large circulation among the working class. He was a gifted writer who could translate Marxist doctrine into messages which were easily understood by the people. In this way he could also attract 'fellow travellers' who were not members of the Communist party, but sympathized with its ideas. Nehru became such a fellow traveller and joined the League Against Imperialism which emerged from the deliberations in Brussels. Nehru was impressed by the many Asian delegates whom he met at the Congress. His contacts with the Chinese and the idea that they were anti-imperialist brothers of the Indians originated at that time. After the Congress, Jawaharlal Nehru joined his father in a tour of the Soviet Union to which they had been invited. This was about the last moment at which people like the Nehrus were welcome guests in the Soviet Union which soon became less hospitable under Stalin's rule. Jawaharlal Nehru was enthusiastic about the achievements of the Soviet Union. He published a report of his trip to this country which to him was an agrarian country like India which had mastered the transition to industrialization. Since his vision of India was that of a modern industrial country, he thought that India should emulate the Soviet Union.

Jawaharlal Nehru returned to India at the end of 1927, just in time for the annual National Congress which was held in Madras (Chennai). Gandhi did not attend this congress, otherwise he and Nehru would have clashed even there, because Nehru used this Congress as a forum for his Marxist ideas. He also supported a resolution demanding the immediate independence of India. Gandhi was against such a resolution because he considered it to be premature as there was no strength for an agitation to back up this demand. After the congress session, Gandhi wrote a letter to Nehru in which he urged him to start a party of his own ('to unfurl his own banner'). If he felt that he was right and Gandhi was wrong it was his duty to break with him and fight him. Nehru was shocked by this letter, apologized for his rash behaviour and called himself an 'errant child'. Although he avoided to break with Gandhi, he continued to speak of socialism and did not give up his Marxist ideas. He stressed, however, that these were his personal convictions which did not affect the policies of the National Congress. Nevertheless, Nehru emerged as a mentor of a generation of young Marxists in India who later on attained great prominence. Among them was E.M.S. Namboodiripad (1909-98), who later on became the first elected Communist Chief Minister of Kerala.

Gandhi believed in the power of individual commitment, he rejected all ideas of social forces which guided human destiny. Nehru had lost his faith in the power of individual commitment after the end of the non-cooperation campaign and had turned to Marxism which would explain the forces of imperialism which held India in bondage. The experience of the Great Depression seemed to confirm Nehru's belief.

THE SALT MARCH AND THE GREAT DEPRESSION

At the end of 1929 Gandhi finally endorsed the independence resolution which Nehru had advocated since 1927. The Congress empowered Gandhi to design a campaign of Civil Disobedience which would back up this demand. As an opening gambit of this campaign, Gandhi published eleven points which he called the 'Substance of Independence'. Nehru was not impressed by these eleven points. He did not see why such a catalogue of specific grievances would inspire the Indian nation. He did not understand that each point appealed to a section of the Indian people, e.g. the peasantry would welcome the reduction of the land revenue, the poor would be benefited by the abolition of the salt tax, the commercial circles would back the demand for the reduction of the exchange rate of the Indian currency etc. Moreover, if the British would have conceded all eleven points, they might have as well quit India as it was not worth ruling it any longer.

Gandhi finally picked one of these points, the abolition of the salt tax, as the issue on which he based his Civil Disobedience campaign. He organized a Salt March from his Sabarmati Ashram near Ahmedabad to the coast at Dandi. Only well trained satyagrahis were permitted to accompany him. This Salt March which took about a fortnight was a great public relations event. It was covered by the international press. By collecting salt at the seaside, Gandhi broke the salt law and thousands followed his example all over India. The prisons could not accommodate the many people who had to be arrested in the course of this campaign. Gandhi had staged a symbolic revolution. At that time the Great Depression had not yet hit India. It was only in July 1930 that the price of wheat was halved after the summer harvest. The peasants were in distress, because the land revenue was not reduced and those indebted to moneylenders were burdened with the same debt service even though their income had dwindled. Jawaharlal Nehru organized peasant campaigns in northern India which spread like wildfire. The fall of the rice price followed in January 1931. Wheat had been overproduced in America, but there was no such overproduction of rice in Asia. The fall of the rice price was triggered by a domestic event in Japan. This country had rejoined the gold standard only recently and followed a deflationary policy in order to maintain it. This affected the rice price in October 1930 when there was a good harvest in Japan. The rice traders in Liverpool felt that rice was now following wheat and the rice price in this port was halved in November 1930. When the winter harvest reached the market in Kolkata and Rangoon in January, the price of rice fell there, too. The peasantry was severely hit by this fall and in Burma there ensued a peasant rebellion which the British put down in a bloody campaign.

The Viceroy, Lord Irwin, feared that he would have to face a similar rebellion all over India. But he found an ally in Gandhi who was afraid that his Civil Disobedience campaign may end in a orgy of violence. In the meantime the first Round Table Conference on the impending constitutional reforms had been held in London. The National Congress had boycotted it, but Indian Liberals had attended it and they now came back with positive reports. They felt that the Labour Premier, Ramsay MacDonald, was genuinely interested in India. At the same time, Indian industrialists who had supported the National Congress financially informed Gandhi that due to the Great Depression they could no longer spare much money. Gandhi thus had several motives for responding to Irwin when he was invited by him for talks in March 1931. Irwin treated Gandhi with great respect and Gandhi felt that the Viceroy showed a 'change of heart'. The Gandhi-Irwin Pact which they concluded contained very few concessions to Gandhi but very substantial concession by him. He suspended the Civil Disobedience campaign and agreed to attend the Second Round Table Conference to be held in London in September 1931. Jawaharlal Nehru was furious about this pact as it meant that the peasants would be left in the lurch who were just then smarting under the impact of the Great Depression. He even said that Gandhi would not have dared to conclude this pact if Motilal Nehru had been still alive. Motilal had died in February 1931 a few weeks before Gandhi had begun his talks with Irwin.

Irwin left India soon after the pact. His time was up and he was succeeded by Lord Willingdon, the Governor-General of Canada, who seemed to be well suited for ushering in constitutional reforms in India. But Willingdon had earlier served as Governor of Madras and of Bombay and his image of India was that of this earlier period. To him, Gandhi was a 'little humbug' with whom he would never have concluded a pact. He hated to be compelled to treat Gandhi well so that he would not cancel his attendance of the Second Round Table Conference. He showed his true colours only after Gandhi had returned from London. Willingdon then ruled India with a iron fist.

IN NEHRU'S WORDS: GANDHI'S 'BOLSHEVIST SPEECH' IN LONDON, 1931

Gandhi attended the Round Table Conference as the sole representative of the National Congress. He did not take a delegation of experts along as he did not know that he would be involved in endless meetings of committees dealing with minority affairs and financial safeguards, etc. He only wanted to present India's national demand. Premier MacDonald's sympathetic attitude had encouraged him and his secret hope was that he would conclude a pact with him as he had done with Irwin in India. But he did not even get an interview with the premier when he arrived in London. MacDonald was in political difficulties, because he could not deal with the impact of the Great Depression. When he finally did grant an interview to Gandhi, he was the helpless head of a national government dominated by the Conservatives and the Liberals. They had retained him as premier only so as to please the working class. He was a hostage in the hands of those who had always opposed him. To Gandhi he appeared as a 'sphinx', he was bitterly disappointed by this encounter with a powerless premier.

Instead of presenting a 'national demand' Gandhi was forced to participate in the deliberations of big committess such as that for financial safeguards. Gandhi was fighting for India's freedom, he had never thought of what he would do if he were to govern a free India. He had long talks with Nehru before he left for London and had obviously taken note of his views. Because in his speech before this committee, Gandhi seemed to argue in Nehru's words for strong action of a future Government of India in the interest of the poor. He sounded so radical that the press called his statement 'a Bolshevist speech'.

Gandhi stressed that a free Indian government would have to work for many years for the uplift of the poor who had been downtrodden by the rich. He was not for racial discrimination against British capitalists in India, but if the rich would have to be discriminated against, the British could not be excluded. It could not be tolerated that the privileged would hold a pistol at the head of the nation, saying 'You will not get a national government unless you guarantee our property rights'. He also advocated the management of key industries by the state. Not only the British will feel that there is no fair play in this respect. But what does 'fair play' mean when dealing with a state?

Sir Tej Bahadur Sapru, the doyen of the Indian Liberals, was shocked by this speech and said that under Gandhi's government there would be no security of property at all. Gandhi gave evasive replies to Sapru's questions, pointing out that everything would be done in a legal way and that he had not yet thought about the details.

It was obvious that he was out of his depth when dealing with such questions. He had certainly made a valiant effort to defend Nehru's views which he had adopted in this radical speech.

NEHRU'S TRIUMPH AND DEFEAT: ELECTIONS AND OFFICE ACCEPTANCE, 1937

While Nehru could be pleased with Gandhi's defence of his economic policies, he had reasons to differ from him when the constitutional reforms of 1935 finally led to the formation of Congress ministries in seven out of nine provinces of British India in 1937. Nehru had led the election campaign in all provinces and had been extremely successful. But he had not regarded this campaign as a pathway to office acceptance. He felt that these elections were a plebiscite against British rule. Under the extended franchise (10 per cent) many substantial peasants had got the right to vote and they had voted for the Congress which had become a party of the peasants under the impact of the Great Depression. These peasants expected tangible legislative benefits from provincial Congress ministries.

Gandhi had suggested Nehru for the office of Congress president for 1936. In this capacity he also spread his socialist messages. The 'Old Guard' was dismayed and Gandhi had to admonish Nehru that he was 'in office but not in power'. Nehru had then toned down his radical messages. But after his triumph in the election campaign he was bound to clash with the 'Old Guard' which pleaded for office acceptance. There was a constitutional hitch about office acceptance. The British governors retained their emergency powers and could suspend an elected government at any time. Gandhi had asked them to promise that they would not use these powers, but even if they had wanted to do this they could not abrogate their constitutional rights. When the Congress did not accept office, other parties formed governments. The Congress politicians then had to watch helplessly how others implemented their programme. Finally the Governor of Madras promised that he would not use his emergency powers if he was not forced to do so. Gandhi accepted this and permitted the formation of Congress governments. For Nehru this was a defeat after his great triumph. He did not join any ministry but became part of the High Command which supervised the ministries on behalf of the Congress party which defined office acceptance as a continuation of national agitation by other means.

GANDHI, NEHRU AND BOSE: THE BREAKUP OF THE TRIUMVIRATE

Nehru had been elected Congress president twice in 1936 and 1937. As his successor Gandhi selected Subhas Chandra Bose who became president in 1938. Bose and Nehru were good friends. They both had been members of the League Against Imperialism. In 1938 Gandhi, Nehru and Bose still appeared to be a triumvirate, working as a good team. But this changed suddenly in 1939 when the Second World War loomed on the horizon. Bose saw in the coming war a great chance for the Indian freedom movment. An Indian rebellion coinciding with war would help to gain India's independence. Gandhi was, of course, fundamentally opposed to such a policy and when Bose hoped to be re-elected as Congress president in 1939, Gandhi did not recommend him and saw to it that another candidate would be put up against him. Even then, Bose won the election. Gandhi announced that he considered it to be a personal defeat. Prompted by this, the 'Old Guard' resigned from the Working Committee, leaving Bose high and dry. Nehru played a sorry role in these machinations. Bose expected his support, but Nehru prevaricated. In his re-election Bose had benefited from a strange rule which the Congress had adopted at the time of office-acceptance: all Congress ministers had to vacate their positions in the Provincial Congress Committees which were then taken up by junior members who had often been rivals of their seniors who had been preferred to them when the ministerial berths had to be filled. The Congress was thus split into a 'ministerial' and an 'organizational' wing. The members of the 'ministerial' wing were no longer represented in the annual Congress which was now dominated by the 'organizational' wing. This had been Bose's constituency.

Bose wanted to regain his power by resigning and getting re-elected, but this did not work. The All-India Congress Committee (AICC), of which the Old Guard was still in control quickly elected another president: Dr. Rajendra Prasad. The AICC was entitled to do that in an emergency. Bose then withdrew to Bengal where he was elected president of the Bengal Provincial Congress Committee. Since Congress had not been able to form a ministry in Bengal, Bose was free to attack the 'ministerial' wing throughout India from his new position. Gandhi then launched a counter-attack. He saw to it that Bose was removed from his position and was debarred from holding any office in the Congress for a number of years. Being convinced that Bose followed a wrong path, Gandhi thus put an end to the triumvirate for good.

Bose then fled to Germany where he expected help from Hitler. Bose was certainly not a fascist, but he believed in the old Indian saying that the enemy of your enemy is your friend. He did not know that Hitler admired British rule in India and was not interested in putting an end to it. He sent Bose off to Japan and the Japanese helped him to recruit an Indian National Army from among the Indian prisoners of war in Malaya. Bose's military adventure failed. He returned to Japan and from there he wanted to fly to the Soviet Union. He is supposed to have died in an aircrash over Taiwan. People in India missed him and many did not believe that he was dead. He was a tragic hero of the Indian freedom movement.

'QUIT INDIA' AND THE 'AUGUST REVOLUTION'

When the Second World War began, the Viceroy, Lord Linlithgow, declared that India was at war without consulting Indian politicians. Had he been a good diplomat he could have persuaded Gandhi and Nehru to back the British at this trying time. Gandhi shed tears when he thought what would happen to his beloved London during this war. Nehru was an ardent anti-fascist and was keen to support the British aganist the Nazis. The British not only failed to ask for Indian support, they also refused to announce what they would do for India after the war. All Congress ministries resigned and Gandhi finally designed a campaign of 'individual satyagraha'. One prominent Congressman after the other would hold speeches against the British war effort and get himself imprisoned for this. Nehru was one of the first to do so. There was no scope for more than this symbolic demonstration. Linlithgow had prepared plans 'to crush Congress' – and he could have done it, if Congress had launched a campaign of mass agitation.

In 1942 the rapid advance of the Japanese threatened India. President Roosevelt urged Churchill to make concessions to India so as to get its support for the war effort. At this critical juncture, Stafford Cripps, a member of the the British war cabinet, offered to fly to India for negotiations with the Congress leadership. Cripps was a socialist and an old friend of Jawaharlal Nehru. He felt that he could win over the Indian leaders. Unfortunately the 'Cripps Offer' which he took along was too vague. There would be a grant of

Dominion Status after the war and provinces which did not want to stay with India would have a right to secede. A national government would be formed immediately but there were doubts about its real powers. Cripps tried to convince his Congress interlocutors that this national government would have all powers and the Viceroy would act like a constitutional monarch in dealing with it. For this Linlithgow's cooperation was needed, but he refused to cooperate. He wrote to Churchill that Cripps wanted to deprive him of his powers. Churchill backed Linlithgow and the Cripps mission failed. Cripps was peeved and blamed his failure on Gandhi who had actually left it to Nehru to handle Cripps. Churchill benefited from the failure of the Cripps mission. Cripps was his rival in British politics and he was glad to see him fail. Moreover, Roosevelt had to keep quiet now. The Cripps mission had provided Churchill with an alibi in dealing with the American President who championed the cause of the Indians. Churchill had run no risk in sending Cripps to India, he knew that Linlithgow would hold the fort and frustrate Cripps' efforts.

After the failure of the Cripps mission, Congress had to take some action, the more so as the Japanese seemed to be on the verge of entering India. Gandhi felt that the British were not in a position to defend India and asked them to 'Quit India' as long as they still had a chance to do so before the Japanese would drive them away. Gandhi stressed that the Japanese had no reason to fight the Indians. He drafted a Congress resolution which appeared to be too pro-Japanese to Nehru. Gandhi then agreed that Nehru should draft a more acceptable resolution. At the last minute, Gandhi also dropped his insistence on the withdrawal of all Allied troops from India. The discussions with his future biographer, the American journalist Louis Fischer, convinced Gandhi that he would lose American sympathies if he insisted on the withdrawal of the troops. Nehru had introduced Fischer to Gandhi. While Nehru had tried in vain to induce Gandhi to give up the demand for the withdrawal of troops, Gandhi finally conceded it to Fischer. It is likely that this is what Nehru had in mind when he asked Gandhi to talk to Fischer.

The 'Quit India' Resolution passed by the National Congress in July 1942 had been phrased by Nehru in diplomatic terms. Gandhi was requested to design a campaign, but there were no concrete indications about what was to be done. We shall never know what Gandhi planned to do, because Linlithgow immediately arrested all Congress leaders. He even wanted to deport them to South Africa for the duration of the war, but his governors advised him against this, because it would have appeared to be a desperate move. The young generation of Congressmen who were not wedded to non-violence, then staged the 'August Revolution' which actually did not last longer than one month. They cut telegraph wires, disrupted railway lines, occupied police stations, etc. If the Japanese had actually entered India at that time, this would have been a fatal challenge of British rule. But the British were lucky, the tide of the war had turned in their favour in 1942. The Japanese had lost the great naval battle near Midway Islands in the Pacific in June 1942 and later that year the German offensive in Soviet Russia ended at Stalingrad. The British did not need to quit India and could wait until the war was over. But after the war, the British faced enormous problems. Great Britain was almost bankrupt, it was heavily indebted to the USA – and to India which had produced goods for the war effort which the British had procured on credit. Moreover, two million soldiers had fought for the British in Europe, Africa and Asia. They had to be repatriated and most of them had to be demobilized. Churchill had lost the elections in 1945 and Great Britain was now governed by the Labour Party. The new Premier, Clement Attlee, had been chairman of the India Committee in the War Cabinet. He was familiar with India and could have made a bold move of granting independence to India. But he prevaricated and it seems that he was influenced by the idea that Great Britain should retain at least some outposts overseas. Pakistan would be such an outpost and Attlee seems to have favoured the partition of India. But he wanted that the Indians should do this partition themselves and the British should not have a hand in it.

'PLAN BALKAN' AND THE 'VIVISECTION OF INDIA'

Mohammed Ali Jinnah who championed the creation of Pakistan had become more powerful during the war. Churchill was his friend and supported him in every respect.

Lord Wavell, the Viceroy whom Churchill had appointed in 1943, was a taciturn soldier. He had not much sympathy for the Congress leadership and tended to favour Jinnah without showing it too much. He regarded Pakistan as a bastion on which the British could fall back if they could not hold on to India any longer. As early as February 1946, Wavell had sent a map to London which clearly showed the contours of Pakistan. In this he had allocated the crucial Gurdaspur district to India. This district is imporant because it provides the only connection between India and Kashmir. The Radcliffe Award at the time of the partition of India closely followed Wavell's map. Later commentators have speculated that Radcliffe gave Gurdaspur to India for this strategic reason. They could not know that Radcliffe merely copied Wavell's map in this respect. Wavell, however, was convinced that Kashmir would have to join Pakistan. He could not yet know about the Radcliffe Award and that the princely states would be excluded from it.

Attlee's hope that the Indians would divide India themselves informed his policy throughout. But there were serious obstacles to it. Gandhi was against a 'vivisection of India' and if he had stuck to this point of view, this could have caused major problems. But he gave it up when Lord Mountbatten, the last viceroy, and Nehru urged him to do so in order to ward of the final 'Plan Balkan' which had come back from London as reply to Mountbatten's 'Plan Balkan' which envisaged a partition of India by the British. The plan as revised in London was a reflection of Attlee's desire of letting the Indians partition India themselves. The British would grant independence to the British-Indian provinces and the princely states and these various units could then decide what kind of states they wished to form. Mountbatten, who was not an expert in constitutional affairs, saw no harm in this deviation from the plan which he had sent to London, but Nehru was furious when he showed it to him. He could see immediately that this new plan would certainly lead to a Balkanization of India. There would be not be a central government any longer which could negotiate with the provinces and the princes. India would dissolve into a welter of states. A partition by the British was to be preferred to this chaos. As much as Attlee may have disliked it, he had to order a partition when Mounbatten demanded it – and Gandhi had to accept the 'vivisection' as much as had deplored it earlier. Mountbatten and Nehru had persuaded him. He not only acquiesced in it but even asked the Indian people to trust Mountbatten.

On the advice of V.P. Menon, the civil servant who had worked on 'Plan Balkan', Lord Mountbatten ordered that the details of the border between India and Pakistan would be revealed only after both states had celebrated their independence on 14 and 15 August 1947. Menon and Mountbatten obviously hoped that the 'vivisection' could be done painlessly while the people were absorbed by these celebrations. Mountbatten even went off to the mountains for a well-earned leave.

But the vivisection proved to be a bloody operation. Millions crossed the new borders in both directions. Delhi was crowded with refugees and the new Government of India headed by Nehru was at a loss when dealing with this disaster. Mountbatten had to return immediately. Nehru was glad that Mountbatten had agreed to stay on as Governor-General of India. When Gandhi was shot on 30 January and Mountbatten rushed to the place, he was asked by people in the crowd whether Gandhi had been shot by a Muslim or a Hindu. Without knowing who had done it, Mountbatten answered that it was a Hindu, because he wanted to prevent a pogrom. Mountbatten's presence of mind was an asset to Nehru in this terrible time. There was another aspect of Mountbatten's staying on as Governor-General: Nehru could continue as Prime Minister and set the pace for India's parliamentary democracy. In Pakistan, where Jinnah had insisted on becoming Governor-General, parliamentary democracy never got a chance.

NEHRU AS INDIA'S FIRST PRIME MINISTER

Nehru had been appointed interim Prime Minister by Lord Wavell in August 1947. His official designation was Vice-President of the Viceroy's Executive Council. Jinnah had protested against his appointment and when the Muslim League finally decided to join the interim government, Jinnah had refused to join the cabinet, as he did not want to play second fiddle to Nehru. Gandhi had tried to establish good relations with Jinnah in 1944. He had been released from prison earlier than the other Congress leaders. In the series of talks with Jinnah he had even conceded Pakistan to him but had suggested that before partition the two states should conclude a treaty regulating their peaceful coexistence. Jinnah had replied that partition had to be done first, because only sovereign states could conclude treaties. Gandhi was caught on the wrong foot, he could not contradict Jinnah whose knowledge of public law was greater than Gandhi's. After this experience, Gandhi avoided all encounters with Jinnah and left it to Nehru to deal with him.

Soon after partition, Nehru had to face the Kashmir problem. He was attached to Kashmir as his ancestors had come from there to settle in northern India. The Maharaja of Jammu and Kashmir was faced with the option of joining either India or Pakistan, but he would have preferred an independent state, a kind of Himalayan

Switzerland. Therefore he prevaricated until tribesmen from Pakistan invaded his state, soon to be followed by regular Pakistani troops. The Pakistan army was at that time still commanded by British officers who connived at this venture. The Maharaja asked India for help, but this was granted to him only under the condition that he would accede to India as Indian troops would otherwise not be entitled to take action in Kashmir. He acceded at the end of October 1947 and Mountbatten went to see Jinnah in Lahore at the beginning of November. He did not like to do this as he detested Jinnah who had given him much trouble, but he felt he must try his best to solve the conflict. Jinnah pretended not to know anything about what was going on in Kashmir and Mountbatten returned with empty hands. Nehru appealed to the United Nations. They should see to it that Pakistan vacated the territory which it had occupied, after that a plebiscite could be held. Gandhi had advised Nehru not to approach the United Nations. He felt that the Western powers still dominated the United Nations and that India could not expect justice from them. Nehru believed in the United Nations and rejected Gandhi's advice. The United Nations then disappointed Nehru, Great Britain sided with Pakistan on this issue. The influential British delegate at the United Nations, Philip Noel-Baker, argued that India and Pakistan were equal contending parties and that a plebiscite should be held as soon as possible under UN-supervision. Since Pakistan did not withdraw its troops, the plebiscite was never held. The UN established a United Nations Commission on India and Pakistan which later on continued as Military Observers Group. Nehru's decision to take the Kashmir issue to the United Nations thus had consequences which extended far beyond his lifetime.

When Gandhi was assassinated, Nehru said farewell to him in moving words. He had been deeply attached to the Mahatma and felt a real loss. But in the task of governing India, Nehru would not have followed Gandhi's guidance. Inspite of his 'Bolshevist' speech in London, Gandhi held liberal views with regard to economic policy and would have disagreed with Nehru's ideas of economic planning. He would have also criticized Nehru's neglect of rural India, a failing which Nehru himself admitted in a speech in Parliament in April 1963, but at that time it was too late for him to make amends for it. Gandhi had worked for development from below, whereas Nehru thought in terms of development from above. In this respect their visions of India differed. During the freedom movement these differences appeared only occasionally. Nehru admired Gandhi's intuitive insight into the feelings of the Indian people and Gandhi appreciated Nehru's dedication to the aims of the freedom movement. Once the freedom movement had come to an end, their differences were bound to become more obvious.

BIBLIOGRAPHY

General

Kulke, Hermann and Dietmar Rothermund, *A History of India* (5th edn.), London: Routledge, 2010.

Moore, Robin James, *Churchill, Cripps and India, 1939-1945*, Oxford: Oxford University Press, 1979.

Moore, Robin James, *Escape from Empire: The Attlee Government and the Indian Problem*, Oxford: Oxford University Press, 1983.

Rothermund, Dietmar, *Die politische Willensbildung in Indien, 1900-1960*, Wiesbaden: Harrassowitz, 1965.

——, *Krisenherd Kaschmir. Der Konflikt der Atommächte Indien und Pakistan*, München: Beck, 2002.

Sarila, Narendra Singh, *The Shadow of the Great Game: The Untold Story of India's Partition*, Delhi: HarperCollins, 2006.

Sitaramayya, Pattabhi, *History of the Indian National Congress, 1885-1947*, 2 vols., Bombay: Padma Publications 1935, 1947.

Wolpert, Stanley, *Jinnah of Pakistan*, New York: Oxford University Press, 1984.

Gandhi

Bondurant, Joan V., *Conquest of Violence: The Gandhian Philosophy of Conflict*, Princeton: Princeton University Press, 1958.

Brown, Judith, *Gandhi: Prisoner of Hope*, Delhi: Oxford University Press, 1990.

Fischer, Louis, *The Life of Mahatma Gandhi*, New York: HarperCollins, 1950.

Gandhi, Mohandas Karamchand, *Collected Works of Mahatma Gandhi*, 90 vols., New Delhi: Government of India, Publications Division, 1958-84.

Iyer, Raghavan N., *The Moral and Political Thought of Mahatma Gandhi*, Oxford: Clarendon Press, 1973.

Kumar, Ravinder (ed.), *Essays on Gandhian Politics: The Rowlatt Satyagraha of 1919*, Oxford: Clarendon Press, 1971.

Nanda, Bal Ram, *Mahatma Gandhi: A Biography*, London: Allen and Unwin, 1959.

Panter-Brick, Simone, *Gandhi contre Machiavel*, Paris: Denoel, 1963.

Pyarelal (Nayyar), *Mahatma Gandhi: The Last Phase*, 2 vols., Ahmedabad: Navajivan, 1958.

Rothermund, Dietmar, *Mahatma Gandhi. Der Revolutionär der Gewaltlosigkeit*, München: Piper 1989.

Rothermund, Dietmar, *Mahatma Gandhi*, München: Beck, 2003 (Beck Wissen).

NEHRU

Brecher, Michael, *Nehru:. A Political Biography*, London: Oxford University Press, 1959.

Gopal, Sarvepalli, *Jawaharlal Nehru: A Biography*, 3 vols. (1975, 1979 and 1984). Reprint of all volumes: Delhi: Oxford University Press, 2011.

Brown, Judith, *Nehru: A Political Life*, New Haven: Yale University Press, 2003.

Gopal, Sarvepalli and Uma Iyengar (eds.), *The Essential Writings of Jawaharlal Nehru*, Delhi: Oxford University Press, 2003.

Nanda, Bal Ram, *The Nehrus: Motilal and Jawaharlal*, New York: John Day, 1962.

——, *Jawaharlal Nehru: Rebel and Statesman*, Delhi: Oxford University Press, 1998.

Nehru, Jawaharlal, *An Autobiography*, London: The Bodley Head, 1936.

——, *A Bunch of Old Letters*, Delhi: Oxford University Press, 1989.

——, *The Selected Works of Jawaharlal Nehru, First Series*, 15 vols. (ed. S. Gopal), Delhi: Oxford University Press, 1988.

——, *The Selected Works of Jawaharlal Nehru, Second Series*, 39 vols. (ed. S. Gopal et al.), Delhi: Oxford University, Press 1984-2007.

Pandey, Bishwa Nath, *Nehru*, New York: Stein & Day, 1976.

Zachariah, Benjamin, *Nehru*, London: Routledge, 2000.

CHAPTER 6

The Rural Roots of Jharkhand

The history of Jharkhand was primarily determined by various tribes which initially practised swidden cultivation, also called 'slash and burn', and then turned into a settled peasantry while still preserving their tribal organization and adapting it to changing circumstances. 'Slash and burn' has been stigmatized as a barbarous and wasteful type of cultivation by economists and government officers of modern times, but given a favourable land/man ratio, it was actually a very reasonable procedure. The tribal cultivators moved on and the forest recovered very soon. The fertility of the soil was restored in this way, and this benefited those who would return to the same spot after many years. Under such conditions there was, of course, no idea of a fixed property in land. Manu's ancient rule "The land belongs to him who first cleared it" should have the additional proviso "and did not move on". Some tribes, however, were very good at reclaiming land from the forest and then moving on. They were not used to buying land, but when peasants who needed land were following them, they were not averse to selling the land to them which they wanted to quit anyhow. But this turned out to be an endgame. Once settled peasants controlled the land, it would not turn into forest once more. Tribal people who learned this lesson then did not move on any longer and founded villages which they defended against newcomers. But this defence could be broken down in various ways. The history of Jharkhand provides object lessons of the transition to settled agriculture and then of the breakdown of defences which led to quiet suffering or violent protest. Whether it was to be the one or the other depended on specific historical conditions.

The process of transition, defence and reaction was neither linear nor uniform in Jharkhand. There were striking instances of a co-existence in time of different stages of the evolution of agrarian relations. Thus the Mundas of Ranchi district who had already a long tradition of settled cultivation were contemporaries of the Santals of the Santal Parganas who had only reclaimed land from the forests around the Rajmahal Hills in the early nineteenth century. The Mundas and the Santals rose in rebellion at different times and for somewhat different reasons. But that they did rise at all and did not suffer quietly as most settled peasants would do, was due to the same reason: They still had some kind of tribal solidarity.

Karl Marx once compared the peasantry to a bag of potatoes. This was not meant to be a gratuitous insult to all peasants. He only wanted to indicate that in contrast with the proletariate which is faced with similar conditions as each worker has to sell his individual labour in a market which he does not control, the peasantry is made up of all kinds of marginal, middle and rich peasants. The proletariate, so Marx thought, can therefore attain class solidarity whereas the peasantry can not. The idea of proletarian solidarity and its necessary triumph in a class struggle may have been rather utopian, but the assessment of the problem of peasant solidarity was correct. Many historical examples show that peasants could only rarely be propelled to joint action and in such instances their solidarity was brought about by extraordinary highhandedness affecting many of them at the same time. In articulating their resistance they then often resorted to religious or quasi-religious ideas. If this resistance turned into violence their opponents could then speak of superstition and fanaticism which must be ruthlessly suppressed – and as the opponents were usually better equipped in every way, they invariably vanquished the peasants.

The rural history of Jharkhand provides many examples of this type of reaction. Before returning to the sources of peasant solidarity in this region we should first analyse the particular manifestations of highhandedness and oppression with which the peasants were faced. They were all related to constructions of agrarian relations which benefited the 'landlord' and/or the government. Originally the tribal cultivator was a free man who was subject only to tribal custom. As long as swidden cultivation prevailed, the rights in land were more or less equal – and temporary. With settled agriculture some stratification came about. The lineage of the founder of the village claimed precedence over other lineages, and all those legitimized by descent from the first settlers would have rights superior to those who were permitted to join the village at a later stage. This pattern was typical for the Mundari Khuntkattidars in those villages which still preserved their customary tribal structure. 'Munda' was intially the title of the administrative head of a village, like that of a 'Patel' or 'Patil' in western India. The tribal people who were referred to as 'Mundas' actually called themselves 'Horos'. But in due course 'Munda' became a generic term. 'Khunt' referred to a Munda-lineage, and a 'khuntkattidar' was a landholder who held his property as member of such a lineage.

Originally the tribal people were not interested in state formation and kingship. Such ideas slowly penetrated tribal society due to cultural contact with the Hindu society of the Gangetic plains which had supported empires and royal splendour for many centuries. As tribals turned into settled peasants they produced their own 'Rajas'. Initially this was probably a measure of self-defence, and there are legends about the election of such 'Rajas' by the tribal people. The Raja of Chotanagpur who 'ruled' the Mundas was such a tribal king. The Mundas supported him with contributions called 'chanda' which were collected in the villages and passed on by the local Munda to a Manki who was in charge of several villages. The Manki then transferred whatever he had collected to the Raja. Mundas and Mankis were entitled to a share of the 'chanda'. This type of contribution was neither a rent, nor a tax, nor even a tribute. A rent is paid by a tenant to his landlord, a tax is levied by a superior authority after some kind of assessment, a tribute is demanded more or less arbitrarily by a ruler or conqueror, 'chanda', however, was freely contributed by the tribal peasants. It could not be enhanced unilaterally by the Raja and he received it through 'proper channel', i.e. Mundas and Mankis, and could not collect it by appointing agents of his own choice. There was no scope for highhandedness in this customary structure.

Even before the British came in, the Rajas had tried to subvert this customary structure by introducing 'feudal' relations. Their feudal minions were mostly Bengali and Bihari Hindus who tried to lord it over the tribal peasants. The Rajas indulged in fights amongst each other. When the British appeared on the scene, they got roped into these conflicts. The Raja of Chotanagpur declared at a very early stage – in the 1770s – that he considered himself to be a British 'vassal', hoping that he could score a point over his rivals in this way. The British acknowledged him as a tributary chief. But he did not retain this special position for a long time. When the British introduced the 'Permanent Settlement' of Bengal in 1793, he became a 'zamindar' like most of the petty Rajas of this region.

THE BRITISH LAW OF LANDLORD AND TENANT

There has been a great deal of speculation about what Governor-General Lord Cornwallis had in mind when he imposed the Permanent Settlement. Did he want to establish a 'rule of property' as Ranajit Guha has argued? The historical constellation of this measure has usually been neglected by those who have tried to find out about the motives of Lord Cornwallis. He had lost the American War of Independence in 1781 but had vanquished Tipu Sultan of Mysore in 1792. The war against Tipu Sultan had strained British resources. Cornwallis could finance it only with the revenue of Bengal. But ever since the terrible famine of 1771 which had swept off about a third of the population, the Bengal peasants had been in a strong bargaining position. If a zamindar was too efficient in collecting the revenue they could move on to the estate of a more lenient one. Thus many zamindars often reported that their peasants had deserted them and that they could not pay the revenue. Thus Cornwallis finally decided to cut the Gordian knot by imposing the 'Permanent Settlement' on the zamindars whose estates would be subjected to compulsory sale if they failed to pay up. It was left to them how to deal with their peasants.

The 'permanence' of this settlement was initially not much of a benefit to the zamindars, because the assessment was high and they were left with only a small margin, provided they did manage to collect enough from the peasants. The new legal construction that the zamindars were now 'landlords' and the peasants were 'tenants' whose payment to the zamindar was considered to be 'rent' was initially not much of a consolation to the zamindars. They could sue their 'tenants' in a civil court just as a creditor could sue his debtor, but the court could at the most empower the 'landlord' to 'evict' his 'tenant'. At a time when the main complaint was that peasants were 'absconding' this was hardly a suitable remedy. But Cornwallis could hold the zamindars to ransom and extracted enough from them to cover the cost of his expensive Mysorean war.

With the increase of population which made land a valuable property, the Permanent Settlement did benefit the zamindars. Moreover, successive government regulations had provided more remedies to them than the threat of eviction. They were entitled to distrain the harvest of a tenant who was in arrears of 'rent', etc. But except for arming the zamindar in this way, the Bengal administration preferred not to interfere with 'landlord' and 'tenant' and to leave the adjustment of agrarian relations to the civil courts.

It took some time before this new dispensation affected the tribal peasantry. But the Rajas – or rather their clever Hindu minions – soon found out ways and means to oppress the peasants by making use of the new legal provisions. In the hilly region the peasants used to extend cultivation by converting up-land into rice terraces, thus adjusting production to an increasing population. According to the law of landlord and tenant, this was an 'improvement' which required the permission of the landlord. The reason for this was that the landlord would have to compensate the tenant for improvements if he wanted to evict him. If the landlord did not watch out, he was running the risk of being deprived of his property rights by such 'improvements'. Instead of permitting them, he rather claimed as much land as possible as his 'bakasht', i.e. land under his own cultivation, and then getting it tilled by the peasants from whom he could demand 'begar', i.e. unpaid forced labour on his land. The tribal peasants felt bottled up in this way. Not only were they prevented from extending their rice terraces, they also had to till the fields of the landlord at a time when they also had to till their own land. This was bound to lead to bitter conflicts, the more so as the Rajas created 'tenureholders' who emerged as the actual landlords with whom the peasants were confronted. These tenureholders were usually 'outsiders' who were hated by the tribal people. It seems that Sikhs and Pathans were particularly notorious in this respect. There were several violent uprisings of the oppressed tribal peasantry in the early nineteenth century. The most widespread peasant revolt occured in 1831/2 when the Hos of Singhbhum turned violent and the Mundas of Ranchi joined them. The butchered victims were marked with seven lethal slashes, one for each type of exaction which the peasants resented. Forced labour was one of these exactions, but there were also fines and fees collected by the landlords or their agents.

The British suppressed this revolt ruthlessly. The Hos or Kols of Singhbhum were then benefited by a special arrangement. The British created the Kolhan government estate in which the feudal tenures were eliminated and the peasants paid their dues directly to the government. The tribals of Southern Singhbhum were called Larka Kols (fighting Kols), they showed this fighting spirit in the revolt of 1831/2. Therefore the British were eager to pacify them by making the Kolhan a tribal reserve. But no such arrangement was made in

Ranchi where the Mundas were left to the tender mercies of their rapacious landlords.

THE FATE OF THE SANTALS IN NORTH-EASTERN JHARKHAND

At about the same time when the British had suppressed the agrarian revolt in Ranchi and Singhbhum, they fostered land reclamation by the Santals in a region called Daman-i-koh which was later on called 'Santal Parganas'. This region South of the Rajmahal Hills was covered with dense forest at that time. The Santals who were very good at reclaiming forest land due to their earlier tradition of 'slash and burn' were invited by the British to settle in the Daman-i-koh. The idea was to convert this 'useless' tract into a revenue paying district. The Santals of Birbhum and Manbhum and other adjacent areas where Hindu peasants had followed them on their heels and taken up the land which they had reclaimed made a beeline for the Daman-i-koh and established prosperous villages in the fertile valleys which they had cleared. The local forest dwellers could hardly keep up with this development, there were anyhow very few of them and the Santals multiplied rapidly in their new abode. There were no landlords around. Thus the Santals were initially not oppressed like the Mundas of Ranchi. But wily moneylenders and corrupt subaltern government officers soon got the better of the gullible Santals. Experiencing the arbitary power of the most lowly government servants, the Chaprassis or messengers, the Santals even created a new god, the Chaprassi Bonga, whom they propitiated in order to be saved from the exactions of those people.

The moneylenders were an even greater headache. They would sue their Santal debtors in a court of law. The nearest courts were in Deogarh and Bhagalpur at that time. For the poor Santal it was a long journey to those courts and if he did go there he was anyhow duped, because he could not defend himself properly. But if he did not attend the court, the creditor could get an ex-parte decree from the judge who only needed to examine the bonds presented to him. The creditor could thus tighten the noose around the debtor's neck. The British officers who had invited the Santals to settle in this area were stationed at a distance and they hardly toured the area. Thus they were not aware of the tension which was building up over a long time and finally erupted in the bloody Santal revolt of 1855.

Several Santal headmen had petitioned the government and drawn attention to the practices of the moneylenders in 1854. But this petition was shelved and nothing was done until the revolt broke out.

The epicentre of this revolt was the village Bhagnadhi near Barhait. Four Santal brothers, Sidhu, Kanhu, Chand and Bhairab emerged as leaders of the rebellion. Sidhu and Kanhu declared that they were now governors of the area. The brothers also claimed that a god had appeared to them and they built a shrine for him which consisted of a cartwheel placed on a mound. The rebels killed some Indian police darogahs and several moneylenders. They also destroyed an indigo factory. The extent of tribal solidarity could be seen from the rapid spread of the uprising to distant Hazaribagh in the west and Birbhum in the east. However, it remained a Santal affair and was later on called the 'Santal Hul'. Other tribes were not drawn into this movement. This was a saving grace for the British who were in a position to quell this revolt by quick military action.

Though some observers commented on the religious fanaticism of the rebels, the British administrative officers were convinced that economic distress was the real cause of the revolt. The petition of 1854 was taken off the shelf and examined only after the violent outbreak. As a result the Santal Parganas were created as a new district with a Deputy Commissioner who had civil and criminal jurisdiction. This district included the sub-districts of Dumka, Godda, Deogarh and Rajmahal. In this area the old police manned by outsiders was abolished and a new Santal police established. This helped to restore 'law and order' and the British could soon note with satisfaction that during the great revolt of 1857 the Santal Parganas remained quiet.

GROWING UNREST AMONG THE MUNDAS OF RANCHI

Whereas the Santals could be pacified by this new arrangement, the Mundas were frustrated in their attempts to get a similar administrative structure. Their leaders sent innumerable petitions to government in which they stated again and again that the Mundas wished to pay their dues directly to the British revenue officers rather than to rapacious landlords and tenureholders. This the British were unable to grant, because the law of 'landlord and tenant' had created vested interests in Ranchi. In the Santal Parganas this type of agrarian relations had not existed. Curbing the activities of the police and of moneylenders was easier than changing the law of landlord and tenant, the more so as 'permanence' had been promised in 1793. The continuous operation of this law whittled away the customary tenure of the Mundari Khuntkattidars. In many areas this type of tenure had already degenerated to a so-called 'Bhuinhari'-tenure. A 'Bhuinhar' was a Munda peasant who lived in a village whose customary organization had vanished, but who still would lay claim to his privileged status as a descendant of an ancient lineage. His privileges included the payment of dues akin to the old 'chanda' which was now termed 'rent'. In the terminology of the law of landlord and tenant prevailing elsewhere in British India, one could refer to the Bhuinhar as an occupancy ryot holding his land at a customary rent rate. It was, of course, in the interest of the landlords to doubt this status. The revenue officers were therefore called upon to ascertain and record it. A Chota Nagpur Tenures Act was passed to this effect in 1869. Under this act a Special Commissioner conducted the Bhuinhar Survey which took about a decade to complete. In Bengal and elsewhere, occupancy rights were usually determined by stipulating a period – usually twelve years – in which prescriptive rights accrued to the tenant. In Chota Nagpur the respective officers were originally so confident about finding out about customary tenure that they spurned the idea of resorting to prescription. In the process of recording those rights they found out that it was not at all easy to ascertain those customary rights and the act was amended to allow for a period of twenty years in which prescriptive rights would accrue.

The Bhuinhar Survey had two major flaws. First of all it did not cover the villages in which Mundari Khuntkattidars were still in control. Actually the customary structure of those villages was decaying rapidly and a timely record of rights could have prevented that. Even more disastrous was the second flaw: the act did not provide for a prohibition of alienation of the Bhuinhari land. Once recorded this land became a valuable commodity which would fetch a good price in the market. Instead of preserving tribal rights in land, the act thus facilitated the acquisition of such land by outsiders or by landlords eager to increase their 'bakasht'. Tribal unrest was therefore enhanced rather than curtailed in this way.

In the meantime the frustration of tribal peasants had found a safety valve in increasing migration to the newly established tea plantations of Assam. Many peasants hoped to earn enough money in Assam in order to be able to buy land at home later on. But the main reason for this migration was not this hope but grinding poverty and oppression. Whenever rice prices rose and those who owned no or only a little land could not make both ends meet, the tide of migration increased. In addition to this 'push'-factor which encouraged emigration, there was, of course, also the 'pull'-factor of increasing tea production in Assam. Around 1870 only about 6 mill. kg of tea had been produced there, this increased to about 41 mill. kg in 1900 and about 80 mill. kg in 1930. The Census of 1901 recorded a migration to Assam from all districts of Chota Nagpur of about 1,80,000 labourers, according to the Census of 1921, there were 3,08,000 at that time of which 1,34,000 came from Ranchi district which probably had always contributed the major share of the migrants. At the end of the nineteenth century, the newly opened mines of the Jharia coalfield in what is now Dhanbad district provided jobs closer to Ranchi, but the Mundas did not like to work underground, whereas the Santals did not mind to do that and eagerly flocked to the mines.

Just like the Santals had petitioned the government before starting their 'Hul', the Mundas also did so and even sent delegations to Calcutta. Sometimes they were taken advantage of by clever Bengali lawyers who collected their fees without being able to help the Mundas. One such lawyer even introduced a fake Lieutenant Governor to the gullible Mundas who duly promised to remove their grievances.

Unlike the Santals who had hardly any education and no European friends, the Mundas resorted to the European missionaries, attended their schools and tried to enlist their support for their cause. The missionaries had come to the tribal region to make converts and not in order to support agrarian movements. Their reactions were mixed at best when their flock turned to them for help against the landlords. Some refused to have anything to do with this problem, others took note of it and supported the petitions to government. The Mundas finally realized that they had to rely on their own strength, but Christianity did provide them with a new type of solidarity which they needed because their customary tribal solidarity crumbled under the impact of British law. As one British officer observed: 'They go up to the Ranchi Mission . . . and they return with their hair puritanically cropped, and ready to assert their rights and defy their landlords'. Further reports indicate that it was not even necessary to go to the mission for a haircut, the new converts eagerly cut the hair of their neighbours at home. The old tribal solidarity was thus revived in terms of a new solidarity of Christian 'Roundheads'.

BIRSA'S REBELLION AND THE CHOTA NAGPUR TENANCY ACT

The missionary schools produced a new generation of Munda rebels who only needed a leader to raise the banner of violent revolt. They found this leader in Birsa Munda whose father was a teacher in a mission school and who had himself attended such a school. He was a charismatic leader who told his followers not to be afraid of British guns as their bullets would turn into water. In doing this he spread the same message which rebellious tribesmen in East Africa eagerly followed only a few years later in the famous 'Maji-Maji'-rebellion against German colonial rule. 'Maji' means water and the Africans trusted that their battle cry would convert bullets into water, just as Birsa's followers did. But in both instances the rebels were mowed down mercilessly and the colonial rulers could proudly proclaim that they had restored 'law and order'.

Just like after the 'Santal Hul', the British administrators reacted to Birsa's rebellion of 1899 by adopting remedial measures. In this case new administrative structures would not suffice, legislation was required which would change the law of landlord and tenant in accordance with local conditions. This was very difficult, because Bengal precedent had accentuated the role of the civil courts. They could deal with individual rights but not with the group rights of tribal communities. The alternative was that of entrusting the British revenue officer with greater powers of protecting tribal custom. It took the British several years and acrimonious debates among different schools of thought before they introduced the Chota Nagpur Tenancy Act of 1908. A first attempt of 1903 failed, because the Act passed at that time had obvious flaws. It had provided for the protection of the rights of Mundari Khuntkattidars which were made inalienable. But Bhuinhari land could still be alienated as before. The contentious issue of the reclaiming of rice terraces by the peasants was not settled by this Act. The Act did make adequate provisions for the commutation of the demand for forced labour into the payment of reasonable fees to be added to the rent. But the Act did not stop the civil courts from issuing decrees in favour of the landlords which practically torpedoed the new legislation.

The new act of 1908 plugged these loopholes by giving even more powers to the revenue officer. As the last great Tenancy Act of British India which could draw on the precedent of such legislation in other provinces passed in the preceding decades, the Chota Nagpur Act had the greatest affinity with the Central Provinces Tenancy Act of 1898 which was the very opposite of the Bengal Tenancy Act of 1885. The Central Provinces Act was the acme of tenancy protection under administrative tutelage, whereas the Bengal Act continued the tradition of entrusting the civil courts with holding the balance between landlord and tenant. The crucial provision of the Bengal Act of 1885 which limited rent enhancements for occupancy ryots to a maximum of 12 per cent after a period of fifteen years, i.e. less than 1 per cent per year, was not included in the Chota Nagpur Act. The landlords of Chota Nagpur had submitted to the dictatorship of the revenue officer enshrined in the Chota Nagpur Act, because they had been assured that the revenue authorities would be more flexible in adjusting rent to rising prices. On the other hand they had to acquiesce in a firmer protection of their tribal tenants. In a way this Act did for Chota Nagpur after Birsa's rebellion what the creation of the Santal Parganas had done for that area after the Santal Hul.

The inalienability of tribal land and the special powers of the revenue officer survived in the Jharkhand region even after India achieved independence. This has sometimes tempted the respective officers to use their administrative discretion in a way not quite intended by the Act. But it did serve the purpose of restoring 'law and order'.

ZAMINDARS, MINES AND PEASANTS IN MANBHUM (DHANBAD DISTRICT)

So far agrarian relations in Ranchi, Singhbhum and the Santal Parganas have been discussed here. We shall now turn to another area which was not affected by tribal unrest, but showed some rather peculiar features as far as agrarian relations were concerned. At present this area is characterized by the Jharia coalfield, the great Sindri Fertilizer complex and Dhanbad as a major administrative centre. The British referred to this area as 'Jungle Mahals' when they first encountered it. Later on it was called Manbhum district. The whole district consisted of a few large zamindari estates. These zamindars had been recognised as such even in Mughal times, they claimed to be Rajputs and called themselves Rajas. They practised linear primogeniture and their estates were regarded as impartible and inalienable. The British accepted this and tried to preserve these estates. The Rajas were not 'improving landlords' and loved feudal splendour. Like the Raja of Chota Nagpur they also created tenureholders – and they soon enough were heavily indebted to moneylenders who readily provided credit to them on the security of their huge estates. This created a problem for the British rulers. On the one hand they had to uphold British law which protected the creditor, on the other hand they wished to preserve those impartible estates. Thus a Chota Nagpur Encumbered Estates Act was passed in 1876 which empowered the government to entrust such estates to the Court of Wards. A government administrator was appointed who would run the estate until it was free of debt and could be returned to the respective Raja. Very often the Raja encumbered his estate again and the whole procedure was repeated. However, the estates could survive in this way and they still existed when coal was discovered in this area.

Jharkhand is rich in iron ore and coal deposits. Tribal iron smelters had made use of the ore for a long time. In fact, the axes used for clearing the forest of the Gangetic plains and the iron weapons used by the empirebuilders of ancient eastern India were probably produced in Jharkhand. But the tribal iron smelters had always used charcoal which they could produce in abundance in the forests of Jharkhand. Coal was made use of only by the British for their railways and river-steamships and for the jute mills of Calcutta. Initially the Raniganj coalfield in Bengal supplied sufficient coal for this purpose. But as the demand for coal increased and the expanding railway network reached Manbhum in 1884, the first mines of the Jharia coalfield were opened.

Almost everywhere else, subsoil rights are vested in the state, but under the 'Permanent Settlement' even such rights were vested in the zamindar. For some of the Manbhum zamindars, particularly the Rajas of Jharia and Katras, this was a great boon. If they had been entrepreneurs they would have explored this new wealth themselves. But instead of this they admitted British managing agencies as tenure holders who would pay a licence fee to them on the amount of coal raised. The Bengal Coal Co. operating in the Raniganj field had also acquired such agrarian rights and then forced the peasants to work as miners or settled newly recruited miners on service tenures. By the time the Jharia coalfield was opened such arrangements would no longer suffice to cope with the rapidly increasing demand for labour. Migrants would flock to the mines from other parts of Jharkhand. In those days an average of 20,000 coolies from Jharkhand would migrate to the tea plantations of Assam every year. This migration receded somewhat when the mines provided alternative jobs. But, as pointed out earlier, only the Santals did not mind working underground whereas others would only go the the open-cast mines. In the first years of the twentieth century the growth of coal mining soon exceeded the supply of local labour. The managing agents running the mines would employ 'raising contractors' who recruited their own labour force and turned to distant areas for that purpose. From 1905 to 1908 coal production in the Jharia field increased from 3.3 millon tons to more than 7 million tons. The number of miners increased in those years from 40,000 to 70,000. Labour from distant Gorakhpur would then be recruited by the raising contractors.

The large labour force had to be fed and one would have expected that agricultural production in the adjacent area would have been stimulated by this rising demand. But this did not happen at all. The railways brought grain and vegetables from distant places and the agricultural production in the area close to the coalfield declined instead of increasing. This was due to the fact that peasants would prefer temporary work in the mines to their work in the villages. There was a special feature of the coalfield which encouraged this shift from one type of work to the other. There were many open-cast mines where the work was not unlike that of making rice terraces. Anybody could come and extract some coal and would be paid accordingly.

The coalfield thus became an enclave with only marginal relations with the area where it was located. Mineowners and miners, food suppliers and merchants were all outsiders, except for the casual workers mentioned above. Only the Rajas of Jharia and Katras were really benefited by all this, but they wasted their income from coal royalties by indulging in conspicuous consumption. They built splendid palaces and bought expensive cars. At the most they hired some more local servants, but otherwise they created no additional employment. Rural Jharkhand would not have lost anything if the coalfield enclave had suddenly vanished. There was hardly any change in these conditions in subsequent decades except for the fact that the wealth of the zamindars disappeared.

KAMIAUTI: A SPECIAL KIND OF AGRARIAN RELATIONS IN WESTERN JHARKHAND

The north-western rim of the Chota Nagpur Plateau from Hazaribagh to the river Son had come under the influence of the agriculturists of the Gangetic plains much earlier than the southern and eastern parts of Jharkhand. Enterprising warriors, including Rajputs, Pathans and other north Indian communities had ventured into the 'jungle' and had established themselves as 'maliks'. They spread irrigated rice cultivation, but for this they required labour. Elsewhere, as for instance in Ranchi, tribal people had themselves adopted rice cultivation and had turned into settled peasants. The rise of the Mundari khuntkattidars is a good example of this process. But this did not happen in Hazaribagh and Palamau. Here the tribal people were so to speak 'de-tribalised' and converted into low caste serfs (kamias) under the control of the 'maliks' who literally 'lorded it over' these poor people. This was a gradual process spread over several centuries.

The Bhuinyas who lived in these areas were such low caste labourers whose communal memory reflected their peculiar relationship with the maliks. Their mythical ancestor, Tulsi Bir (bir = hero), according to their legend followed the request of a malik to repair a breached embankment which nobody else could do. Thousands of villages and innumerable maunds of paddy would have been lost. But Tulsi Bir managed to close the breach and was praised for it. Subsequently, however, he experienced a polluting encounter which depressed him to the lowest strata of the caste hierarchy. This myth portrays in a nutshell the emergence of the special agrarian relationship between low caste kamia and high caste malik and the crucial maintenance of embankments which are necessary for irrigated rice cultivation. The name of the mythical ancestor being derived from the sacred tulsi plant shows that he was a Hindu and no longer a tribesman. At the same time the myth mirrors the interdependence of malik and kamia. The malik can tell the kamia to repair the embankment, but he would be lost without his strength and skill.

In pre-colonial times when labour was scarce, the kamia was in a relatively good bargaining position. The ploughing and harvesting of the rice fields was very labour intensive but it was limited to a few months in the year. During the off-season the kamia had to rely on the support of the malik who had a natural interest in maintaining his labour force. In a region where rice cultivation was rather precarious, this patron-client relationship was of mutual advantage.

When population increased and the British colonial rulers determined the rules of agrarian relations, the bond between malik and kamia was redefined in contractual terms. The malik was conceived of as a creditor and the kamia as an indebted 'bonded' labourer. Such contractual bonds were actually executed and served as legal instruments which colonial courts could handle. The customary advances given to the kamia, particularly at marriage, were construed as 'loans'. As the kamia did not repay such 'loans' he was kept in debt bondage forever.

When kamiauti acquired these new features, it did become what it was supposed to be – a system of debt bondage. Even rich peasants whose caste status was not much higher than that of the kamias could become maliks by means of the cash nexus. In a way this type of arrangement mimicked the evolution of capitalist agriculture in which the landlord cultivates his fields with hired labour. The difference was, of course, that the capitalist landlord would have to pay competitive wages to free labour whereas the keeper of kamias could dictate his terms to 'bonded' labour. Laws were passed to break this bondage, but the kamias rarely availed themselves of these legal remedies, because they were too poor to get along without their malik.

The striking peculiarities of kamiauti which were so characteristic for Western Jharkhand should not detract from the fact that it was not as widepread as it appeared to be. In 1920 about 9 per cent of the population of Palamau were kamias. But their number did not decrease in subsequent years. Under the impact of the depression of the 1930s indebted peasants who had lost their land to their creditors joined the ranks of the kamias.

ECOLOGICAL CONDITIONS, POPULATION PRESSURE AND AGRARIAN RELATIONS

The Chota Nagpur Plateau did not provide much scope for agricultural growth. Rice cultivation was precarious and required terracing which was labour intensive. Nevertheless population increased in this region as it did everywhere else in India. As has been discussed in detail, agrarian relations in many instances encouraged exploitation rather than equitable development. This turned the region into a supplier of migrant labour. The remittances of the migrants which flowed into Chota Nagpur helped to keep the families alive whom they had left in their villages, but they certainly did not amount to a transfer of capital which was invested in the improvement of local agriculture.

The rich natural resources of the region were exploited by outsiders. With very few exceptions they were sent out of the region and helped to develop industry elsewhere. In most parts of the world coalfields attract industry as the transport of coal for the generation of energy or the smelting of iron is more expensive than the transport of other inputs for industrial production. But this did not happen here. The Jharia coalfield did not become an industrial centre. The only exception was Tata Iron and Steel Co. (TISCO) at Jamshedpur in Singhbhum which made use of the local iron ore deposits and of some of the coal mined in deep-shaft mines in the Jharia field which was suitable for being converted into coking coal for the TISCO-furnaces. But in terms of employment the steel mill at Jamshedpur did not make much of a difference to the labour market of this region. Most of the skilled labour was recruited elsewhere. But at least this modern industrial centre was a beacon of hope for this otherwise extremely poor area.

BIBLOGRAPHY

Biswas, A.K., *Understanding Bihar*, Delhi: Blumoon Books, 1998.

Bradley-Birt, F., *Chota Nagpore: A Little Known Province of the Empire*, London: Smith, Eldes & Co., 1903.

Macpherson, T.S. and M.G. Hallett, *Ranchi (Bihar and Orissa Gazetteers)*, Patna: Government Printing Press, 1917.

Prakash, Gyan, *Bonded Histories: Genealogies of Labour Servitude in Colonial India,* Cambridge: Cambridge University Press, 1990.

Rothermund, D., *Government, Landlord and Peasant in India: Agrarian Relations under British Rule, 1865-1935*, Wiesbaden: Steiner, 1978.

Rothermund, D. and D.C. Wadhwa, eds., *Zamindars, Mines and Peasants: Studies in the History of an Indian Coalfield*, Delhi: Manohar, 1978.

Rothermund, D., E. Kropp and G. Dienemann, *Urban Growth and Rural Stagnation: Studies in the Economy of an Indian Coalfield and its Hinterland,* Delhi: Manohar, 1980.

Roy Choudhury, P.C., *1857 in Bihar (Chotanagpur and Santhal Parganas)*, Patna: Government Printing Press, 1959.

Singh, K.S., *Duststorm and Hanging Mist*, Calcutta: K.L. Mukhopadhyaya, 1966.

Schwerin, D., *Von Armut zu Elend. Kolonialherrschaft und Agrarverfassung in Chota Nagpur, 1858-1908*, Wiesbaden: Steiner, 1977.

CHAPTER 7

The Self-consciousness of Post-Imperial Nations: A Cross-national Comparison*

INTRODUCTION: THE SPECTRUM OF SELF-CONSCIOUSNESS

Gordon Brown made a speech in Tanzania before he became Prime Minister, in which he asserted that the times when the British had to apologize for their colonial rule are over.[1] This was a self-conscious statement. You become self-conscious when you feel that you are under scrutiny. In such a situation you may remain quiet and introspective or adopt a defiant posture preempting whatever criticism you expect. Post-imperial nations often have such feelings with regard to their colonial past. Of course, the majority of the respective nations may have no such feelings at all. These nations tend to suffer from a general amnesia concerning their colonial past. But the political elite articulates such self-consciousness – as Gordon Brown did in Tanzania.

The academic elite, however, is affected by another type of self-consciousness which expresses itself in terms of post-colonial sensibilities. Scholars nowadays wish to avoid the hegemonic discourse emanating from the metropolitan centres of power. The beginnings of this sensibility can be traced to Edward Said's analysis of 'Orientalism'. He had shown that Orientalist scholarship of imperial nations had served the purpose of defining and controlling the 'Oriental' – a subtle power game played by academics who pretended to study the 'Orient' in an objective manner. Ever since the publication of Said's book,[2] Western scholars who deal with non-Western societies have become extremely self-conscious about their work. Do they unwittingly

*The author wishes to thank the following colleagues who commented on an earlier draft of this paper: Margaret Frenz, Olivier Le Cour Grandmaison, Gert Oostindie, Antonio Costa Pinto, Wolfgang Schwentker, Jean-Luc Vellut.

follow a hegemonic discourse? Have they really done justice to the subject they study? In the meantime post-colonial studies have projected a discourse of their own in which terms like 'hybridity', 'de-centering' , 'asymmetry', etc., play an important role. Post-colonial studies are prominent in the anglo-saxon sphere, they are less conspicuous elsewhere. There are also differences with regard to academic disciplines in this respect. Studies of literature are in the vanguard of this new field because literary texts lend themselves to 'discourse analysis'. 'Self-conscious' scholarship of this kind sometimes becomes somewhat esoteric, but it is certainly a useful antidote to the self-confident 'hegemonic' pronouncements of earlier days.

Another type of self-consciousness has arisen from the encounter of European nations with ex-colonial immigrants who have settled in great numbers in European countries. These encounters are not a matter of academic sensibility but are part and parcel of everyday life. To the extent that these immigrants form identifiable communities they induce a self-consciousness of distinctiveness or even hostility – the 'us' and 'them' confrontation. This phenomenon is highly differentiated according to the variety of national policies and the intensity of migration. In the six national case studies which follow, this phenomenon will be highlighted. It has made a greater impact only in recent years and has contributed to a new self-consciousness concerning the colonial past. Much that had remained dormant in the years after 'decolonization' has suddenly become a matter of public debate.

A comparison of six nations in terms of post-imperial self-consciousness faces many problems. The starting point of comparison is the shared experience of post-war decolonization. But this experience was highly differentiated both in time and space as well as in terms of the national policies followed. 'Shared experience' is therefore a misnomer. In fact, even at present the six nations discussed here know very little about their respective experiences. Public debates on the consequences of the colonial past are hardly taken note of even in neighbouring countries. The problems discussed here are eminently 'national'. For this reason the comparison attempted here has been called a 'cross-national' one. 'Trans-national'[3] would imply that the matters dicussed transcend national boundaries, and 'international' refers to the intercourse of nations with each other – therefore these terms were not adopted for the present study.

Two nations have been omitted from this study: Germany and

Italy. The German colonies were lost after the First World War and German reactions to this loss were confined to the inter-war period. After the Second World War Germany was concerned with internal problems. Only in recent years some German historians have delved into German colonial history once more. But their findings have hardly interested the German public. Italy lost its colonies after the Second World War and it should have been discussed here. But studying six cases was difficult enough, therefore Italy has been neglected here.

GREAT BRITAIN: INDIFFERENCE AND AMBIVALENCE

Great Britain had by far the largest empire and apparently decolonized it rather smoothly after the Second World War. Prime Minister Macmillan who had to deal with this process of decolonization did not think that it was a rather smooth one. He once said that it was much more difficult to get rid of an empire than to build one.[4] The British political leaders who had to do this difficult job were helped by two phenomena which reduced national resistance to the loss of empire. There was first of all a widespread national indifference with regard to the empire. Public opinion polls conducted in 1948 and in 1997 showed more or less the same degree of glaring ignorance of the empire and of the colonial past.[5] Dealing with the empire had always been left to the 'Establishment' which included the colonial administrators, the civil servants at home and the political elite. They shared more or less the same social and educational background. The Establishment was neither ignorant nor indifferent as far as the empire was concerned, but its attitude to the empire after the war showed a high degree of ambivalence. There was a mixture of realism and delusion. Granting independence to India in 1947 was due to a realistic assessment of the situation. India had changed from a debtor into a creditor of Great Britain after the war.[6] Two million Indian soldiers had been enlisted during the war and the majority of them had to be demobilized immediately after the war. Continuing to rule India would have been an impossible task. A 'Transfer of Power' was necessary – and it was achieved and celebrated as such – conveniently forgetting the tragedy of the partition. The British saw to it that shortly before becoming independent, India granted a moratorium to them. India did not claim the reserves accumulated during the war immediately as this would have driven Great Britain into bankruptcy.

Inspite of the realism shown by the British Establishment in this case, there was also a great deal of imperial delusion. In 1948 Parliament passed a Nationality Act which granted the right of citizenship to all people of the empire.[7] This has to be understood in the context of the support of the Commonwealth of Nations into which the empire was supposed to be converted. The British King/ Queen remained the head of the Commonwealth and although India had become a republic in 1950 it remained in the Commonwealth. This flexibility was adopted so as to preserve the illusion of post-imperial unity. In subsequent years this illusion was wearing thin, but it helped to soften the blow of the loss of empire.

The empire had been a green pasture for the British elite. Careers were made in imperial service and there were many British families which produced veritable dynasties of colonial civil servants.[8] After the loss of empire, the British Establishment was no longer able to absorb all educated young men and it was then subjected to criticism which became more and more virulent. The young playwright John Osborne was just 26 years old in 1956, when his play *Look Back in Anger* became a huge success in London. It became emblematic for the 'angry young men' of that time.[9] The impotent rage of the main character in this play reflected their feelings. Osborne made him say: 'The people of our generation are not able to die for good causes any longer. There aren't any good causes left.' In the same year when this play was staged, Prime Minister Eden, a quintessential representative of the Establishment, implicated Great Britain in the disastrous Suez affair which sounded the death knell of the British role as a 'great power'. Under American pressure, Eden had to resign and his cabinet colleague Macmillan became Prime Minister. Inspite of the Suez disaster he led his Conservative Party to an astounding victory in the elections of 1959.[10] This enabled him to go ahead with decolonization in Africa at a rapid pace in 1960.

Macmillan's fame diminished subsequently and he was ridiculed by young comedians who ushered in a veritable boom of satire in the 1960s. The rage of the 'angry young men' had turned into the sardonic humour of 'Beyond the Fringe'.[11] In a more serious vein, contemporary authors addressed the question 'What's Wrong with Britain?' *The Stagnant Society* by Michael Shanks appeared in 1961.[12] Its title became emblematic for this period. At the end of the 1960s an alarming voice attracted attention: Enoch Powell. This highly intelligent man was a professor of classical languages and had his eyes on becoming a Viceroy of India in his youth. He became an ardent critic of the delusions of empire and wanted to combat the prevailing ambivalence. He saw Britain as a homogenous nation and wanted to restrict immigration. In his sensational 'rivers of blood' – speech he warned against racial conflicts.[13]

Powell's bloodcurdling intervention highlighted the new type of British self-consciousness precipitated by an increasing wave of immigration. As mentioned earlier, the 1948 Nationality Act was practically an invitation to all empire citizens to come and settle in Great Britain. By 1961 about 1,00,000 immigrants arrived annually, most of them coloured people. Successive governments had considered amending the Nationality Act but hesitated to include racial criteria. When a new Commonwealth Immigration Act was finally passed in 1962 it tried to avoid racial criteria by making immigration dependent on employment permits.[14] There was no limit for general permits, only those for unskilled jobs were limited. In this way one hoped to keep out coloured migrants without adopting racial criteria. This proved to be insufficient and in 1968 a new Act was introduced. The aim of this Act was to keep 'Asians' out who lived in Africa but held British passports and could use them for coming to Britain. Again open racial restrictions were avoided by making previous British family connections a criterion for admission. In 1971 the Act was further amended by defining the family connections as 'patrial' and in a new Act of 1981 this was narrowed down to those whose parents or grandparents had been born in Great Britain.[15] The laws governing immigration had thus come closer and closer to Powell's idea of preserving a homogenous British nation without mentioning race as a criterion of exclusion.

While this helped to stem the tide of immigration, it did not diminish the large number of immigrants who had settled in Great Britain in the meantime. Several million people from Africa and South Asia live in Great Britain now, among them many members of the second generation. In general they have remained peaceful and there is no evidence of Powell's 'rivers of blood'. Of course, these 'coloured' people often congregate in specific suburbs where they live among themselves. Integration cannot be achieved in this way, but perhaps the 'homogenous' British population prefers to live at some distance from the immigrants without much intermixing.

As a strange irony of fate, the issue of citizenship caught up with the British and forced them to wage their last imperial war over the Falklands Islands in 1982. The few thousand inhabitants of those islands are British citizens and want to remain British and not join Argentina. Prior to the seizure of the islands by Argentina all kinds of compromises had been discussed, e.g. the British could transfer the sovereignty over the islands to Argentina and then arrange for a 99-years lease. The government of Argentina obviously presumed that the British would not wage a war for retaining the islands, but Britain was forced to protect its citizens and thus the war became inevitable. It was accompanied by some unfortunate imperial jingoism. But Mrs. Thatcher's government profited from taking a stand and winning the war.[16]

In a way this war compensated for British impotence in dealing with Southern Rhodesia where the white minority had seized power by means of a Unilateral Declaration of Independence in 1965. There were demands for a British military intervention, but the British government did not want to take the risk. Ian Smith, the leader of the white minority, managed to defy the British government for a long time.[17] In 1980 free elections led to the victory of Rob Mugabe who was then involved in a civil war against his African rivals which came to an end only in 1987. Thus ended the most controversial chapter of British decolonization.

By now, the British empire is only an object of nostalgia, particularly with regard to the British Raj in India. An exhibition entitled 'The Raj: India and the British, 1600-1947' was shown in the National Portrait Gallery in 1990 which also produced a magnificent catalogue[18] edited by Sir Christopher Bayly who holds the Chair of Imperial and Naval History at Cambridge University. About 80,000 people visited this exhibition which was generally well received.[19] A decade later Britain could have celebrated the Fourth Centenary of the founding of the East India Company, but instead of a public celebration the British Library only organized an exhibition concerning the East India trade without any trace of imperial triumphalism.

THE NETHERLANDS: CELEBRATION AND APOLOGY

Dutch self-consciousness about the imperial past of the Netherlands is somewhat different from that shown by the British. This is due to the fact that the decolonization of that empire was beset with problems which the British did not have to face. After recovering from Nazi occupation, the Dutch considered it to be a matter of national honour to recover their empire. This led to a protracted war with the Republic of Indonesia proclaimed in 1945 when the Japanese left Indonesia.[20] The bitterness of this war later on caused the Indonesians to break off all contacts with the Dutch and also to eradicate all traces of the Dutch language which had once been the language of instruction for the Indonesian elite. In the tortuous process of Indonesian decolonization, the Dutch had conceived of a Union which was supposed to encompass the Netherlands and their colonial empire.[21] The Indonesians had rejected this Union but it did survive in the West Indies, i.e. Suriname and some small Caribbean Islands. Just like the British with their Nationality Act of 1948, the Union granted citizenship rights to those remaining within it. This was bound to cause some embarrassment to the Dutch later on.

Dutch Guyana (Suriname) was a multi-ethnic colony. Initially it was a destination for African slaves. After the abolition of slavery, Indian indentured labour was imported and when that system ended, the Dutch brought Javanese labourers from Indonesia. By 1941 the colony had about 1,80,000 inhabitants of whom 70,000 were of African descent, 50,000 of Indian descent and 35,000 of Javanese origin.[22] Initially the political relations between these ethnic communities were fairly harmonious but this changed when the Dutch practically imposed independence on Suriname in 1975. The reason for this course of events was that the Dutch had been forced to suppress violent labour unrest in their Caribbean colony Curacao in 1969 at the request of the local government. The Netherlands got a bad press for this intervention which was interpreted as a relapse into imperialism. Therefore a decision was made to get rid of these troublesome vestiges of colonialism. Actually the Dutch were stuck with the small islands whose inhabitants did not want to be decolonized, but they did manage to push Suriname into independence. When the communities which were not of Afro-American origin realized that they would be dominated by the Afro-American majority, there was a sudden exodus to the Netherlands, because everybody was afraid that the Dutch might soon revoke the right of citizenship which guaranteed free access to the 'home'-country.[23] Many people of Afro-American descent also joined this exodus. Thus the Netherlands had to face the sudden immigration of about 1,00,000 people. Afro-

Americans from the small Caribbean islands which remained colonies by their own choice also used their free access to the 'home'-country to a significant extent. The Netherlands already hosted another ethnic minority, about 50,000 people of Moluccan descent, who had played a role similar to that of the 'harkis' of Algeria in Indonesia. More about the 'harkis' will be said later on. The Moluccans in the Netherlands had some angry young men among them who staged violent protests, whereas the people from Suriname and the Caribbean islands did not cause much trouble. But they did emerge as a community to which Dutch politicians had to pay some attention.

The differences in political self-consciousness with regard to such contrasting aspects of the Dutch imperial legacy was strikingly demonstrated in very recent times by two public events. In 2002 the Netherlands celebrated the Fourth Centenary of the foundation of the Dutch East India Company with pomp and circumstance.[24] This was in contrast with the low-key British commemoration of the East India trade mentioned earlier. Indonesia resented this celebration, but it seems that the Dutch government did not feel that it had to listen to Indonesia in this matter. In the same year the Dutch publicly apologized for their participation in the Atlantic slave trade. A monument commemorating the sufferings of the slaves was inaugurated in Amsterdam.[25] The solicitude for the establishment of this momnment was obviously due to the strong support for this gesture by the West Indies minority in the Netherlands.

The Dutch are proud of their tolerance and in general the immigrant communities have lived well in the Netherlands. But there are radical currents just below the placid surface which can occasionally erupt and create a public stir. This was shown by the political career of Pim Fortuyn who attracted great attention before the elections of 2002. He was a professor of sociology who in his younger years had taught Marxism and had sympathized with the Communist Party. He had later veered to the right and led a small party of his own. He attacked Islam and also sneered at those who campaigned for the protection of animals. A militant animal rights activist shot Fortuyn before the elections of 2002 in which his party then won many seats and was even included in the government coalition. This party then disintegrated very soon. Fortuyn had flashed like a meteor accross the political sky of the Netherlands. Fortunately there has been so far no repetition of this kind of fireworks.

BELGIUM: HAUNTED BY KING LEOPOLD'S GHOST

Neighbouring Belgium has hardly taken any notice of Dutch problems concerning the imperial past and it has also tended to forget its own past in this respect. The number of immigrants from ex-colonial countries in Belgium is relatively limited. Thousands of people from Rwanda, Burundi and the Congo have attained Belgian citizenship but they do not constitute a politically relevant minority. Thus a political element is missing here which has been so important in Great Britain and the Netherlands – and also in France as we shall see.

There has been a great deal of solid historical research by Belgian scholars in which also the negative aspects of Belgian colonial rule have been shown.[26] Unfortunately nobody in Belgium took much interest in this kind of academic work. Jean-Luc Vellut who held the only chair of African history in Belgium (at the university of Louwen La Neuve) published several pioneering studies in this field and also trained young Congolese historians. But when he retired, his chair was abolished which obviously shows the indifference of his university to this subject.

The Belgian public was shocked when an American writer, Adam Hochschild, published a book with the title *King Leopold's Ghost* in 1998 in which he highlighted the 'Congo atrocities' which had been revealed by American and British missionaries and other observers at the end of the nineteenth century.[27] At that time the Belgian public had become used to the denial of these atrocities, a denial which became an integral part of Belgian nationalist ideology in earlier years. In recent years Belgian researchers had fully documented these atrocities and Hochschild´s book was based on their research and did not contain anything new. But his book became a bestseller and a film and a television show were based on this. Ever since, the Belgium people have been haunted by King Leopold's ghost and this has given rise to a self-consciousness of a special kind. In 2005 an impressive exhibition on 'The Memory of the Congo: The Colonial Era' was shown by the Royal Museum of Central Africa at Tervuren in Belgium. Jean-Luc Vellut acted as an advisor and edited the catalogue of the exhibition.[28] Taken by itself this was quite a courageous and innovative venture of confronting the Belgian people with their colonial past. It did not exclude the negative aspects such as the brutal system of forced labour and even provided estimates of the loss of human lives due to this system. But, of course, some of those who had read Hochschild's book found this exhibition somewhat apologetic. Hochschild himself reviewed the exhibition in the epilogue to the second edition of his book and criticized its understatements. It seems that he had expected an exhibition which would serve as an illustration of the arguments presented in his book. Perhaps these controversies helped to attract more visitors to the exhibition. The organizers had expected only about 70,000 visitors and were surprised when this figure was nearly doubled.[29]

Soon after King Leopold had started to haunt the Belgians, the fate of another political figure had come into the limelight of public consciousness: Patrice Lumumba, the first Prime Minister of the independent Congo, who had been assassinated in January 1961. In 1999 the Belgian sociologist, Ludo De Witte, had published his account of Lumumba's assassination in which he had clearly established Belgian complicity in this murder.[30] This had created such a stir that the Belgian Parliament had ordered a commission of enquiry into this matter. The verdict of this commission confirmed De Witte's arguments to a large extent. Although the commission denied official Belgian complicity in the murder of Lumumba it recognized the part played by individual Belgian citizens and the moral responbility of officials who did not try to prevent the murder. So here was another ghost to haunt the Belgians. Presumably these two experiences gave rise to a Belgian self-consiousness about their country's colonial past and put an end to the amnesia which had prevailed in earlier years. But it is difficult to assess this at present.

FRANCE: 'LA FRACTURE COLONIALE'

The present French state, the Fifth Republic, arose from the turmoil of the Algerian war. The powerful position given to General De Gaulle as President in 1958 has continued to shape French politics until today. The wounds inflicted by this war have also been festering ever since. France is not only a post-imperial nation, it is even more poignantly a 'post-Algerian' nation. De Gaulle decolonized the French possessions in Africa with breathtaking speed in 1960. The mandate which he had received from the French people enabled him to do this almost unchallenged.[31] He set the pace for the British in this way as Macmillan's 'Wind of Change' followed close on the heels of De Gaulle's African whirlwind. But it was far more difficult for De Gaulle to put an end to the Algerian war. Many French were passionately attached to Algeria. When I visited Paris as a student in 1955, I saw the slogan 'L'Algerie francaise' on many walls. Talking to a young French student at that time, I told him that this cannot go on much longer. He reluctantly agreed and then said mournfully: "C'est la decadence de la France". I did not know at that time – and I guess he did not know either – that the great French political thinker, Alexis de Toqueville, had used the very same words when he stressed more than one hundred years earlier that France should never give up Algeria.

The Algerian war was faught with great brutality on both sides. The French tortured may Algerians and even today this war is remembered in France for this torture. More than 3,00,000 young Frenchmen were sent to fight in Algeria, among them Jacques Chirac who later on became President of France and asserted that he had done his duty in that war. De Gaulle faced stiff resistance and even had to put down a mutiny of some French officers before he finally ended the war in 1962. Negotations were held with a provisional Algerian government in Evian in France in that year. The agreement which was signed in March 1962 seemed to satisfy both sides.[32] Unfortunately the provisional government soon collapsed in Algeria – and with it all the guarantees which it had given to the French. The military dictator, Houari Boumedienne, seized power and unleashed a reign of terror and revenge. It was an irony of fate, that Boumedienne and his troops had been spared the ravages of war and could only now play a role in independent Algeria. These Algerian nationalist troops had been stationed in neighbouring Tunisia and throughout the war the French had prevented them from crossing the border.[33] Since the Evian agreement was by now a dead letter, 1.6 million French settlers fled from Algeria to France. These so called 'pieds noirs' had to be re-settled in France and in due course they emerged as a group with some political clout.

While the French government had to receive the 'pieds noirs', another group of refugees was not at all welcome: the 'Harkis', i.e Algerian soldiers serving as auxiliaries in the French army.[34] The French officers had instructions to disarm them before leaving for France and to leave them to the tender mercies of the Algerians. About 1,00,000 or more of these soldiers and their families were exterminated by the Algerians. Approximately an equal number of Harkis and their families managed to flee to France although secret insructions had been issued by the French government to turn them back if they were apprehended. This was not easy, so finally the government had come to terms with these refugees many of whom were interned in old military camps. They were not the only Algerians who managed to get to France. Even during the war, many Algerian workers had come to France and this stream of migration continued after Algeria had attained independence.

The French call the thirty years after 1945 the 'Glorious Years' (Trente glorieuses). These were the years of reconstruction and rapid economic growth. It was the old type of growth which required plenty of workers, among them many unskilled ones. The labour market could absorb many immigrants, but this was no longer possible when the industrial economy experienced a structural change in the subsequent decades. By now the second generation of the immigrants had grown up. Many of them felt rejected by the majority and stressed their own identity. The term 'beur' (a slang word for Arab) became current in the 1980s for the people of this second generation. A group inspired by Martin Luther King and Gandhi organized a long march for equality in 1983 which became known as 'Marche des Beurs'.[35] Only a few people started from Marseilles in October 1983, their ranks swelled when they reached Lyon and by the time they arrived in Paris in December about 60,000 'Beurs' assembled there and President Mitterand met their leaders. He promised to grant them permits of residence for 10 years and also said that he would think about their rights to vote. Ever since, many Beurs have been active in politics but only very few got elected. The economic position of this minority did not improve. The identity politics which emerged from this situation was condemned as 'communalism' by the representatives of the majority.

The French republic has always condemned the communalism of minorities, but it has encouraged it by pretending that such minorities do not exist at all because all citizens of France are equal and there is no need to acknowledge minority rights. In 1978 the Italian judge, Francesco Capotorti, was commissioned by the United Nations to prepare a report on minority rights. The answer he received from the French government in the course of his study was characteristic for the French approach to this matter: 'France cannot recognize the existence of ethnic groups, whether minorities or not.'[36] Accordingly the French have always insisted on complete integration of immigrants although in practice these immigrants have often been treated as second class citizens. Moreover, an implicit racism has dominated French immigration policy for along time. Whereas European immigrants could be easily assimilated, African and Asians were better to be kept out of France. There was a great deal of official xenophobia which was backed up by supposedly scientific studies.[37] French colonial policy was a reflection of this attitude. Assimilation was emphasized as the aim of this policy, but in fact the majority of the colonized could never aspire to citizenship rights. In Algeria only about 50,000 indigenous people were granted French citizenship whereas the majority had to live under the discriminatory 'code de indigènat'.[38] This discrimination was so to speak 'cited' by groups of second and third generation immigrants in 2005 who published an 'Appel des indigènes de la Republique' (Appeal of the Natives of the Republic).[39] This appeal emphasized that France has a colonial past which it tends to forget, that it still has some colonies and that it practises discrimination. The appeal also demanded social policies which would benefit the disadvantaged minorities.

It was an irony of fate that soon after this appeal the French Parliament passed a law which stressed the positive effects of French colonial rule particularly in North Africa and even obliged the universities to concentrate on this in their research and teaching. Obviously President Chirac wished to please the 'pieds noirs' and their descendants. This law caused a vigorous public debate, about thousand historians signed a petition for its repeal. It so happened that this law was passed at a time when a renewed interest in the Algerian war had been noticed in France. For a long time this war had officially not been recognized as one, it was only in 1999 that this 'war without a name' was permitted to have its proper name. In the next year the nation was shocked by the memoirs of Louisette Ighilahriz, an Algerian freedom fighter, who had been tied naked to a bed and tortured and raped for several days by French soldiers during the war.[40] A year later a French intelligence officer published his memoirs and openly admitted his participation in Acts of torture in Algeria.[41] While all this referred only to the recent past, Olivier Le Cour Grandmaison showed in his book *'Coloniser. Exterminer. Sur la guerre et l'État colonial'*, that even in the nineteenth century the French had adopted very brutal methods in order to control Algeria. Between 1830 and 1872 the Algerian population of about 3 million had been reduced by about one third. Torture was a standard practice. Even the great Alexis de Toqueville had advocated the brutal suppression of the Algerians in a report for the French government written in 1847.[42] Le Cour Grandmaison's book was published in

2005, a few weeks before the law was passed which obliged historians to study the 'positive' aspects of French rule in North Africa. Presumably none of the legislators had read it.

The year 2005 was a time of great turmoil. At the end of the year there were riots in the suburbs (banlieu) of Paris. Young people left a trail of destruction. Most of them were black and white Christians and not Muslim Beurs. Social marginalization rather than 'communalism' caused these riots. Nicolas Sarkozy who was soon to be President of France made a populist speech in which he threatened to 'flush out' those young people. This perhaps reflected the prevailing mood of the majority but was certainly not a contribution to the solution of the social problems which plagued the ghettoes of the poor.

At the height of the debates of 2005, three French historians edited a book with the provocative title *'La fracture colonial'* (The colonial break).[43] The break which they and their contributors analysed was a multiple one. There was a break between those who adored the colonial past and those who deplored it. There was a break between those who had experienced this past and those who knew nothing about it any longer but had to live with its consequences. Being historians, the editors of this volume advocated a national history which encompasses all aspects of the past and does not hide some of them while highlighting others. They had conducted a kind of opinion poll of their own and were appalled at the evidence of ignorance of the colonial past.[44] This French evidence, by the way, parallels the British evidence mentioned earlier.

'Places of Memory' (Lieux de Memoire) are powerful symbols of a nation's past and they could remind the people of the colonial past. The French historian Pierre Nora has been a pioneer in the field of the retrieval of such places in France, but he had to admit that the colonial past has not played a role in his work. However, the French government has thought of filling this gap with the reconstruction of museums in Paris. At the centre of these initiatives is the former Museum of the Arts of Africa and Oceania. It was opened in 1931 in order to house the great colonial exhibition with which France celebrated its position in this world. Replete with contemporary allegorial art work which showed France dominating Africa and Asia, it must have impressed the 33 million visitors who attended this exhibition in the 1930s. It has now been converted into the 'Cité nationale de l'histoire de le l'immigration' obviously to please those citizens who are immigrants themselves or children of immigrants.[45] It remains to be seen whether this will be accepted as a suitable 'place of memory'.

In 2007 the great orator, Nicolas Sarkozy, has added a new dimension to French post-imperial sensibilities. In a speech in Toulon in February 2007 he provided surprising reasons for his advocacy of a Mediterranean Union. He recalled French greatness in its dealings with that region and mentioned the crusaders, as well as Napoleon and General Lyautey in one breath, asserting that they all had not been interested in conquest but only in the spread of civilization. Those who may have thought that the Mediterranean Union was projected as a partnership would have been struck by Sarkozy's hegemonic discourse. But in December 2007 when making a speech in Constantine, Algeria, Sarkozy asserted that the colonial system was unjust by its very nature.[46] Maybe that post-imperial self-consciousness with extraordinary statesmen like Sarkozy actually turns into schizophrenia.

PORTUGAL: IMPERIAL NOSTALGIA AND LUSOPHONE SOLIDARITY

The Portuguese empire was huge as compared to Portugal itself. It had once included Brazil, but even in the twentieth century it had enormous dimensions. In 1934 the Portuguese government circulated a map with the caption 'Portugal nao é um país pequeno' (Portugal is not a small country). It showed a map of Europe with Angola and Mozambique projected on it.[47] These two colonies taken together could rival Europe in its dimensions. Actually Portugal regarded its colonies as 'overseas provinces' and thus as integral parts of Portugal. The loss of these 'provinces' would greatly diminish Portugal and as long as the Portuguese dictator Salazar was in power, there was no idea of decolonization, even after all other European nations had disbanded their empires. Salazar's intransigence exasperated the Indian government which had to tolerate the Portuguese enclaves of Goa, Daman and Diu on its soil. African nationalists taunted Nehru for this 'tolerance' and finally Indian troops occupied these territories in December 1961.[48] Salazar had to accept this defeat, but he tried to ignore it. Representatives of Goa sat in the imperial parliament long after India had taken over this territory.

Attributing the longevity of Portugal's empire to Salazar's strong political will probably gives too much credit to him. Boaventura de Sousa Santos has argued that the Portuguese colonial empire was a subaltern one, always subjected to British hegemonic power.[49] This hegemonic position was taken up by the NATO of which Salazar's Portugal was a trusted member. At the time when other colonial empires were dismantled while the Cold War created new problems in Africa, the Portuguese empire served as a useful proxy. But this also depended on Portugal's ability to control its colonies which became more and more difficult. Colonial resistance flared up in the African territories in the 1960s. Guinea-Bissau set the pace under the able leadership of Dr. Amilcar Cabral, a disciplined revolutionary who managed to liberate most of this colony by the end of 1964. In 1965 he visited Cuba and since then Castro got deeply involved with the wars in Portuguese Africa. Cabral was grateful for Castro's help but did not wish to acknowledge it openly – and Castro was discreet and kept a low profile.[50] Cabral was assassinated in 1973 at the time when General Spinola was Governor of Guinea-Bissau. But Cabral's followers continued the war very successfully and Spinola was so disillusioned by the course of this colonial war that he became an advocate of decolonization.[51] In the meantime a group of young Portuguese officers who had fought in Africa had secretely formed a 'Group of Captains' which then turned into the Movimento de Forcas Armadas (Movement of the Armed Forces = MFA).

The careers of two officers who led this movement, Ernesto Melo Antunes and Otelho Sarvaia de Carvalho, reflected the typical experience of their generation. Antunes grew up in Angola where his father served as a military officer, Carvalho was born and brought up in Mozambique.[52] Both loved the countries in which they had grown up and were convined that the wars in which they had to fight there had to come to an end. These two men had very different temperaments. Antunes was a taciturn scholar in uniform, responsible for the ideology of the movement which was summarized as 'democratize, decolonize, develop'. He later on conducted most of the negotations with African leaders. Carvalho was a charismatic leader who headed the MFA when it seized power on 25 April 1974. He later on drifted to the left and spent many years in prison. But in the early days of the revolution he was a powerful figure. The bloodless coup of April 1974 became known as the 'Carnation Revolution'. The carnations were just then blossoming in Portugal and a young girl stuck a carnation into the barrel of the gun of a soldier. This caught on and soon all guns were decorated with carnations. But after the carnations withered away, the revolution got into trouble. Struggles for power had erupted and it took some time before Portugal attained political stability.

On the day of the revolution, Salazar's successor Caetano had abdicated and had handed over power to General Spinola. The officers of the MFA accepted him although they did not sympathize with him.[53] But at that time he was the most obvious choice. Three days after the revolution, Mario Soares, the exiled leader of the Socialist Party had returned home. Spinola made him Foreign Minister and he tried his best to get ahead with decolonization with the support of the officers of the MFA. In another coup in 1975, Spinola was overthrown and finally Soares headed a democratic government. He appointed Antunes as his foreign minister who completed the process of decolonization.

After getting rid of its empire rather swiftly, Portugal could look ahead and aim at becoming a member of the European Union. Its ex-colonies, however, plunged into civil wars.[54] One of the reasons for this unfortunate development was the lack of constitutional preparations for the transfer of power to independent governments. In many ways the situation in Portuguese Africa resembled that of Algeria in 1962. There was also an exodus of large numbers of Portuguese settlers who had initially hoped that they could stay on when Spinola became president.[55] But in the 'hot' summer of 1975 they realized that they had to leave Africa. For a long time Portugal had been a country of emigration and not of immigration. This changed very drastically in 1975.

The Portuguese tradition of race relations which was praised for its tolerance and flexibilty was deeply affected by this change. 'Luso-tropicalism' had been the product of an 'expansive' mood. Portuguese could settle anywhere and marry locally, producing mixed families who blended well with the local environment. Speaking of Brazil, the famous writer, Gilberto Freire, even praised 'racial democracy'[56]as the greatest achievement of his country. It was part and parcel of the Portuguese heritage. In fact, Salazar's government had made use of Freire's ideology so as to justify Portuguese rule in Africa. In 1951 Freire was sent on a lecture tour to Portuguese colonies. Critics accused him of myth-making. They also pointed out that his ideas of the cultural benefits of racial hybridization would not apply to Portugal itself. For a long time this did not matter as Portugal did not yet harbour black ethnic minorities. But this changed when Portugal which had usually experienced an outflow of people was faced with a sudden inflow. Luso-tropicalism could not be easily adapted to the European climate. A Portuguese professor of literature, Inocencia Mata, poignantly remarked that even thirty years after the revolution of 1974 black Portuguese citizens were still regarded as 'the others'.[57] She also stated that in earlier times such black people had remained a silent minority whose members were regarded as 'students' or people living in exile, but not as permanent residents of Portugal.[58] Becoming a country of immigration while also entering the European Union changed the fate of Portugal to a great extent.

'Contar o imperio' (narrating the empire) became more difficult as Portuguese intellectuals were also affected by post-colonial self-consciousness. Nevertheless, a great wave of imperial nostalgia swept through Portugal at the end of the twentieth century during the celebrations of the fifth centenary of the 'descubrimentos', first of Vasco da Gama's passage to India (1498) and then of Cabral's discovery of Brazil (1500). The many texts produced in the course of these celebrations lend themselves to 'discourse analysis'. Miguel Vale de Almeida who had just returned from fieldwork in Brazil when the celebrations were going on in Portugal 'felt uncomfortable with the persistence of an imperial and expansionist rhetoric' at that time.[59] When the preparations for these celebrations were in full swing, Portugal founded the Comunidade dos Países de Língua Portuguesa (CPLP) in 1996. This organization has held annual summit meetings in different member states ever since. It prides itself on encompassing about 230 million people.[60] Almeida has called this lusophone region 'novo imperio da geolinguistica compensatoria'.[61] The sovereignty of language has replaced imperial domination. Throughout the period of colonial rule the Portuguese had always stressed the importance of their language and had looked down upon the vernacular languages which they encountered in Africa and elsewhere. They could now continue this policy in their new geolinguistic empire.

But post-imperial lusophone solidarity is not just an obsession of intellectual memory-makers, it can suddenly produce a popular movement. A striking incident of this kind of mobilization was the reaction of the Portuguese public to the events in East Timor in September 1999.[62] This tiny colony had never been officially decolonized by Portugal, it had simply been deserted and was taken over by Indonesia in 1976. The anti-colonial movement of East Timor then turned against the new rulers and its small Portuguese-speaking elite used Portugal as an outpost for its international propaganda. In September 1999 a referendum was held in East Timor in which a majority opted for independence from Indonesia. The Indonesian army was not ready to recognize this verdict and unleashed a reign of terror. The United Nations were unable to stop this and it was at that point that the people in Portugal literally took to the streets and organized spontaneous demonstrations in which large crowds participated. In fact, most of the people of East Timor did not speak Portuguese and therefore there was hardly any reason for lusophone solidarity. But the Portuguese had listened for a long time to the pleas of the Portuguese-speaking Timorese elite, including the leaders of the Catholic church.[63] The demonstrations were certainly spontaneous, but the ground for this kind of solidarity had been prepared for a long time. When the Indonesian government relented and East Timor finally achieved its independence, Portuguese involvement in the affairs of East Timor receded. But in September 1999 the concern for this distant island united the Portuguese nation in its resistance to the sufferings of the Timorese at the hands of the Indonesian army. Conservatives who still felt an imperial nostalgia could at that time join hands with leftwingers who support the self-determination of nations.

Lusophone solidarity has also become more important due to changes in the structure of the European Union. Initially EU-membership had helped Portugal to overcome the loss of empire. In fact, decolonization was seen as a precondition for acquiring this coveted membership. The recent expansion of the EU, however, has enhanced a fear of 'peripheralization' in Portugal. Therefore the renewed emphasis on Portugal's ties with Brazil and other members of the CPLP is not so much a compensation for the loss of empire than it is due to a balancing act with regard to the relative loss of weight in the EU.

JAPAN: FROM 'FROZEN MEMORIES' TO DEFIANT NATIONALISM

Japan had a fate which was very different from that of all other post-imperial nations. It lost its colonies, Korea and Taiwan, immediately after the Second World War without any process of decolonization. Japan had ruled these two colonies for more than four decades with a heavy hand. Their products were of strategic importance for the Japanese economy.[64] Taiwan supplied rice and Korea rice as well as industrial products. By 1945 Korea accounted for a quarter of the total industrial production of the Japanese empire. There was substantial Japanese investment, particularly in the North Korean industrial regions. Due to this there were also many Japanese in Korea. By the end of the war there were about 7,00,000 Japanese in Korea and about 6,00,000 Koreans in Japan. These Japanese in Korea held comparatively well-paid positions whereas most of the Koreans in Japan had been imported as forced labourers. The Japanese were repatriated to Japan while most of the Koreans remained in Japan, eking out a living at the lowest level. In addition to the older colonies, Korea and Taiwan, Japan acquired a quasi-colony in Manchuria in the 1930s. This part of China became a kind of laboratory of industrial modernization for the Japanese. Many Japanese scientists worked there. This Manchurian experiment was also terminated at the end of the war.

There were more than 3 million Japanese stationed abroad by the end of the war as civilians or soldiers. When they were repatriated they brought back memories of places where they had often spent many years of their lives. But as well informed observers have remarked, these were 'frozen memories'[65] which were never articulated and died with the generation of the repatriated people. Colonial rule over Korea and Taiwan was thus erased from Japanese consciousness and initially there was no self-conscious reflection on Japan's position as a post-imperial nation. Marxism dominated the social sciences in Japan after the war. Its leading representative was Maruyama Masao.[66] Some attention was also paid to the theories of the German sociologist Max Weber.[67] These influences led to intensive debates on the role of imperialism in Japan's recent past and its supposedly deviant modernity. These debates remained at a highly abstract level and they focussed Japanese self-consciousness on its internal national history and to some extent also on its role in world history. But there was no interest in Japan's rule over Korea and Taiwan. It is only in recent years that colonial history has emerged as a field of scholarly attention in Japan. Eight volumes devoted to the history of modern Japan and its colonies edited by Oe Shinobu and Asada Kyoji (Tokyo: Iwanami, 1992-3) are an impressive testimony to the emergence of a field of historiography which had been neglected for a long time.[68] In this context the impact of Japanese educational policy on the colonies has also been studied. Komagome Takeshi, a specialist in this field, has worked on this aspect of Japanese rule in Korea. Even post-colonial studies have been taken note of in Japan in recent years and Komori Yoichi has published a book on this subject in 2001.[69] However, all these academic studies do not necessarily influence Japanese national consciousness. Writers who spread their views in the popular media are more likely to reach a mass audience.

The Manga is such a popular medium in Japan. It is designed in the style of comic books. Most Manga texts are novels aimed at young people, but there are also authors who are producing more serious Mangas. One of these authors is Kobayashi Yoshinori who published in 2001 a Manga with the title 'On Taiwan' in which he praised the effects of Japanese colonial rule and maintained that the Taiwanese had imbibed Japanese values so very well that they now surpass the Japanese in this respect. The book became a bestseller in Japan and there was a Chinese edition in Taiwan which created quite a stir. Kobayashi supports an association devoted to the reform of Japanese history textbooks whose guiding light is Fujioka Nobukatsu of Tokyo University. This 'revisionism' is anti-American and promotes a defiant Japanese nationalism. It denies that the Japanese army committed a massacre in Nanjing during the war and it also holds that the so-called Korean 'comfort women' who were used as prostitutes by the Japanese army were not forced but volunteered to do this service.[70] This kind of tampering with history has, of course, given rise to the protest of many historians. After the earlier years of 'frozen memories', there is now a veritable 'civil war of memory' in Japan as Kang Sang Jung has pointed out who happens to be the only professor of Korean origin at Tokyo University.

The Koreans are the oldest and the largest ethnic minority in Japan. They had to face a great deal of discrimination although they cannot be easily identified at sight as their physical features hardly differ from those of the Japanese. Many second-generation Koreans have grown up speaking Japanese, adopting Japanese names so as to escape discrimination. Only very few – like Kang Sang Jung – have dropped their Japanese names and reclaimed their Korean ones. The North Korean government had sponsored many Korean schools in Japan and they were permitted to operate but their certificates obtained no official recognition. For getting on in life, this was a dead end and therefore the attendance of these schools dwindled.[71] Unlike the minorities in other post-imperial nations, the Koreans in Japan do not constitute a challenge which gives rise to self-consciousess.

There are at the most individual challengers like Kang Sang Jung who opposes the defiant nationalism propagated by people like Fujioka and Kobayashi. He has emerged as a valiant fighter in the 'civil war of memory', but in this he is not alone. There are many Japanese colleagues who share his views in this respect.

CONCLUSION: SIMILARITIES AND CONTRASTS OF NATIONAL EXPERIENCES

The memory makers and memorykeepers of the six nations discussed here faced very different tasks according to the specific process of decolonization and its aftermath in their respective countries. Whereas many other historical processes in our times would require analyses which would follow the 'transnational turn' of research, the study of the phenomena discussed here concerns national history with a vengeance. Decolonization and its consequences have reconfirmed national histories in an unexpected manner. They have etched new features into the national profile which may not have added to its beauty but which have certainly revealed important aspects of the national character.

The work of professional historians has contributed a great deal to the discovery of the colonial past, but the effect of much of this work has remained restricted to scholarly circles. Sometimes the publication of a bestseller such as Hochschild's book on King Leopold was needed to wake up the nation and has forced it to take note of what scholars had known for a long time. Kobayashi's Mangas played a similar role in Japan. Scholars may take issue with the views of such popular authors, but at least these authors have helped to raise a debate.

An absolutely crucial factor in the debates on the post-imperial experiences of nations was the presence of immigrants from the ex-colonies in the midst of the respective nations. The origins of such immigration were very different. In Great Britain this immigration was a gradual inflow of people who were looking for better chances to make a living. Most of these immigrants retained good relations with their countries of origin. Their experience was very different from the political refugees who hastily left Algeria in order to save their lives by settling in France. Accordingly the challenges which emerged from dealing with immigrants were different for the British and the French. The challenges faced by the Dutch were akin to those faced by the French. Belgium had comparatively few ex-colonial immigrants and the Portuguese case resembled that of the British experience. There were, of course, a few hundred thousands of returning Portugese settlers, but many of them had settled in the African colonies only in recent times and still had family connections in Portugal. On returning home they blended with the majority and did not form a minority with a distinctive identity of its own. The Koreans in Japan had come as forced labourers and certainly had an identity of their own which was reconfirmed by the discrimination which they had to face in Japan. Even the second generation was not easily absorbed by the majority, but as time went by integration increased, the more so as it is impossible to distinguish Koreans physically from Japanese. As these few remarks show, even a common feature such as immigration from the ex-colonies does not necessarily imply the same kind of experience for post-imperial nations.

Another common feature is the recent surge of interest in the colonial past in several countries. However, those recent debates on the imperial past have ususally concentrated on very specific issues, therefore they have been restricted to the nation concerned. They have not had a trans-national impact as yet. Two French authors have made a plea for a comparative study of what they call 'Mémoires grises' (Grey Memories) of the colonial past.[72] They have been influenced by the debates in France in 2005 which have been described above. They recall that Pascal Blanchard, one of the editors of *La Fracture Coloniale*, had hinted at parallels of French and Japanese experiences and they then devote considerable attention to what had happened in Belgium after the ghost of King Leopold had been conjured up. In discussing the relations between the post-imperial nations and their former colonies they speak of the 'diplomacy of repentance'. Finally they argue for a worldwide memory. This is a very valid plea, but as the six case studies presented here have shown, it is not easy to revive national memories and even more difficult to transcend them.

The cross-national comparison attempted here has been a study in contrasts. The loss of empire has induced a certain self-consciousness in the nations concerned, but this feeling has been articulated in different ways. There is, however, a surprising coincidence in the fairly recent revival of interest in the colonial past. The ice in which frozen memories were embedded seems to have melted and the fog of amnesia has lifted here and there. Surviving witnesses have recorded what they remember. At the same time a new generation born after the loss of empire is trying to understand the past. This is an encouraging atmosphere for further research in this field.

NOTES

1. George Steinmetz, 'Empire et domination mondiale', in *Actes de la recherche en sciences sociales*, nos. 171-2, March 2008, pp. 4-19.
2. Edward Said, *Orientalism*, New York: Vintage Books, 1978.
3. Mico Seigel, 'Beyond Compare: Comparative Method and the Transnational Turn', in *Radical History Review*, Issue 91, Winter 2005, pp. 62-90
4. Gerhard Altmann, *Abschied vom Empire. Die innere Dekolonisation Großbritanniens, 1945-1985*, Göttingen: Wallstein, 2005, p. 219.
5. Jeffrey Richards, 'Imperial Heroes for a Post-imperial Age: Films and the End of Empire', in Stuart Ward, ed., *British Culture and the End of Empire*, Manchester: Manchester University Press, 2001, p. 128.
6. Hermann Kulke and Dietmar Rothermund, *A History of India*, London: Routledge, 2004 (4th edn.), pp. 317, 330
7. Kathleen Paul, 'Communities of Britishness: Migration in the Last Gasp of Empire', in Ward, *British Culture*, pp. 181 f.
8. Elizabeth Buettner, *Empire Families: Britons and Late Imperial India*, Oxford: Oxford University Press, 2004.
9. Dan Rebellato, 'Look Back at Empire: British Theatre and Imperial Decline', in Ward, *British Culture*, pp. 82 f.
10. Richard, 'Imperial Heroes', in Ward, *British Culture*, p. 135.
11. Stuart Ward, '"No Nation Could be Broker": The Satire Boom and the Demise of Britain's World Role', in Ward, *British Culture*, pp. 91 f.
12. Michael Shanks, *The Stagnant Society*, Harmondsworth: Pelican, 1961.
13. Shompa Lahiri, 'South Asians in Post-imperial Britain: Decolonisation and Imperial Legacy', in Ward, *British Culture*, p. 206.
14. Paul, 'Communities of Britishness', in Ward, *British Culture*, pp. 193 f.
15. Ibid., p. 195.
16. Altmann, *Abschied vom Empire*, p. 397
17. Dietmar Rothermund, *The Routledge Companion to Decolonization*, London: Routledge, 2006, p. 192.
18. Christoper Bayly, ed., *The Raj: India and the British, 1600-1947*, London: National Portrait Gallery Publications, 1990.
19. Christopher Bayly, personal communication.
20. Rothermund, *Routledge Companion*, pp. 71 f.
21. Ibid., pp. 76 f., 205 f.
22. Gert Oostindie and I. Klinkers, *Decolonising the Caribbean: Dutch Policies in a Comparative Perspective*, Amsterdam: Amsterdam University Press, 2003, pp. 94 f.

23. Ibid, pp. 177 f.
24. Gert J.Oostindie, 'Squaring the Circle: Commemorating the VOC after 400 years', in *Bijdragen tot de Taal-, Land- en Volkenkunde*, vol. 159, 2003, pp. 135-61.
25. Ibid., pp. 151 f.
26. Guy Vanthemsche, 'The Historiography of Belgian Colonialism in the Congo', in Csaba Levai, ed., *Europe and the World in European Historiography*, Pisa: Edizioni Plus – Pisa University Press, 2006, pp. 89-119.
27. Adam Hochschild, *King Leopold's Ghost: A Story of Greed, Terror and Heroism in Colonial Africa*, New York: Houghton Mifflin, 1998.
28. Jean-Luc Vellut, ed., *La Memoire du Congo: Les temps colonial*, Ghent and Tervuren: Editions Snoeck/Musee royal de l'Afrique central, 2005.
29. Jean-Luc Vellut, personal communication.
30. Ludo De Witte, *De moord op Lumumba*, Leuven: Editions Uitgiveri van Halewyck, 1999; English edition: *The Assassination of Lumumba*, London: Verso, 2001.
31. Rothermund, *Routledge Companion*, p. 127.
32. Ibid., p. 182
33. Ibid., p. 183
34. Mathew Connelly, *A Diplomatic Revolution: Algeria's Fight for Independence and the Origins of the Post-Cold War Era*, London: Oxford University Press, 2002, p. 269.
35. Said Bouamama, *Dix ans de marche de Beurs. Chronique d'un mouvement avorté*, Paris: Desclée de Bouwer, 1994
36. Dietmar Rothermund, 'Individual and Group Rights in Western Europe and India', in D. Rothermund, *The Role of the State in South Asia and Other Essays*, Delhi: Manohar, 2000, p. 80.
37. Olivier Le Cour Grandmaison, 'Colonisés-immigrés et, périls migratoires': origines et permanence du racism et d'une xénophobie d'Etat (1924-2007)', in *Cultures et Conflicts*, Mo. 69, 2008, pp. 19-32.
38. Olivier Le Cour Grandmaison, *Coloniser. Exterminer. Sur la guerre et L'État colonial*, Paris: Fayard, 2005, pp. 247 f.
39. www.indigenes-republique.org
40. Joshua Cole, 'Intimate Acts and Unspeakable Relations. Remembering Torture and the War for Algerian Independence'; in Alec G. Hargreaves, *Memory, Empire and Postcolonialism. Legacies of French Colonialism*, Lanham MD: Lexington Books, 2005, pp. 128, 132 f,
41. Paul Aussareses, *Services Spéciaux: Algerie 1955-1957*, Paris: Perrin, 2001.
42. Le Cour Grandmaison, *Coloniser. Exterminer*, pp. 98 f.
43. Pascal Blanchard, Nicolas Bancel et Sandrine Lemaire, eds., La fracture

colniale. La société francaise aus prisme del'héritage colonial, Paris: La Découverte, 2005.

44. Ibid., pp. 263 f. (Annexes 1 and 2)
45. Arnauld Le Brusq, '"Épilogue. De'notre" memoir à "leur" histoire: les métamorphoses du Palais des colonies', in Blanchard et al., *La fracture coloniale*, pp. 255 f.
46. Olivier Le Cour Grandmaison, 'Passé colonial et identité nationale: sur la rhétorique de N. Sarkozy', in *La Journal Lignes*, no. 25, March 2008, pp. 150-9.
47. Manuela Ribeiro Sanches,ed., *Portugal nao é um país pequeno; contar o 'imperio' na pós-colonidade,* Lisboa: Livros Cotovia, 2006, p. 22.
48. Rothermund, *Routledge Companion*, pp. 226 f.
49. Boaventura de Sousa Santos, 'Between Prospero and Caliban: Colonialism, Postcolonialism and Inter-identity', in *Luso-Brazilian Review*, vol. 39/2, 2002, University of Wisconsin, pp. 9-43.
50. Piero Gleijeses, *Conflicting Missions: Havana, Washington and Africa, 1959- 1976*, Chapel Hill NC: University of North Carolina Press, 2002, p. 187.
51. Rothermund, *Routledge Companion*, p. 229.
52. Ibid., pp. 235-7.
53. Ibid., p. 225.
54. Ibid., pp. 231 f.
55. Ibid., p. 236
56. Bea Gomes, 'O mundo que o portugues criou – Von der Erfindung der lusophonen Welt', in *Stichproben. Wiener Zeitschrift für kritische Afrikastudien*, vol. 1, 2/2001, pp. 27-43.
57. Inocencia Mata, 'Estranhos en permanencia: a negociacao da identidade portuguesa na pós-colonialidade', in M. Sanches, *Portugal*, p. 289.
58. Ibid., p. 295.
59. Miguel Vale de Almeida, *An Earth-colored Sea: Race, Culture and the Politics of Identity in the Post-Colonial Portuguese-Speaking World*, New York: Berghahn, 2004, p. 45.
60. www.cplp.org.
61. Miguel Vale de Almeida, 'Comentário', in M. Sanches, *Portugal*, p. 364.
62. Almeida, *An Earth-colored Sea,* pp. 83 f.
63. Rothermund, *Routledge Companion*, p. 80.
64. Ibid., pp. 97 f.
65. Kang Sang Jung, 'The Imaginary Geography of a Nation and its De-Nationalized Narrative: Japan and the Korean Experience' (trsl. Trent Maxey), www. japanfocus.org/products/topdf/1997.
66. Maruyama Masao, *Denken in Japan* (trsl. W. Schamoni and W. Seifert), Frankfurt/Main: Suhrkamp, 1988.

67. Wolfgang Schwentker, *Max Weber in Japan. Eine Untersuchung zur Wirkungsgeschichte*, Tübingen: Mohr Siebeck, 1998.
68. Anneli Wallentowitz, 'Grundzüge der Diskussion über Imperialismus in Japan', in Hans Martin Krämer, Tino Scholz, Sebastian Conrad, eds., *Geschichtswissenschaft in Japan*, Göttingen: Vandenhoeck & Ruprecht, 2006, p. 83.
69. Ibid., p. 84
70. Rebecca Clifford, *Cleansing History, Cleansing Japan: Kobayashi Yoshinori's Analects of War and Japan's Revisionist Revival.* Nissan Occasional Papers, no. 35, 2004.
71. Toru Umakoshi, 'The Education of Korean Children in Japan', in Dietmar Rothermund and John Simon, eds., *Education and the Integration of Ethnic Minorities*, London: Frances Pinter, 1986, pp. 36-47.
72. Christine Deslaurier et Aurélie Roger, "Mémoires grises". Apports d'une comparaison des recompositions mémorielles due passé colonial en Europe et an Afrique', in *Politique africaine*, no. 102, June 2006, pp. 1-13.

CHAPTER 8

The De-Industrialization of India*

THE MEANING OF DE-INDUSTRIALIZATION

The English term 'industry' refers not only to modern industry organized in factories and using machinery, but also to the production by artisans such as handloom weavers and spinners. The term 'de-industrialization' as used in the debates concerning the destructive impact of British colonial rule on India tends to have a complex meaning. It refers first of all to the decline of production by Indian artisans to the extent that they could not compete with the products of British industry after the Industrial Revolution, but it also implies that there were obstacles to transferring the achievements of the Industrial Revolution to India.

The Indian debate has often been conducted in rather sweeping terms. The adverse impact of colonial rule has been seen as uniform and linear. Actually there were at least three distinct phases to this impact. The first was the eighteenth century, which was characterized by a rapid rise of Indian exports followed by a sharp decline. The second was the phase of severe deflation in India in the early nineteenth century. And the third was the second half of the nineteenth century, which was marked by slow but steady inflation and the rise of some modern industrial enclaves in India. Anticipating some of the explanations that will be detailed later on, we can conclude that during the first period, certain regions – Bengal in particular – were stimulated by British demand and then suffered most when this demand receded, whereas during the second period general deflation affected the whole country, preserving Indian cottage industry at a low level due to the availability of cheap food and cheap raw materials, but preventing the rise of modern industry. In the third phase, when silver flowed once more into the country, prices of food and raw materials rose. This rise reduced the 'comparative advantage' of

*I would like to thank Tirthankar Roy for reading an earlier draft of this article and making suggestions for its improvement.

cottage industry and thus favoured the growth of modern industry. But this modern industry remained restricted to a few industrial enclaves and had hardly any linkage effects. The term 'de-industrialization' would have different meanings in these three historical contexts.

De-industrialization was also debated very intensively in Great Britain in the late 1970s and the 1980s, when there was a growing concern about the decline of British industry. Economists then defined this problem as 'a failure of the manufacturing industry to earn enough to pay for the full employment level of imports'.[1] Actually similar problems were already being debated in the nineteenth century, when Walter Bagehot, the editor of The *Economist*, remarked that the population of the British Isles would soon consist of moneylenders and their servants only. In other words, the service sector would predominate and the primary and secondary sectors of the economy would dwindle to insignificance. De-industrialization has generally been interpreted in this way, but in colonial India the path of development seemed to follow the opposite direction: the primary sector re-emerged as the leading sector, while the secondary one receded. Accordingly, the Indian debates have been concerned with the question of whether employment in manufacturing in the broadest sense of the term declined under British rule, leading to a 're-ruralization' of India.

Most Indian economic historians who have been concerned with these problems have tended to focus almost exclusively on the production of cotton textiles. In this field India had been a leading producer and exporter since the days of the Indus civilization. It is said that in the mid eighteenth century India still produced about a quarter of the world's textiles. It lost this position within a few decades due to the Industrial Revolution in England. We shall therefore discuss the textile industry in detail before turning to the traditional small-scale industry in other fields of production.

COTTON TEXTILE PRODUCTION IN INDIA AND EUROPE

In the 1830s the British Governor-General of India, Lord Bentinck, commented on the 'bones of the weavers bleaching in the plains of Bengal'. Later, Karl Marx repeated this statement and it gained wide currency among Indian nationalists as well as Indian Marxists. For a long time it was taken for granted that this statement reflected the fate of Indian artisans in general, but in recent decades revisionist studies have asserted that Indian artisans could survive. These revisionists initially concentrated on the handloom weavers. The American economic historian Morris D. Morris, who worked mostly on western India, argued that the production of the handloom weavers was actually given a new lease of life as they were able to use imported industrial yarn and could thus compete with imported textiles.[2] The Swiss scholar Konrad Specker, studying the southern Indian weavers in the first half of the nineteenth century, proved that they were able to make both ends meet even without using industrial yarn, as long as food and raw cotton were cheap and thus local hand-spun yarn was available at a low price. They also profited from the proximity to the rural consumers.[3] Taking a broader look at the production of Indian artisans in different fields, Tirthankar Roy has recently shown that small-scale industries did not decline and that commercialization led to a wider distribution of their products.[4] A more nuanced 'revisionist' account is Douglas Hynes recent study of western India, 1870-1960.[5] He has traced the emergence of 'weaver capitalists' who benefited from the migration of weavers to towns such as Bhiwandi and Sholapur. Migrant weavers had no means of production and had to work as wage labourers. The 'weaver capitalists' were innovative both in terms of their production and in marketing it. Haynes also argues that so far too much attention has been paid to production and not to consumption and the demand for textiles. He stresses that while male attire was increasingly made of imported cloth, the women remained attached to handloom fabrics. Weaver capitalists were quick to adjust to new trends, whereas the mills were tied to mass production. These weaver capitalists later on also made the transition to powerlooms, which ushered in a wave of 'secondary industrialization'[8] and contributed to the rise of the 'informal' sector of the Indian economy.

Such revisionist studies seemed to imply that Lord Bentinck's observations concerning the weavers of Bengal were perhaps somewhat exaggerated. But in fact there was a great difference between Bengal and other regions of India in this respect. In order to understand this we must examine the rather dramatic shifts in the procurement of Indian textiles for export in the course of the eighteenth century.

The export trade in Indian textiles had been very brisk even in earlier centuries. Hand-printed Indian textiles with colourful patterns were in great demand in many countries around the Indian Ocean. When the European East India Companies started to participate in the Indian Ocean trade (the British called it 'country trade'), they soon found that they could sell Indian textiles at a good profit in Southeast Asia but also along the African coast. The Dutch earned so much from this trade that they could buy the goods to be shipped to Europe from the profits made in the country trade. Since they sold their wares in auctions in Amsterdam, they could also use this method for testing the market for Indian textiles in Europe. From the middle of the seventeenth century textile sales increased so much that they soon surpassed the trade in spices. The British quickly followed this precedent, and their auctions in London then rivalled those of Amsterdam.

In the course of the late seventeenth century cotton-printing shops were established in many European countries, and these imitated the Indian fabrics. They found it difficult to match the quality of the Indian products, but being closer to the consumers they could adjust to changes in fashion more quickly, whereas the Indian printers used to repeat traditional designs. Initially, Indian prints were mostly used for bedspreads and tapestry, but once they had conquered the field of women's dresses they became a great craze and were, of course, subjected to the trends of changing fashions.

This was the age of mercantilism, and British artisans threatened by these imports were quick to ask for protective measures. The Dutch, who were international traders with a comparatively small home market, were not inclined to opt for such protectionism, but the British had a substantial home market and powerful guilds engaged in the production of various textiles. This caused the British Parliament to pass an Act in 1700 which prohibited the import of printed Indian textiles except for the purpose of re-export to America or the European continent. The producers who benefited most from this legislation were the London cotton printers, who now invested heavily in their booming industry and captured not only the home market but also contributed a great deal to British exports. They depended to a large extent on the import of white Indian cotton textiles procured for them by the East India Company. This type of cloth, which became a semi-finished input for the London cotton printers, had to be carefully bleached to their specifications in India because otherwise it would not be fit for printing. The servants of the East India

Company had to employ bleachers as wage labourers. This was initially resented by the directors of the company in London, who argued that a trading company should not employ such labourers. But the requirements of the London printers had to be met.[9] In fact, this became an extremely profitable business and the servants of the company showed great acumen in finding new supply lines for the white cloth needed by the printers.[10]

The major region of India known for the production of fine white cloth was Bengal. Accordingly, exports of such cloth from Bengal increased enormously in the first half of the eighteenth century, while exports from other regions of India receded. In the early 1720s exports from the Bombay and Madras presidencies still surpassed those from Bengal, which were valued at only £2,00,000 at the time. In the early 1740s Bengal exports amounted to £5,00,000 per annum, whereas the total for the Bombay and Madras presidencies had declined to less than £2,00,000.[11] This steep increase in export demand must have led to a growth in the numbers of weavers working more or less exclusively for export production and thus being much more vulnerable than the weavers elsewhere in India, whose production was predominantly geared to the home market.

In the 1750s, exports of Bengal cloth declined. By 1760 the value of those exports had fallen to about £3,00,000. Political turmoil obviously contributed to this decline. The Maratha raids had cut supply lines in Bengal and the British confrontation with the nawab of Bengal, which culminated in the battle of Plassey in 1757, also obstructed trade. All this must have encouraged import substitution in Europe. In many parts of Europe cotton spinning and weaving were well established in the eighteenth century.[12] With the booming business of the London cotton printers, British spinners and weavers could also find a ready market for their products. But the scarcity of labour was a major problem, the more so as the production of woollens had a much greater claim on British industrial activity. The artisans and traders in this field had complained about the competition they faced due to the craze for cotton textiles. But, in fact, they had not suffered at all. They had improved their production by introducing light woollens (worsteds), and from the early 1720s to the early 1770s the value of annual exports of British woollens had increased from £3 to £4 million.[13] There was thus no reason why spinners and weavers should shift from woollen to cotton textile production. Spinning was the chief bottleneck, as on average one weaver required the production of six to seven spinners. The invention of the spinning jenny by James Hargreave in 1764, the waterframe by Richard Arkwright in 1775 and the spinning mule by Samuel Crompton in 1779 marked the rapid progress of mechanization, which paved the way for the Industrial Revolution. The use of water power gave rise to the 'textile mill', as British factories were called even after the steam engine had replaced water power.

Economic historians have been puzzled by the fact that the Industrial Revolution started in an industry which was a minor one in Great Britain, whereas it was much more prominent on the European continent.[14] The scarcity of labour in Great Britain was the main reason for this. Its population stood at about 5 million in the mid-eighteenth century. Great Britain was a small country even by European standards, but a pigmy when compared to India, which had a population of at least about 150 million at that time. It was the ample supply of labour which prevented the transfer of the Industrial Revolution to India. The early spinning machines that helped to save labour in Great Britain could easily have been reproduced in India, but they were not required there. On the contrary, as British productivity increased, unemployment spread in India and labour-saving machinery was the last thing one would have needed there.

Continental Northwestern Europe provides an interesting contrast to both Great Britain and India in this respect. Labour was not as scarce there as in Great Britain. Therefore there was no indigenous motive for the invention of labour-saving machinery. But once such machines had been introduced in Great Britain, competition increased as British imports became cheaply available. It was not the scarcity of labour on the continent but the higher productivity of British competitors that induced continental entrepreneurs to adopt the new methods of production. The British machines were reproduced in Northwestern Europe with a time lag of about ten years.[15] At this early stage, when the spirit of mercantilism still prevailed, the British were not at all eager to export their machines, and prohibited their transfer to the continent. They even tried to prevent British mechanics from migrating to the continent. But all this was of no use. Northwestern Europe did catch up with Great Britain in due course. Why did this not happen in India? The answer is that the supply of labour was greater in India than in Europe and the impact of competition due to higher productivity was not as quick and pervasive as in Europe.

In India it was the export market whose loss was felt – particularly in Bengal – whereas in Northwestern Europe it was the production for the respective home market, which was at stake. The Indian home market was affected by other problems caused by colonial rule, which we shall discuss later on.

As far as the export market was concerned, it is interesting to note that the proverbial weavers whose bones were bleaching in the plains of Bengal were not actually made redundant by the progress of mechanization in Great Britain, but by the increasing productivity of British handloom weavers. Edmund Cartwright had invented a mechanical loom in 1786, but it did not work very well. Cartwright was a theologian with no practical experience in the textile industry.[16] His loom required such expert handling that it could not compete with the handloom at that time; the more so as British handlooms were already semi-mechanized. The flying shuttle invented by John Kaye in 1733 had greatly speeded up handloom weaving since the mid-1750s. Further improvements had been added. An advanced handloom, called a 'dandy loom', enabled the handloom weaver to work at half the speed of a powerloom in the early nineteenth century. Moreover, handloom weavers were more flexible in adjusting to changes in design than powerloom operators. Thus there was a reluctance to invest in powerlooms in the early nineteenth century.[17] Until 1830 the number of British handloom weavers increased by leaps and bounds, whereas powerlooms were still comparatively rare. By 1820 there were only 14,000 powerlooms in Great Britain, but 2,40,000 handlooms. While the number of handlooms did not increase any further after that date, it took until 1850 for the number of powerlooms to increase to more than 2,40,000.[18]

The surprising surge in handloom weaving in Great Britain and the initially rather slow spread of the powerloom may also be explained by referring to the evolution of industrial organization. While mechanical spinning implied economies of scale, which favoured the setting up of factories, weaving could be extended in terms of a decentralized putting-out system. Of course, the scarcity of labour referred to above should also have impeded the expansion of handloom weaving. But it seems that Irish migrants joined the ranks of weavers in England.[19] Moreover, population increased in general in Great Britain in the early nineteenth century. The expansion of gainful employment bred 'proletarians'.

Whereas weaving could expand in a decentralized way, since it did not require the organization of factories, cotton printing had from the very beginning encouraged the establishment of centralized workshops that resembled factories. Some London cotton printers of the early eighteenth century had up to 400 workers in their workshops and owned rather expensive equipment,[20] but mechanization was a fairly late development in this line of production. Printing with rotating cylinders was introduced in the mid-1750s, but this was still done by hand. As soon as it became possible to drive these cylinders by water power or steam engines in the late eighteenth century, productivity increased enormously. Thomas Bell introduced such a rotating press in 1783.[21] With the speeding up of production at both ends – spinning and printing – weaving was under pressure to keep pace. This actually put a premium on the further development of powerlooms, but this required advances in the construction of machine tools capable of producing high-precision metal parts for such looms. In 1822 an advanced powerloom made almost completely of metal parts was introduced and rapidly improved in subsequent years.[22] By the 1830s powerlooms could compete with the handlooms in terms of quality and flexibility of production. It was only then that the Industrial Revolution literally moved into high gear. Again, all this was transferred to other parts of Europe with a time lag, but it did not reach India before the second half of the nineteenth century.

THE IMPACT OF THE DEFLATION OF THE FIRST HALF OF THE NINETEENTH CENTURY

In addition to the ample supply of labour, which we have mentioned earlier, there was another reason for India's 'de-industrialized' state of affairs, and this was the severe deflation that affected the country in the second period mentioned above. The diagnosis of 'de-industrialization' shifts from the destructive impact of the decline in demand for Indian exports to the obstructive impact of macroeconomic conditions. In fact, the latter was probably more serious than the former. As pointed out earlier, only specific regions had been stimulated by the rapid increase in British demand for Indian white cotton cloth. Even referring to Bengal would be too general in this respect. Only certain districts produced the type of cloth that the British required,[23] and their weavers were affected by the decline in export demand. In general statistical terms and with regard to the whole of India, this impact was marginal. But those who suffered would have seen it differently.

In contrast with such a sharp but marginal impact, deflation spread like a wet blanket over the whole of India and suffocated all but the most elementary economic activities. The art of survival was the distinctive feature of this period. In the first half of the eighteenth century the British had pumped large amounts of silver into India. The value of the silver paid for the exports of white cotton cloth from Bengal from about 1720 to 1750 alone totalled no less than £12 million. After 1765, when the East India Company was in control of Bengal's revenues, much of this money was taken out of the country again,[24] though there were occasional spurts of new bullion inflows at times of increased British military activity. Exports of textiles from Bengal also increased once more towards the end of the eighteenth century, but by this time the Bengal weavers were already suffering from the oppression of the British, who used coercive measures to procure cloth, thus depressing the weavers' wages.

By the time the British conquest of India was almost complete in the early nineteenth century, there was no further need to ship silver to India. On the other hand, the outflow of silver continued, and this precipitated severe deflation. We can get an idea of how low prices were at that time by referring to the series of rice prices compiled by Konrad Specker for the Madras Presidency.[25] Except for three famine years prices were well below those of the first decade of the century. In the 1820s and 1830s they were on average 20 per cent below that level, and in the 1840s as much as 35 per cent below. Raw cotton was also cheap at that time and thus weavers could make both ends meet, particularly in the interior of the country where transport was cumbersome and costly before the age of the railways. The export prices for British grey cloth also declined in this period. From 1815 to 1830 they fell by about 65 per cent, and by 1845 they were only 25 per cent of what they had been in 1815. Nevertheless, the weavers of the Madras Presidency could survive this competition not only as far as the home market was concerned but also in terms of exports. In the 1820s and 1830s this region still exported cotton textiles worth 7 million rupees per annum, a figure which receded to between Rs. 3 million and 4 million in the 1840s. Cotton textile imports amounted to only Rs. 0.6 million around 1825 and increased to an average of Rs. 1.5 million in the mid-1840s. If one accepts Morris D. Morris's hypothesis that imported industrial yarn gave a new lease of life to the Indian handloom weavers, then this very positive balance of trade in cotton textiles should have been caused by yarn imports. But the value of yarn imports was rather modest up to 1845, when they averaged about Rs. 0.5 million per annum. It was only in the late 1840s that they increased to about Rs. 1.5 million. Due to the ample supply of cheap food and cheap labour the traditional Indian cotton textile industry could still hold its own rather successfully, and there was no scope for the establishment of modern cotton textile mills in India.[26] These conditions changed only in the second half of the nineteenth century, due to several factors that contributed to a rise in prices.

The art of survival of Indian artisans in this period can be assessed from two different perspectives. It could be cited as evidence to refute the 'de-industrialization' thesis as defined in terms of the first period outlined above, but it could also be interpreted so as to support the claim that low-level survival techniques obstructed modern industrialization. We shall return to these different assessments later on when summing up the debate on India's de-industrialization. We should look first though at the emergence of modern Indian industry, which remained a somewhat isolated phenomenon both in its spatial dimensions and as far as its linkages were concerned. We thus proceed to the third phase mentioned above, in which 'de-industrialization' changed its connotation once more.

THE RISE IN PRICES AND THE GROWTH OF MODERN INDUSTRY

When the British started investing in the railways in India, silver again flowed into the country and this led to an increase in prices. Moreover, wherever the railway appeared it linked the countryside to the wider world and this immediately affected the local price level. In addition, silver depreciated after the mid-1870s and India absorbed large amounts of the metal, which was being demonetized by several European countries at the time.[26] This contributed to slow but steady inflation in India, which contrasted with the deflation that had characterized the first half of the nineteenth century.

In the Madras Presidency, for instance, rice prices almost doubled from 1860 to 1866; they then declined somewhat, but once silver depreciated after 1876 they increased steadily. At the same time, the prices of raw cotton were affected by the American Civil War. They increased almost fourfold from 1860 to 1863; they then declined somewhat, but in the 1870s they were still at a level about twice that of 1860. This meant that the days of cheap food and cheap cotton were gone, and traditional spinners and weavers could no longer make both ends meet. It was only at this stage that modern Indian mills could prosper. At first they were mostly spinning mills, and it was only now that industrial yarn became a major input for handloom weavers. Indian industrial yarn was even exported to East Asia. Only when these exports receded did Indian mill owners establish composite spinning and weaving mills.

So far the phenomenon of de-industrialization and the survival of traditional production have been discussed only in the context of cotton textile production. But there were, of course, many other traditional industries in India which also faced the challenge of the Industrial Revolution.

THE SURVIVAL AND COMMERCIALIZATION OF SMALL-SCALE INDUSTRIES

Tirthankar Roy has promoted the 'revisionist' approach in this field.[27] But it is perhaps wrong to speak of 'revisionism' in this context. It was rather a neglect of this field which had hitherto characterized Indian economic historiography. Highlighting the importance of this neglected field is 'revisionist' to the extent that it challenges the emphasis on textile production. The production of Indian potters, carpenters, ironworkers and makers of leather goods actually covered a wide spectrum of economic activities. Much of this production was only for the home market, or rather for narrowly circumscribed local markets, and it could thus withstand the competition from imported industrial products – at least until the railways penetrated the interior of India and the Suez Canal opened, reducing freight rates for bulk shipments of European industrial goods. But, as Roy argues, it was not only cheap local production but also the benefits of commercialization which helped various small-scale industries to both survive and prosper in India. Village- and household-based production declined. The local artisan who resorted to subsistence agriculture whenever he could not survive on the earnings from his trade disappeared with the progress of commercialization. If he had a chance, he migrated to larger, more specialized centres of production and became a wage labourer. The entrepreneurs who organized such centres of production were often the traders who marketed the respective products, distributing them to distant places.[28] A narrow focus on the decline of the number of village artisans would support the de-industrialization thesis, but it would disregard the growth of new types of small-scale industries.

Such small-scale industries could in due course give rise to very important branches of Indian industry, such as the leather industry.[29] At the village level this had mostly consisted of the activities of 'untouchables', who took care of carcasses and made simple articles from hides and skins. But in time it was transformed into an urban-based small-scale industry producing marketable and finally even exportable leather goods.

Whereas there are certainly some success stories in this field, there is also some evidence of the decline of traditional industries, particularly of the urban-based crafts geared to elite consumption. Before the British took over India, the country was ruled by courtiers and warriors who indulged in conspicuous consumption both in dress and housing and with regard to all kinds of other items. The revenue collected by the elite remained in the country and was to a large extent spent on such items. The British civil servants rarely provided any patronage to Indian craftsmen. They led a comparatively frugal life in India and spent their savings at home, believing that 'Life begins after retirement' – and they retired rather early.

CONCLUSION

The de-industrialization thesis requires several qualifications both in terms of the different regions of India and of the types of industrial activity. The weavers of Bengal, who increased in number due to a rising export demand for white cotton cloth, were certainly very badly affected by British import substitution and export production at the time of the Industrial Revolution, whereas Southern Indian weavers were able to face the challenge of competition. Among small-scale industries the production of leather goods obviously experienced a successful transition from village craft to commercialization, while production for elite consumption declined under colonial rule.

The crucial question of why the achievements of the Industrial Revolution could not be transferred to India has been answered here by referring to the ample supply of labour, which discouraged the introduction of labour-saving machinery. Macroeconomic phenomena such as the long depression of the first half of the nineteenth century have also been mentioned in order to explain the long time lag before modern industrial methods of production were transferred to India.

When railways and steamers linked India to the world market and silver flowed once more into the country – almost with a vengeance – the macroeconomic context changed dramatically. Modern industry did now grow to some extent in India, but it was a fragmented growth without linkage effects. Textile mills were established, but neither textile machinery nor machine tools were made in India as they could be readily imported, and neither Indian mill owners nor the British would have supported the imposition of protective tariffs for 'infant industries' producing such machines in India. The emphasis on the emergence of machine tools during the Industrial Revolution has shown what India missed in this respect under British rule.

Taking up once more the theme of the three periods and the three aspects of 'de-industrialization' outlined in the beginning, we may assert that the first aspect, which has usually been highlighted in the Indian debate, has been overemphasized. Only specific districts in Bengal were actually affected very severely by the decline in export demand. The reversal of the flow of textiles due to the Industrial Revolution was actually not as swift as some economic historians have suggested. Indian artisans could survive, but they adjusted to a low level of survival. Deflation 'protected' them at this low level, but it also prevented any other type of industrial growth. In the third phase we can no longer speak of 'de-industrialization' in destructive or obstructive terms as in the two previous phases, but we would have to characterize the kind of industrial growth which emerged in India as isolated, stunted and fragmented. It was not so much the direct colonial impact, but rather the general consequences of the 'imperialism of free trade' and the nature of global technological development which relegated India to a subordinate position. Karl Marx, writing in 1853, had predicted that the introduction of the railways would inevitably lead to the industrialization of India due to the linkage effects of the production of engines and rolling stock, rails and bridges, etc. He could not know that steamships passing through the Suez Canal would reduce freight rates to such an extent that rails and engines, but also textile machinery, etc., could be sent to India from Great Britain, thus cutting off all linkages within India. Another technological innovation of that time, the telegraph, also contributed to a strengthening of imperial ties. Commercial intelligence, but also the telegraphic transfer of money, would now connect London with India at an amazing speed. Similarly, orders from London would reach the Government of India much more swiftly than in earlier times. India remained at the receiving end rather than being able to take any initiatives of its own. 'De-industrialization' in this third phase, in which some modern industry did actually emerge in India, was characterized by the many subtle ties with which India – like Gulliver, another giant – was held down.

NOTES

1. Ajit Singh, 'Manufacturing and De-industrialisation', in John Eatwell et al. (eds), *The New Palgrave: A Dictionary of Economics*, vol. 3, London, 1987, p. 304.
2. Morris D. Morris, 'Towards a Reinterpretation of Nineteenth-Century Indian Economic History', *Indian Economic and Social History Review*, 5 (1968), pp. 1-15.
3. Konrad Specker, *Weber im Wettbewerb. Das Schicksal des südindischen Textilhandwerks im 19. Jahrhundert*, Stuttgart, 1984.
4. Tirthankar Roy, *Traditional Industry in the Economy of Colonial India*, Cambridge, 1999.
5. Douglas E. Haynes, *Small-Town Capitalism in Western India: Artisans, Merchants and the Making of the Informal Economy, 1870-1960*, Cambridge: Cambridge University Press, 2012.
6. Haynes, *Small-Town Capitalism*, p. 125.
7. Ibid., p, 114.
8. Ibid., p. 252.
9. Sergio Aiolfi, *Calicos und gedrucktes Zeug. Die Entwicklung der englischen Textilveredelung und der Tuchhandel der East India Company, 1650-1950*, Stuttgart, 1987, p. 317.
10. Dietmar Rothermund, 'The Changing Pattern of British Trade in Indian Textiles, 1701-1757', in Sushil Chaudhuri and Michel Morineau, eds., *Merchants, Companies and Trade: Europe and Asia in the Early Modern Era*, Cambridge, 1999.
11. Dietmar Rothermund, *Asian Trade and European Expansion in the Age of Mercantilism*, Delhi: Manohar, 1981.
12. See Serge Chassagne, Le coton et ses patrons. France, 1760-1840, Paris, 1992; Ulrich Pfister, *Die Zürcher Fabriques. Proto-industrielles Wachstum im 16.-18. Jahrhundert*, Zurich, 1992, and J.K.J. Thomson, *A Distinctive Industrialization: Cotton in Barcelona, 1728-1832*, Cambridge, 1996.
13. Rothermund, *Asian Trade and European Expansion*.
14. Ralph Davis, *The Rise of the Atlantic Economies*, London, 1973, pp. 311-12.
15. Gerhard Adelmann, *Die Baumwollgewerbe Nordwestdeutschlands und der westlichen Nachbarländer beim Übergang von der vorindustriellen zur frühindustriellen Zeit, 1750-1815*, Stuttgart, 2001, p. 72.

16. Akos Paulinyi and Ulrich Troitzsch, *Mechanisierung und Maschinisierung, 1600 bis 1840* [Propyläen Technikgeschichte Bd. 3], Berlin, 1997, pp. 307-9.
17. Ibid., p. 312.
18. Adelmann, *Die Baumwollgewerbe Nordwestdeutschlands und der westlichen Nachbarländer*, p. 65.
19. Ibid.
20. Aiolfi, Calicos und gedrucktes Zeug, pp. 162-74.
21. Paulinyi and Troitzsch, *Mechanisierung und Maschinisierung*, p. 314.
22. Ibid., p. 310.
23. Rothermund, 'The Changing Pattern of British Trade in Indian Textiles'.
24. Om Prakash, 'Trade and Politics in Eighteenth Century Bengal', in Leonard Blussé and Femme Gastra, eds., *On the Eighteenth Century as a Category of Asian History*, Aldershot, 1998, pp. 248-57.
25. Specker, *Weber im Wettbewerb*, pp. 278-9.
26. Dietmar Rothermund, 'India's Silver Currency: An Aspect of the Monetary Policy of British Imperialism', *Indian Economic and Social History Review*, 7 (1970), pp. 351-67.
27. Roy, *Traditional Industry in the Economy of Colonial India.*
28. Tirthankar Roy, *The Economic History of India, 1857-1947*, New Delhi, 2000, p. 131.
29. Roy, *Traditional Industry in the Economy of Colonial India*, pp. 161-5.

CHAPTER 9

Mumbai: From Fishing Village to Metropolis*

A NODE IN MANY NETWORKS

Mumbai has been a node in many networks in the course of its history. Some traces of these nodal points are still visible in its cityscape. Its modern history began in the 1660s when it graduated from a fishing village to a fortified port of the East India Company. For a long time it remained an outpost of the British factory in the Mughal Port of Surat. The Maratha empire controlled its hinterland throughout the eighteenth century and condemned it to a marginal position. It profited from the decline of Surat after 1730 but its position remained tenuous nevertheless. When the British defeated the Marathas in 1818, Mumbai emerged as the capital of a vast territory. It now controlled its hinterland and became the centre of a network of political and commercial relations extending into the interior of India while at the same time increasing its maritime outreach. But its real breakthrough came only in the period from 1850 to 1870 when several developments converged which added up to a sudden transformation of the role of Mumbai. The railways linked the port with the hinterland just at the time when the American Civil War led to an Indian cotton boom. Mumbai became very wealthy in a short time. Building activity increased, the fort was dismantled, the sanitation of the city was improved and a textile industry grew up at what were then the outskirts of the city. The opening of the Suez Canal in 1869 cut the distance between London and Mumbai by

*This paper was presented as a keynote address at the conference 'Between Global Aspirations and Local Realities: India's Cities in Interdisciplinary Perspective', jointly held by the South Asia Institute of Heidelberg University and the Jawaharlal Nehru University, New Delhi, 26-8 March, 2012. The conference was supported by grants of the German Research Foundation and the German Federal Ministry of Education and Research.

half. Telegraph and steamers helped to invigorate maritime trade. Mumbai was now *Urbs Prima in Indis* as its new logo proudly announced.

In 1885 the first session of the Indian National Congress was held in Mumbai and the city then supported the Indian freedom movement financially throughout the subsequent decades. It also provided many leaders to the freedom movement in its early phase.Thus Mumbai became an important nodal point also in the nationalist network. Two world wars and the inter-war depression made an impact on Mumbai. But its most trying time came after independence when the huge Bombay Presidency of which Mumbai was the capital had to be divided along linguistic lines. 'Cosmopolitan' Mumbai which harboured speakers of many languages was claimed by the Maharashtrians who fought for it in the streets of the city until they won their battle in 1960. The subsequent two decades witnessed a further development of the city, but then the great textile workers strike of the 1980s killed the city's premier industry. Mumbai had to re-invent itself as a centre of services and software production. This process is still going on. It is accompanied by a fierce struggle for the reclamation of the land of the mills. Similarly the lands of the Port Trust which is the greatest landlord in Mumbai are coveted by many 'developers'. While these contestations are going on, Mumbai also harbours the largest slum in Asia at Dharavi. In the meantime Mumbai has become 'Greater Mumbai', a conurbation extending far beyond the island city and deserving to be called a 'megalopolis'.

In discussing the history of Mumbai which has been briefly outlined here, we can only study some significant episodes in detail. In each case we shall highlight the features which were crucial for the further development of the city. The nodal points occupied by the city in different networks will be of special interest to us. The cultural history of Mumbai will not be covered here, although it is of great importance. However, some remarks on the tensions between 'urbanity' and 'cityness' may conclude this introduction. 'Urbanity' refers to the cultural refinement of the city-dweller as distinct from the habitus of the rustic villager. 'Cityness' is a term introduced by the sociologist, Abdoumaliq Simone, who has studied several urban centres of the Global South from Jakarta to Dakar. It refers to the frequent intersections of many lives in the give-and-take of daily survival in the big city.[1] Mumbai is certainly characterized by intense cityness. Suketu Mehta has captured this atmosphere very well in his *Mumbai:*

Maximum City.[2] But there are also many traces of urbanity in the vigorous cultural life of this cosmopolitan metropolis.

A FORT SURROUNDED BY FISHERMEN

The Portuguese had controlled the island of Mumbai and the adjacent small islands as well as the immediate vicinity since 1534. The British in their factory at Surat had eyed these possessions for quite some time before King Charles II received them when he married the Portuguese princess Catherine of Braganza in 1661. The Portuguese did not give up Mumbai lightly and created all kinds of difficulties for the royal governors dispatched by Charles II. The king then let Mumbai in perpetuity for a small rent to the East India Company which took over the islands in 1668. Mumbai became an outpost of the British factory at Surat. It so happened that in 1664 the Maratha king, Shivaji, had sacked Surat and the British could well have opted for Mumbai as a suitable alternative for their base at Surat. But Surat was the main port of the Mughal empire. It had a good access to the hinterland via the Tapi valley and its great Muslim merchants had excellent connections with the Red Sea trade. Surat as the main node of this great trading network recovered from Shivaji's brazen attack very quickly, as the network was not destroyed and the trade did not suffer.[3] Thus the British had no reason to shift to Mumbai at that time as Surat flourished for several decades until the Marathas under Peshwa Baji Rao I who ruled from 1720 to 1740 ruined the Mughal empire and occupied Surat's hinterland. It was then that Mumbai became more important for British trade. However, the Marathas now also controlled the hinterland of Mumbai and even the island of Salsette which the British had claimed as part of the Portuguese dowry. Salsette had been retained by the Portuguese until 1739 when it was conquered by the Marathas. The British got it only in 1802.

When Gerald Aungier became Governor of Mumbai on behalf of the East India Company in 1669, he constructed a fort on this island. This helped to defend the port against the Marathas later on. The local Kolis (fishermen) were not a serious threat for the British. They supplied them with fish and could be recruited for all kinds of work. They also paid a poll tax to the British as they had earlier done to the Portuguese. A Parsi family was in charge of collecting this tax under the Portuguese and continued to do so under the British. They were considered to be hereditary 'headmen' of the Kolis and retained this office until the 1830s.[4] The Kolis still supply the inhabitants of Mumbai with fish today and in the early twentieenth century they even defended their right to land their boats on Chowpatty Beach in the heart of the city. Aungier had not disturbed the symbiosis with the fishermen. He had also tried his best to attract other useful settlers to the island. More Parsis came from Gujarat in his time and he permitted them to construct a Tower of Silence for the disposal of their dead. This Tower of Silence still exists on Malabar Hill where it was built in Aungier's time. The first Parsi temple was also established in Mumbai at that time. In due course the Parsis became one of the most important communities of the city. Aungier had also made a great gesture of establishing the first British court in Mumbai. He had proclaimed that it would be devoted to impartial justice and even he himself could be tried in this court if the law would require it.[5] After this impressive beginning, Mumbai seemed to have a bright future. But it remained a neglected place throughout the eighteenth century. The Bombay Presidency was a poor cousin of the Bengal and Madras Presidencies. There were even plans to deprive it of the rank of a presidency as it was dependent on subsidies from Kolkata. By 1750 the city of Mumbai had only 70,000 inhabitants rising to 1,14,000 by 1780. Many Indian traders had left Surat and settled in Mumbai by that time. But the network commanded by Surat had withered away and could not be inherited by Mumbai which had to wait for the nineteenth century to come into its own.

THE CAPITAL OF A CONQUERED TERRITORY

In 1818 British troops under the command of Mountstuart Elphinstone vanquished the Maratha army in the battle of Khadki near Pune. Elphinstone was a civil servant of the East India Company, but he was also a brilliant military strategist. Early in his career he had served as assistant to the British resident at the court of the Peshwa in Pune and was an aide to Sir Arthur Wellesley (the Duke of Wellington) at the time of the battle of Assaye (1803) against the Marathas. In 1811 Elphinstone was sent as British Resident to Pune, observing the conduct of the Peshwa at close quarters. He was thus well equipped to vanquish him in 1818. In the following year he was appointed Governor of Mumbai and held this office until 1827. Unlike his predecessors he was now in charge of a vast territory and Mumbai flourished as his capital. Many people flocked to this capital and by

1830 its population had risen to 2,30,000. The magnificent Townhall (completed in 1833), which looks like an ancient Greek temple, commenmorates this splendour of the new capital. At present it houses the Asiatic Society of Mumbai.

Elphinstone believed in the benefits which Indians would derive from modern education and initiated state-aided education. The government college of the Bombay Presidency was named Elphinstone College in his honour. It was formally established only in 1856, but it had a predecessor, the Elphinstonian Institution.[6] Mumbai's first generation of Western educated Indians grew up in the new capital at that time. The commerce of Mumbai also increased in this period. The great Parsi merchant, Jamshedji Jeejeebhoy, made a fortune in the Opium trade with China. He embarked on several voyages to China and set the pace for his community in this enterprise. Jeejeebhoy was a great philanthropist and donated funds for hospitals and schools in Mumbai. The Sir J.J. School of Arts was endowed by him. Queen Victoria made him a knight and then a baronet. He was the first Indian to receive this high honour.

Prosperous Mumbai attracted many migrants and its population doubled from 1830 to 1846. But overcrowding and insanitary conditions in the 'native' quarters to the North of the Fort became major problems. By 1864 Mumbai had more than 8,00,000 inhabitants and called for urgent attention as far as civic administration was concerned.

GLOBAL PORT AND EMERGING INDUSTRIAL CENTRE IN THE MID-NINETEENTH CENTURY

The most important event for Mumbai in the mid-nineteenth century was the coming of the railways. It finally provided the port city with an easy access to its hinterland. Crossing the mountains which rose steeply behind Mumbai had been difficult. Pack animals had to carry heavy loads up and down the mountain passes. The coming of the railway age would deliver Mumbai from these constraints. A discussion of railway schemes started in 1843.[7] Some leading citizens of Mumbai established an Indian Railway Association in 1845. Jamshedji Jeejeebhoy and the leading Hindu merchant, Jagannath Shankerseth, sponsored this association and then became members of the board of the Great Indian Peninsula Railway (GIPR)(now Central Railway) which was incorporated in London by an act of Parliament in 1849.

In 1853 the first train steamed from Mumbai to Thane. Further work on the track proceeded swiftly. By 1858 Pune was reached and by 1860 Sholapur became the railhead in the heart of the cotton country. Another track of the same railway connected Mumbai with places like Nagpur and Jabalpur. Slightly later than the GIPR, the Bombay-Baroda and Central Indian Railway (BBCIR) (now Western Railway) started its operations and reached Baroda (now Vadodara) in 1861. Running along the coast, it did not have to cross mountains. It opened up the way to the cotton fields of Gujarat.

The cotton tracts had hardly been reached by the railways when the American Civil War disrupted the supply of American cotton to British mills. Indian cotton was suddenly in great demand and Mumbai emerged as the major port for the export of raw cotton. Enormous fortunes were amassed by the Mumbai cotton traders. The richest of them was Premchand Roychand, a Gujarati Jain whose parents had settled in Mumbai.[8] Born in 1831 he had received an English education and became a stock broker who attracted British as well as Indian clients. Known as 'King Cotton' he was at the centre of the share mania which befell Mumbai at that time. He did not only deal in cotton but also sponsored land reclamation companies. Such companies mushroomed in Mumbai which was bursting at its seams.[9] The end of the American Civil War marked also the end of the cotton boom in Mumbai. Satyendranath Tagore, Rabindranath's elder brother, has written a vivid account of these fateful years in Mumbai. He was among the first Indians who were admitted to the 'heavenborn' service, the Indian Civil Service (ICS), and he was posted to Mumbai in 1864. His *Bombai Chitra* published in Bengali show that he was an acute observer of the boom and bust of Mumbai's economy.[10]

Premchand Roychand and many others lost their fortunes in 1865, but being a great philanthropist he had donated huge amounts to the new University of Mumbai established in 1857.[11] The Rajabai Tower of the university and the university library which he had endowed were built only in the 1870s when his fortune had been lost. But the buildings which he financed remained as a permanent testimony to his munificence. He had also endowed a Premchand Roychand Scholarship at the University of Kolkata which was bestowed on brilliant students who were proud of this mark of distinction.

The University of Mumbai became the node of another important network connecting the city with its hinterland. It was an affiliating university on the pattern of the University of London and supervised college exams throughout Western India.[12] It thus set a uniform standard for higher education in this region. In its early years the university was housed in the Townhall before it could occupy its permanent buildings which were completed only in the 1870s.

The cotton boom had proved to be an ephemeral phenomenon, but it nevertheless left its traces in the city. Even before the boom some farsighted businessmen had laid the foundations for the cotton textile industry which later on dominated Mumbai for more than a century. The first mill was established in 1854 and others followed soon.[13] By 1870 there were 17 mills in Mumbai. The main product of these early mills was cotton yarn which was exported to China in large quantities. Land was available for the mills at the outskirts of the overcrowded city in the Parel-Byculla area which later on became known as Girangaon (mill village) and is nowadays in the heart of the city. The British cotton textile industry was not pleased by this development, but the British manufacturers of textile machinery were eager to sell their products to the Indian industrialists in Mumbai and helped them with technical advice. In the first half of the nineteenth century, cotton mills would not have been profitable in India, because the Indian weavers could produce cotton cloth cheaply as long as both raw cotton and the food they ate were also very cheap due to the deflation which prevailed at that time in India.[14] These conditions had changed very rapidly with the inflow of capital for the building of railways and the rising price of raw cotton during the cotton boom. When the cotton price fell after the boom was over, this then helped the Indian mills while the handloom weavers found it difficult to recover lost ground, the more so as India experienced a slow but steady inflation when the value of silver declined after 1876.[15]

With the cotton boom, the dawn of the railway age and incipient industrialization Mumbai experienced an unprecedented growth which urgently required changes in its municipal administration. Governor Bartle Frere (1862-9) was keen to revamp the city and ordered the dismantling of the old fort, thus creating a larger heart of the city. Frere's term of office partly coincided with those of two other remarkable officers who changed the face of Mumbai: Arthur Crawford, the first Municipal Commissioner[16] and Charles Forjett, Chief of Police. Both spoke Marathi fluently and kept in touch with the people of Mumbai. Crawford literally cleaned up the city and thus reduced the death rate considerably. Forjett toned up the police service and reduced the crime rate. He was a perfect spymaster who often toured the city incognito and in 1857 prevented an outbreak of the Mutiny in Mumbai by spotting the sepoys who were planning it before they could get into action.[17]

Crawford is still remembered for the Crawford Market which he installed. He was highly efficient, though he was only thirty years old when he became Municipal Commissioner. In his youthful ardour he was highhanded, his expenditure transgressed the limits of the municipal budget and he may have also lined his own pockets. The 'ratepayers' who had to pay the house taxes imposed by the municipal corporation emerged as a powerful interest group opposing Crawford who was supported by the big landlords led by Jagannath Shankerseth. The ratepayers raised the slogan 'no taxation without representation' and demanded a revision of the municipal act.[18] Crawford had been defended in the legal case by a brilliant young Parsi lawyer, Pherozeshah Mehta, who had returned from his legal studies in London in 1868 when he was only twenty-three years old. He quickly emerged as the major municipal leader and was entrusted with drafting the new Act of 1872 which provided for a representation of the ratepayers but also retained the strong position of the municipal commissioner. After the dust had settled and Crawford had left, Mehta was appointed municipal commissioner in 1873. He was to earn the sobriquet 'Lion of Bombay'.

Mumbai was a different place after Crawford had reshaped it. But after these years of boom and reform, it experienced a sudden decline in its population from about 8,00,000 to 6,00,000. Many of those who had found work in the city when millions of bales of cotton had to be shipped must have returned to their villages when they lost their employment. The opening of the Suez Canal a few years after the end of the cotton boom did not immediately create much new employment for workers in Mumbai. On the contrary, with lower freight rates British industrial goods were now much cheaper in India. The locomotives and other equipment for the early railways had been manufactured in Mumbai,[19] but once the Suez Canal was opened, locomotives, rails and overbridges could be imported from Great Britain. Even British coal was now cheaper in Mumbai than Indian coal from Bengal. But, of course, Mumbai's imports increased and its Port Trust became a major employer.

Towards the end of the nineteenth century the city had once more as many inhabitants as in 1864 but then the plague struck in 1896. After the plague there were only about 4,00,000 left. Those who could do so had returned to their villages. But the city soon recovered and added new splendour to its impressive cityscape. In 1903 Jamshetji Tata opened his legendary Taj Mahal Hotel. He had to rent the place where he built it, from the Port Trust. Tata had been refused to stay at a British owned hotel nearby and had then decided to build his own hotel which would far surpass the one to which he had not been admitted. Tata was fabulously wealthy. He had also suffered a loss as a young man at the time when the cotton boom ended. But he had then turned himself into an innovative millowner. He was the first to introduce ring spinning in India in 1877. It was an American invention which was adopted in Great Britain only at the time when Tata did this for India. Unlike the earlier Parsi entrepreneurs of Mumbai who were mainly traders, Tata was a visionary industrialist.[20] Whereas the other major industrial centre of India, Kolkata, was in the hands of British firms, the rise of Tata manifested the strength of Indian enterprise in Mumbai.

CHALLENGES OF THE TWENTIETH CENTURY: WAR, DEPRESSION, WAR

The early years of the twentieth century were a period of prosperity for Mumbai. Even the First World War to some extent benefited Mumbai. Maritime trade was curtailed during the war, but for industrial Mumbai which produced goods for the Indian homemarket this had an effect similar to a protective tariff. The British had always denied this protection to India's infant industry, but the war impeded imports and the Mumbai mills could substitute them. They would have liked to expand at that time, but the import of textile machinery was also affected by the war and India could not yet produce this machinery. After the war the Indian millowners who had accumulated a large amount of capital placed enormous orders for new machinery, creating excess capacity which troubled them in the 1920s.[21] The Mumbai mill owners were on the horns of a dilemma. They still controlled about 50 per cent of India's cotton textile production, but the other half was contributed by upcountry mills which were close to the cotton tracts and paid lower wages. In 1919 a large scale strike of the Mumbai textile workers hit the mills. War-time inflation had raised the cost of living in Mumbai and the workers could not make both ends meet. About 1,50,000 millhands are supposed to have struck work at that time, but the strike was not organized by trade-unions which later on played such an important role in Mumbai.[22] In 1919 the strike started spontaneously in one mill, then spread to the next one and so on until all mills were affected. The strike in Ahmedabad in 1918 in which Gandhi had been active may have inspired the Mumbai workers, but Gandhi played no role in the Mumbai strike. His influence spread in Mumbai only during the Rowlatt satyagraha several months later.

The profits of the Mumbai millowners dwindled in the mid-1920s. By 1925 most of them were in the red. At this stage the Mumbai Millowners Association advocated a wage cut of about 10 per cent.[23] This caused labour trouble. In contrast with the strike of 1919, the strike of 1925 was organized by Communist led trade-unions. But it was only a prelude to the much bigger ones of 1928 and 1929. Altogether about 44 million man-days were lost in those two years.

The impact of the Great Depression changed all this very radically. The prices of wheat and rice were halved in 1930 and 1931. This increased the real wages of labour as nominal wages remained sticky. At the same time the mill owners benefited from a protective tariff introduced by the British to ward off the import of cheap Japanese textiles.[24] After a radical devaluation of the Japanese currency, Japanese textiles threatened not only Indian textiles but also the import of British textiles into India. The British imposed a scheme of 'market sharing' on the Indian textile industry by introducing preferential rates for British textiles. The Indian mill owners disliked 'imperial preference' but had to accept it as this was the price of protection.[25] The production of India's cotton textile mills increased in the 1930s. But the Mumbai mills were at a disadvantage, because they faced the increasing competition of upcountry mills and of the handloom weavers who stepped up their production to an amazing extent.[26] Since cotton and food were now very cheap, they could once more make both ends meet. However, agrarian distress caused by the depression also restricted the purchasing power of the masses. Per capita consumption of textiles remained more or less the same, only population growth led to an increasing demand for textiles. Under such conditions the Mumbai mill owners did not prosper during the depression years. The only saving grace was that they did not face any labour trouble. The fact that they invested very little in new machinery in the 1930s shows that they did not accumulate much capital during the depression years. A glance at the contemporary balance sheets of the Standard Mill owned by the Mafatlals indicates that this major firm was close to insolvency and drastically reduced the capital invested in the mill.[27]

During the Second World War the Mumbai mills reaped handsome profits by producing goods for the British. The colonial government dictated the prices according to a 'cost plus' formula, granting a 10 per cent margin of profit to the mill owners.[28] These were not windfall gains, but due to the large orders the mills did very well under this arrangement. No new machinery could be imported during the war and India still did not yet manufacture textile machines. Since hardly any machines had been imported during the depression years, the mills were saddled with antiquated and worn-out equipment at the end of the war. But this time the mill owners could not buy new machines as they had done after the First World War. India had to sign a moratorium on the eve of independence which precluded immediate access to the reserves accumulated during the war in the Bank of England.

Mumbai city had grown a great deal during this period. Dadar, the part of the city to the north of the mills, had by now become a central residential area. Mahim which was still covered by palm trees at the beginning of the twentieth century had become another crowded precinct.[29] Bandra, beyond the Mahim Creek, emerged as the most fashionable suburb and a favourite place of the Bollywood filmstars.

MUMBAI AND SAMYUKTA MAHARASHTRA

After independence Mumbai remained the capital of the huge Bombay State, but it was soon to be affected by 'states reorganization' along linguistic lines. This necessitated a division between Gujarat and Maharashtra which would have caused no problems if Mumbai had not become a bone of contention. It was sourrounded by Maharashtra, but only about half of its population consisted of Marathi-speakers. There was a large Gujarati minority which dominated the economy of the city. Nehru felt that the linguistic reorganization of states would harm national unity and agreed to it only very reluctantly.[30] He particularly annoyed the Maharashtrians and due to his prevarication the Samyukta (Unified) Maharashtra movement gained momentum.

In January 1956 he poured oil into the fire by announcing that the central government would take over Mumbai and make it a Union Territory.[31] Thus in 1956 a Samyukta Maharashtra Samiti was organized by the opposition parties with the eminent Socialist S.M. Joshi as its Secretary General. Joshi had been a freedom fighter attached to Gandhi's ideas. He did not support violent agitations, but when Nehru and the Government of India refused to listen to the Maharashtrians, the agitation took a radical turn. In 1956 C.D. Deshmukh, the Finance Minister in Nehru's cabinet and the most prominent Maharashtrian in the Government of India, resigned in protest against Nehru's policy. This greatly supported the Samyukta Maharashtra Samiti.

Morarji Desai, the Chief Minister of Bombay State, a Gujarati, was relentless in his opposition to Samyukta Maharashtra. In January 1960 the police shot at demonstrators in the heart of Mumbai and killed some of them. The tragic event is commemorated by a monument near Flora Fountain. This central place has been renamed Hutatma Chowk (Martyrs Place). In order to placate the Maharashtrians, Morarji Desai was replaced by Y. B. Chavan, a Maharashtrian, who presided over the division of the state. The Congress leadership had accepted the division, because it feared that it might lose the elections of 1962 in Maharashtra. Having reached its goal, the Samyukta Maharashtra movement faded away and played no role in the elections which were once more won by the Congress party.

'Left unity' had been the driving force of Samyukta Maharashtra. The textile workers, who were mostly Maharashtrians, were the backbone of the agitation which to some extent became a class struggle against the Gujarati millowners and the ruling Congress party. The Communist Party of India (CPI) led by S.A. Dange had great influence on the workers. Since the Communists had to support the British during the war, they were regarded as traitors by Indian nationalists as well as by socialists like S.M. Joshi. It was due to Joshi's initiative that this gulf was bridged in 1956. But after 1960, 'left unity' disintegrated. The Chinese attack on India in 1962 which then led to the split of the CPI in 1964 played a crucial role in this development. Dange, who took a nationalist line, was isolated and lost his hold on the party. His influence on the trade union movement also receded. At the same time, S.M. Joshi's fame also faded and the younger generation of the Maharashtrians looked for other leaders. Even the sons of dedicated Communist textile workers drifted towards a new movement: the Shiv Sena, founded by Balasaheb Thackeray in 1966.[32] He articulated their feelings of frustration and tried to find jobs for the unemployed. Thackeray was a fascist who openly announced his admiration for Hitler. He was a staunch anti-communist and this made him attractive for the Congress leaders who used him and his young followers in order to undermine Communist influence in Mumbai. As Mumbai's woes increased due to the decline of the textile industry, the Shiv Sena's star was rising . It could not do much for the workers, but it articulated the general frustration which spread in Mumbai and occasionally it incited violent riots.

THE 'DE-INDUSTRIALIZATION' OF MUMBAI IN THE 1980S

The textile policy which the Government of India adopted after independence badly affected the Mumbai mills. After an initial experiment of liberalizing the textile market, it introduced strict controls. It also favoured the handloom weavers and discouraged the introduction of modern machinery.[33] Actually the handloom weavers were displaced by powerloom operators producing cheap cotton cloth in small sheds. These operators paid hardly any taxes, could hire and fire their workers and paid them very low wages. The mill owners had clamoured for protective tariffs shielding them from foreign competition, but protection then benefited the powerloom operators. Both protectionism and the textile policy created an atmosphere which did not encourage new investment in the mills. Many mills turned 'sick', but in order to combat unemployment, the goverment did not let them go bankrupt but supported them. Clever mill owners even managed to profit from 'sickness' by using subsidies for other purposes than that of nursing their sick mills.[34] The public sector National Textile Corporation (NTC) established in 1968 then took over mills which were terminally 'sick' and thus amassed valuable real estate in Mumbai about which more will be said later on. By 1974 more than 100 mills had been taken over by NTC and they were all nationalized by a special act passed in that year. Between 1965 and 1979 mill production had stagnated at about 4 billion metres per year whereas powerloom production had increased from 3 to 5 billion metres. The powerlooms were now definitely ahead of the mills.[35]

The frustrated textile workers of Mumbai did not realize that they were doomed when they took the fatal decision to go on strike in

January 1982. They had turned to an independent labour leader, Dr. Datta Samant, as the Congress-led 'official' union (Rashtriya Mill Mazdoor Sabha) could not help them. Under the Bombay Industrial Relations Act of 1946 only one union would be recognized for the textile industry and such a recognized union was prohibited from organizing an 'illegal' strike. When the strike was on in 1982, this 'official' union organized strikebreakers rather than helping the striking workers.

Dr. Samant, whom the textile workers had asked to lead them, had worked as a physician in a working class neighbourhood. He had sympathized with the workers and had successfully conducted a strike in an automobile factory in Mumbai where he had obtained a wage rise related to increasing productivity.[36] This impressed the textile workers who did not see that the hopeless situation of their industry precluded a similar success. They showed extraordinary perseverance when the strike continued for more than a year. The charismatic Samant encouraged them to stand fast. But many workers who had to earn a living after all turned to the powerlooms and the millowners bought cloth from the powerlooms and marketed it as they had no products of their own to sell. Thus the brave strike only strengthened the powerlooms and increased the number of 'sick' mills. The workers who shifted to the powerlooms did not realize that they undermined the effect of the strike in this way. In January 1982, when the strike began, A.R. Antulay was the Chief Minister of Maharashtra and he was inclined to mediate so as to achieve a compromise, but he had to resign due to corruption charges. His successors adopted a hard line. In July 1982, S.M. Joshi went to Delhi and pleaded with Indira Gandhi to intervene, but she refused to do so.[37] The Congress leadership did not want to enable Samant to score a success and would rather starve the workers into submission. Samant was ready for a compromise at that time, but he had no 'exit strategy' and did not want to betray the workers. They respected him for that and did not blame him even when the strike, which he never called off, finally collapsed, leaving the workers in utter distress. Those who had shifted to the powerlooms had to put up with much lower wages. Many left the city and those who remained in the city were unemployed. The *chawls*, their one-room tenements, decayed. In 1989 a Closed Mills Workers Action Committtee was founded by old trade unionists. It campaigned for a reopening of the mills – but it was a losing battle.[38] In July 2011 about 28,000 homeless textile workers marched through the city in a procession in order to call attention to their plight. It was a tragic demonstration highlighting the fate of a 'de-industrialized' Mumbai.

'Girangaon' as the mill area in the heart of Mumbai was called, had been a centre of popular culture. The workers lived near their mills. They ate together in *khanavals*, community kitchens run by housewives of the neighbourhood. They met at *vyayamshalas* for bodybuilding and other exercises, and they attended theatre performances and listened to local poets and singers.[39] 'Cityness' produced a popular 'urbanity' in these quarters. All this disappeared as the mills closed. *Ripping the Fabric* is the title of a book by Darryl D'Monte on the decline of Mumbai and its mills.[40] This title reflects the tearing asunder of the social cohesion which had earlier characterized the life of the city despite all its conflicts and contradictions. A spread of anomie, of socially conditioned lawlessness and frustration, prevailed in the 1990s. Its most obvious symptom were the terrible riots of 1993 which broke out all over the city. These riots were triggered by Hindu-Muslim encounters in the wake of the destruction of the Babri Masjid in Ayodhya, but they quickly went far beyond this source of conflict. The hatred against 'outsiders' nurtured for some years by the Shiv Sena found its expression when hordes of Maharashtrians swept through the streets shouting 'Mumbai hamari hai'.[41] Mumbai was not quite the same again after these violent outbursts although 'business as usual' seemed to prevail once more after some time.

The Shiv Sena prospered in the aftermath of the failed strike. In addition to its earlier campaigns against 'outsiders' it now adopted a militant hatred of Muslims. The first evidence of this were the Bhiwandi riots of 1984. This was then revived with a vengenace in the riots of 1993 which affected all of Mumbai. It is estimated that more than 2,00,000 people fled the city during the riots. Many of them may have never returned.

THE LANDS OF THE MILLS AND OF THE PORT TRUST AND THE SLUM AT DHARAVI

The deserted mills remained as monuments of bygone days in the heart of the city. It would have been sensible to use the mill lands for the construction of affordable housing. Mumbai is 'blessed' by a Rent Control Act passed immediatelly after the Second World War, freezing rents at the level of 1940.[42] This was supposed to prevent rack-renting at a time when people flocked into the city in large numbers. But it also discouraged landlords from improving the existing houses and building new ones. Those who have inherited houses or flats in Mumbai from their parents can enjoy holding them at very low rents. Politicians will hesitate to deprive them of those privileges. A revised Rent Act was passed in 1986. It relaxed rent control for new buildings so as to encourage developers of real estate, but it did not touch the privileges of old tenants. However, these are doubtful privileges if they condemn the people to live in dilapidated buildings as the landlords will not renovate them.

The new high-rise buildings which dominate the sky-line of Mumbai are only providing homes for the rich – and Mumbai attracts many of them. Quite a few of these new buildings have come up on mill lands. But it took some time before these lands could be sold, because the government was initially very reluctant to permit such sales. There were dreams of reviving industry or of providing open spaces which the city urgently needs. Legal restrictions were introduced and then contested and revised.[43] Developers were not sure of what could be done. But finally the dam broke and mill lands flooded the real estate market. A young firm of real estate brokers established in 1999 and appropriately called 'Indiabulls' charged into the arena and grabbed choice pieces of milllands in Girangaon (i.e. Parel, Worli etc.) The NTC which has been mentioned before sold the plots of the nationalized mills and collected huge amounts. Private mill owners followed suit. By now almost all prime milllands have been sold. Attention now turns to the land held by the Port Trust of Mumbai which controls more than 700 acres along the seafront to the east of the city.

The Mumbai Port Trust is a powerful institution established in 1873 as an autonomous corporation. It is now owned by the Government of India. Following British precedent, the Port Trust is not only a landlord but also the employer of a large labourforce which loads and unloads ships. Originally the idea of having a specialized labourforce was a good one, because the handling of ships requires many skills. An efficient labourforce would reduce the turnaround time and thereby save demurrage charges. But this could also be perverted by letting the labourforce 'work to rule' and thus delay the turnaround which enabled the Port Trust to collect heavy demurrage charges.[44] It is said that for a long time the Port Trust saw to it that turnaround time would be 8 days regardless of the size of the vessel. Ships with only a part of their load destined for Mumbai would break bulk in Colombo or Singapore so as to avoid getting delayed in Mumbai. Recently the Port Trust has become more efficient, but as a landlord it is still a monster sitting on a huge pile of prime real estate. I once had a chance to take a ride across the Port Trust lands. I crossed a huge expanse of vacant land cluttered with rusty remnants of what may once have been useful equipment. But the land held by the Port Trust extends beyond those vacant lands. As mentioned before, even the Taj Mahal Hotel has been built on Port Trust land and there has recently been a dispute about the rent which the Tatas ought to pay for it. Just like Bartle Frere dismantled the Fort in the 1860s, the Government of India should now disband the surplus lands of the Port Trust. But it should also take care of providing a masterplan for this land instead of letting the 'Indiabulls' convert it into their arena.

Even all the new land developments discussed here will not help to relocate the inhabitants of Dharavi, which is often called the largest slum of Asia as it houses about 1 million people. This sprawling shanty town is full of economic activity.[45] The 'informal sector' flourishes here. Many slum dwellers are not poor, they have refrigerators and television sets in their huts, but they could not afford to pay the rent for a flat in the city. Dharavi was originally a fishing village and some of the fishermen still live here. Since the fish have become scarce in the polluted water, they have turned to brewing illicit liquor. About a third of Dharavi inhabitants are Tamilian tanners who have upgraded their production to finished leathergoods. Readymade garments and jewellery are also produced in the small shops along the narrow alleys of Dharavi. People in Dharavi estimate that the daily turnover of goods in this industrious slum amounts to one million US Dollars. Only about 10 per cent of the inhabitants are unemployed. Dharavi is still attractive for upcountry immigrants, because some jobs can always be found here. Intense 'cityness' is very much in evidence here. Many of Dharavi's people are literate and education is highly valued. There are many second generation slum dwellers here. In the 1970s the government was still busy demolishing slums, but later on it started recognizing them and has supplied them with basic amenities like water, toilets and drains, etc. Dharavi was also affected by the riots of 1993 which have been mentioned earlier. Half of its inhabitants are Muslims. They used to live with their Hindu neighbours without major conflicts. The identity politics projected by the Shiv Sena had also penetrated Dharavi and upset Hindu-Muslim relations.

Dharavi is not the only large slum in Mumbai. There are supposed to be four more slums in the city which rival Dharavi. It is estimated that half of Mumbai's inhabitants live in slums. In addition to the visible slums there are many small ones tucked away in backyards and between regular quarters. Most families living in regular quarters have servants who live in nearby slums. Many of the resourceful dabbawallas who take food from the home to the office of their middle class customers may also live in slums. There is thus a kind of symbiosis of those who can afford regular housing and the slum dwellers who work for them. The overcrowded island city has reached its limits. Further expansion is possible only on the mainland where the sprawling conurbation of Greater Mumbai grows by leaps and bounds.

THE GREATER MUMBAI CONURBATION AND ITS PARTS

Patrick Geddes coined the term 'conurbation' which is now applied to Mumbai. He intitally thought of contemporary Birmingham and its environment when he invented this word. He was a polymath, taught botany and zoology, worked as a town planner and ended up as a sociologist. He analysed the Mumbai town plan of 1915. It was in this year that he created the word 'conurbation'. He lived in Mumbai for several years and chaired the University of Mumbai's Department of Sociology from 1919 to 1924.[46] He was influenced by the evolutionary thought of Herbert Spencer. When he was in Mumbai it had not yet become a fully developed conurbation. A conurbation emerges when cities and towns which intially have their own distinctive centres converge and their boundaries get blurred. This has happened to Mumbai and Thane to which have been added Kalyan-Dombivli, Ulhasnagar, Bhiwandi and Raigad. Navi Mumbai on the other side of the harbour is somewhat different in this respect. It is a planned satellite city which is at the most an adjunct to the conurbation.

Thane is the biggest town next to Mumbai city and has a population of 2.5 million. It is a very ancient town and was known as a port even to the seafarers of antiquity. It has a diversified industry and many firms which find Mumbai city too crowded have set up their plants here. The process which produces a 'conurbation' can be traced very well by looking at the merger of Mumbai and Thane which still maintain their distinct identity although the boundaries between them are blurred.

Kalyan-Dombivli is a rather new municipal corporation, but Kalyan, its centre, is also a very old town. It covers a large area which harbours many small-scale industries of the 'unorganized sector' which supply parts to the industrial firms located in Greater Mumbai. It has a population of about 1.2 million. Ulhasnagar is a rather young urban community. Refugees from Sindh settled here in an old army camp after the Partition of India. Half of the population of nearly 1 million are Sindhis who are very alert businessmen. They have made Ulhasnagar a thriving economic centre.

Bhiwandi, which by now has a population of one million people, is primarily a powerloom textile centre and has benefited from the decline of the Mumbai mills and may have absorbed a large number of the millhands which left Mumbai in the 1980s. It is also a centre of many godowns in which goods are stored for further transport into Mumbai or to places elsewhere. It thus helps to save storage space in Mumbai city.

Navi Mumbai was established as a satellite of Mumbai City in 1972, it became a Municipal Corporation in 1991. It is supposed to be the biggest planned city on earth. Conceived as a twin city of Mumbai, almost half of its more than 2 million inhabitants have come from Mumbai. The aim of decongesting Mumbai in this way has thus been accomplished to some extent. But it has not yet become a true twin of the metropolis.[47] It is multicentred, Nerul and Vashi are its major settlements. Together they account for about three quarters of the population of Navi Mumbai. At the southern end of Navi Mumbai is the Jawaharlal Nehru Port at Nhava Sheva, India's largest container port. It urgently needs further expansion as its present capacity is strained. To the south of Navi Mumbai is Raigad, a new settlement near the Fort of Shivaji built in the seventeenth century. It is at the outskirts of the Mumbai conurbation but already attracts residents working in Mumbai city. Convenient local transport is a major problem of the expanding conurbation. The island city has a good railway network and in recent years new lines have been constructed which reach the other centres of the conurbation. There were also plans of using hovercraft for providing sealinks across the harbour. With further urban growth all avenues of speedy transport have to be explored.

FUTURE PROBLEMS OF THE 'MAXIMUM CITY'

Mumbai has changed from an old-style industrial city to a global service hub. Tata Consultancy Services, India's leading software firm, has now nearly 2,50,000 employees. Of course, many of them work abroad, but even in Mumbai they are of great importance. Textile workers could not be retrained for employment in the sophisticated service sector. Thus the workforce of Mumbai has changed beyond recognition within a few decades. The knowledge economy spreads while old-style industry recedes. Mumbai is now an important node in a global network of the knowledge economy. Knowledge workers live in high rise buildings and not in slums. Real estate wizards like the 'Indiabulls' are very much aware of this and cater to the new needs of the Maximum City. But the metamorphosis of an old metropolis is a painful process. It requires the patient approach of a physiotherapist rather than the quick operation of a surgeon. City planners face a daunting task in the Maximum City. A new avatar of Patrick Geddes would be helpful in this context. Mumbai's rich industrialists like Mukesh Ambani of Reliance Industries could apply their enormous financial resources to creative projects of urban renewal. But even more essential is the political will of legislators and administrators who have to make proper decisions and back them up with concerted action. The population of Greater Mumbai may double within a few decades. The Maximum City must be prepared for its gigantic transformation.

NOTES

1. Simone Abdoumaliq, *City Life from Jakarta to Dakar: Movements at the Crossroads*, London: Routledge, 2010, p. 117.
2. Suketu Mehta, *Maximum City: Mumbai Lost and Found*, Delhi: Penguin, 2004.
3. Ashin Das Gupta, *Indian Merchants and the Decline of Surat, c.1700-1750*, Wiesbaden: Steiner, p. 7.
4. Peter Reeves et al., 'The Koli and the British at Bombay: The Structure of Their Relations to the Mid-Nineteenth Century', in *South Asia*, vol. XIX, Special Issue, 1996, pp. 97-119.
5. Mariam Dossal, *Mumbai: Theatre of Conflict, City of Hope*, Delhi: Oxford University Press, 2010, p. 17.
6. Teresa Albuquerque, *Urbs Prima in Indis: Bombay 1840-1865*, Delhi: Promilla, 1985, p. 139.

7. Albuquerque, *Urbs Prima*, p. 4.
8. Ibid., pp. 18-20.
9. Mariam Dossal, *Imperial Designs and Indian Realities: The Planning of Bombay City, 1845-1875*, Delhi: Oxford University Press, 1991, pp. 156-63.
10. Ruby Maloni, 'Satyendranath Tagore's *Bombai Chitra*: Bombay Presidency in the Nineteenth Century', in Mariam Dossal and Ruby Maloni, eds., *State Intervention and Popular Response: Western India in the Nineteenth Century*, Bombay: Popular Prakashan, 1999, pp. 187-204.
11. Aroon Tikekar, *The Cloister's Pale: A Biography of the University of Mumbai*, Mumbai: Popular Prakashan, 2006 (2nd edn.), p. 36.
12. Tikekar, *The Cloister's Pale*, p.10.
13. Dietmar Rothermund, *An Economic History of India*, Beckenham: Croom Helm, 1988, pp. 51-3.
14. Rothermund, *Economic History*, pp. 28-9.
15. Ibid., pp. 42-4.
16. Albuquerque, *Urbs Prima*, p. 185.
17. Ibid., pp. 118-22.
18. Christine Dobbins, *Urban Leadership in Western India: Politics and Communities in Bombay City, 1840-1885*, London: Oxford University Press, 1972, pp. 131-52.
19. John Hurd, 'Railways', in Dharma Kumar, ed., *The Cambridge Economic History of India*, vol. 2, Cambridge: Cambridge University Press, 1983, p. 749.
20. Dietmar Rothermund, 'The Industrialization of India: Technology and Production', in B.B. Chaudhuri, ed., *Economic History of India from Eighteenth to Twentieth Century*, Delhi: Centre for Studies in Civilizations, 2005, pp. 450-2.
21. Rothermund, *Economic History*, pp. 85-6.
22. Neera Adarkar and Meena Menon, *One Hundred Years, One Hundred Voices: The Millworkers of Girangaon: An Oral History*, Calcutta: Seagull, 2004, p. 153.
23. Rothermund, *Economic History*, p. 87.
24. Dietmar Rothermund, *India in the Great Depression, 1929-1939*, Delhi: Manohar, 1992, pp. 142-54.
25. Ibid., p. 148.
26. Ibid., p. 159.
27. Ibid., p. 139.
28. Rothermund, *Economic History*, p. 120.
29. Dossal, *Mumbai*, pp. 168-71.
30. Michael Brecher, *Jawaharlal Nehru: A Political Biography*, London: Oxford University Press, 1959, p. 482.
31. Brecher, *Nehru*, p. 457.
32. Rajnarayan Chandavarkar, 'From Neighbourhood to Nation: Rise and

Fall of the Left in Bombay's Girangaon in the Twentieth Century', in Adarkar and Menon, *One Hundred Years*, pp. 51-7, see also Hansen, Thomas Blom, *Urban Violence in India: Identity Politics, 'Mumbai' and the Postcolonial City*, Delhi: Permanent Black, 2001.

33. Rothermund, 'The Industrialization of India', in Chaudhuri, *Economic History*, p. 475.
34. Ibid., p. 497.
35. Ibid., p. 486.
36. Adarkar and Menon, *One Hundred Years*, p. 361.
37. Ibid., pp. 388-90.
38. Ibid., p. 420.
39. Chandavarkar, 'Neighbourhood', in Adarkar and Menon, *One Hundred Years*, pp. 22-6.
40. Darryl D'Monte, *Ripping the Fabric: The Decline of Mumbai and Its Mills*, Delhi: Oxford University Press, 2002.
41. Jim Masselos, *The City in Action: Bombay Struggles for Power*, Delhi: Oxford University Press, 2007, p. 371.
42. Dossal, *Mumbai*, p. 226.
43. Ibid., pp. 218-21.
44. Dietmar Rothermund, *India: The Rise of an Asian Giant*, New Haven and London: Yale University Press, p. 90.
45. Kalpana Sharma, *Rediscovering Dharavi: Stories from Asia's Largest Slum*, Delhi: Penguin, 2000.
46. Tikekar, *The Cloister's Pale*, p. 159.
47. Masselos, *The City in Action*, p. 375.

CHAPTER 10

Nation Building in India under British Rule

INTRODUCTION: BRITISH CHALLENGE AND INDIAN RESPONSE

The British did not conquer India in order to build an Indian nation. On the contrary, most of the British posted in India never conceived of India as a nation and referred to it as 'congeries of nations' which could never be united. They also used the old imperial strategy of 'divide and rule'. And yet, they contributed unwittingly to nation-building in India by their very presence. They imposed a more or less uniform institutional framework of governance on India so as to control it. But even more important was the challenge they provided to the Indians by demonstrating what a nation could do whose power was derived from social cohesion and efficient organization. In the eighteenth century when the East India Company gained territorial control of large parts of India, the British were a small nation of about six million people. The former Mughal empire had approximately 150 million inhabitants. It was a confrontation like that between David and Goliath. The match was even more uneven, because the number of British men sent to India was very small. The British did not invade India, they hired Indian soldiers to conquer India for them and they paid them with the money of Indian taxpayers. The Great Mughals had based their central power on a monetized land revenue. When the British gained the control of the rich province of Bengal they could use its revenue for financing their further operations in India.

British military strength was not based on superior weapons. All weapons used in those times were easily available to Indian rulers, too. But the British introduced modern methods of infantry warfare in India which consisted of making soldiers fire well-timed volleys at the enemy's cavalry with a devastating effect.[1] Traditional Indian musketeers were skilful marksmen, but they were not used to concerted attacks. A few British drill sergeants sufficed to teach them the new methods of warfare. The British were also better military paymasters than their Indian adversaries. Indian military heroes were often inept as far as financial matters were concerned. They might even win a battle and were then unable to pay their troops who promptly deserted them. Officers in the service of a company of traders would calculate their military ventures more carefully. British military leaders in India had also other important characteristics which distinguished them from their adversaries. As members of a bourgeois nation they never succumbed to the feudal temptation of becoming independent warlords after a victorious campaign. Warren Hastings, the first Governor-General who was the founder of the British empire in India even humbly submitted to his recall and his impeachment by the British Parliament.[2] He was accused of conquering large parts of India 'illegally'. But whereas the Parliament impeached him for that, it never considered restoring those territories to their Indian rulers.

Another source of British strength was naval power which had been neglected by Indian rulers. The most powerful rulers of India were landbased and did not care for maritime affairs. The smaller rulers who controlled individual seaports benefited from customs duties and welcomed traders of all nations. They never thought of trying to control or oppress them as they knew that maritime trade could easily shift to other ports. The despotic regime of the monsoon shielded India against maritime invaders as their supply lines would be cut each year. This made Indian rulers complacent as far as the control of India's maritime periphery was concerned. Only the perceptive young ruler of Maharashtra, Madhav Rao, remarked in 1767 that the British had encircled India with a ring of naval power.[3] By that time it was too late to do anything about it even if Indian rulers had stopped their internecine warfare and had turned their attention to naval defence. The British had the best ships of the world at their disposal. In the 1660s the East India Company had closed its own dockyard and had adopted the very modern method of leasing rather than owning ships. Private shipowners then competed with each other to offer state-of-the-art ships to the company.[4] These ships sailed very fast and were heavily armed. They were the pride of the British nation and their captains were expert navigators who earned high salaries. National efficiency was clearly demonstrated by the performance of this impressive mercantile fleet. High freight charges imposed a strict discipline on the operations of this fleet. Timetables had to be closely watched as each day lost at sea meant a loss of much money. Capitalism subjected the British even at this early stage to its rigorous rules.

The Indians noticed the challenge posed to them by the British nation very slowly. Therefore their response to it took a long time. They were not confronted with a large foreign occupation army which could have provoked immediate resistance. The British gradually usurped and transformed Indian institutions. After the decline of the Mughal empire, the commercialization of power had increased in India.[5] Some Indian rulers so to speak mortgaged their states to merchants who organized the collection of their revenues and managed their treasury. In this context the activities of the East India Company were not unsual. This company could adjust much more easily to Indian conditions than an administration manned by royal officers of a foreign power would have done. The servants of the East India Company could play many roles in India. Initially they were hired as commercial employees only. Their salaries were meagre and they had to pay a large deposit when entering their career. It was taken for granted that they would enrich themselves in India, the deposit would be forfeited only if they hurt the company's interest by their machinations. If they served the company well they could quickly rise to high positions.

The career of Robert Clive provides striking evidence of this flexible pattern of company rule.[6] He came to India as a teenager and was first employed as a 'writer', i.e. clerk, in the company's office in Madras. In 1751 he emerged as a military hero in a war waged by the company against Indian rulers. He valiantly defended the fortress of Arcot against an Indian army. He then returned to his commercial line and made a fortune. He retired at an early age and campaigned for a seat in the British Parliament. He lost much money in the election campaign and did not win a seat. So he returned to India after having procured the patent of a Lieutenant Colonel. Back in India he was sent from Madras to Calcutta, commanding troops of the East India Company. The Nawab of Bengal had taken action against the British settlement there as it had been fortified by the British who defied his orders. Clive defeated the Nawab in 1757 and established British rule over this fertile province, becoming its first British governor. The Battle of Plassey which Clive won was a mere skirmish. His success was due to bribery rather than to military valour as the Nawab's general deserted the Nawab and joined forces with Clive. The traitor's name, Mir Jafar, is still a synonym for treachery in India. There was no parallel to his behaviour among the British. Clive was cunning and devious, he lined his pockets with Indian money, but faithfully served the British cause.

When the East India Company became a territorial ruler, the methods of Clive and his contemporaries had to be changed. The commercial servants of the company became 'civil servants' who earned high salaries which were supposed to prevent them from succumbing to corruption. The company established a special college at Haileybury in England where the candidates for the civil service were trained. They followed regular careers, starting as a district officer and ending as a secretary to government or even as a member of the governor's council. They were freely transferable and were expected to cope with any task with which they were entrusted. Indians had earlier been ruled by military commanders who employed scribes to do the administrative work for them, now they were to be ruled by British scribes.

ADMINISTRATION: THE BUREAUCRATIC 'STEEL FRAME'

The comparison of the British civil service in India with a 'steel frame' which kept the country together was made by Prime Minister Lloyd George in 1922. It was not an expression of imperial bravado, but rather a desparate plea at a time when the star of the empire was sinking. Lloyd George wanted to attract young British men to this service who were no longer certain whether they could look forward to a lifetime career in India. After India had gained independence, the powerful Home Minister, Vallabhbhai Patel, used similar words in order to defend the maintenance of the 'steel frame', now manned by Indians. Addressing the Constituent Assembly he asserted that the country had to be kept together by a 'ring of service'. His arguments were accepted, there was a change in name only: the old Indian Civil Service (ICS) became the new Indian Administrative Service (IAS). The rules of the service remained the same, it was centrally recruited and was under the jurisdiction of the central home ministry. The terms of service were enshrined in a special section of the Indian constitution.[7] The officers of this service could be freely transferred. They usually started their career in a district, would then rise to higher positions in the respective state government or could be deputed to a central ministry. They could also be put in charge of a large public sector enterprise. As 'generalists' they were supposed to be able to cope with any task assigned to them.

Vallabhbhai Patel was a staunch nationalist and a close associate of Mahatma Gandhi. He could be expected to hate the civil service whose members had jailed so many nationalists in the course of the freedom movement. In fact, the members of the service themselves feared that Patel might take revenge and disband the service and even prosecute individual members for what they had done under British rule. Instead Patel surprised them by wholeheartedly opting for the 'ring of service' – and they did keep the country together. This was a striking instance of adopting a British legacy and using it in the interest of nation building. Patel's decision was prudent. The Indian national leadership had not attained power in a violent revolution but due to a 'transfer of power' by the departing British. It was thus advisable not to cast aside one of the main instruments of the power transferred by the British.

The British administrative legacy had been greatly enhanced by the need of coping with the pressures of the Second World War.[8] Before the war the British-Indian government was powerful but small. It consisted of few departments which determined rules and regulations but had hardly any executive functions. This changed dramatically during the war. Two million Indian soldiers served in the British-Indian army during the war. They had to be equipped and Indian industries were geared to the British war effort. These industries remained in private hands but the procurement was managed according to a 'cost plus'-rule. The bureaucrats calculated the cost of production and added a margin of profit (usually 10 per cent). Another task faced by the British Indian government was the accumulation of buffer stocks of grain so as to prevent speculative hoarding and an inflationary increase of prices. Initially this was attempted by imposing price controls. But this only encouraged a booming black market. Only a massive accumulation of buffer stocks would enable the government to dominate the market.[9] Procurement and storage of such stocks required a new institution. It still exists as Food Corporation of India and nowadays stores huge buffer stocks. British India was turned into an interventionist state with a vengeance and the instruments required for this were bequeathed to independent India. This creation of an interventionist state could be regarded as another instance of the unintended consequences of British rule over India which contributed to the process of nation building. Jawaharlal Nehru knew this very well. He praised the state which he had inherited as a school of the Indian nation.

Another British legacy which was akin to the inherited state was the colonial legal system which had slowly evolved over a long period of time. Many old British acts are still on the Indian statute book. Hardly any questions are raised when they are applied today. Only very rarely do they emerge into the limelight of public debate. A recent instance is the application of the draconian Land Acquisition Act of 1894 for the establishment of Special Economic Zones in India.[10] In general India is proud of the rule of law but occasionally it becomes necessary to examine the root of laws which have existed for a long time.

JURISDICTION: THE IMPOSITION OF A LEGAL SYSTEM

Even before the British began to build up their civil service system in India, they imposed a new legal system on the territory which they controlled. Having been entrusted with the Diwani of Bengal by the Great Mughal in 1765, they were also responsible for the Diwani Adalat jurisdiction which concerned civil law. This was a kind of customary law which was a mixture of Muslim and Hindu law. It permitted a great deal of judicial discretion and this was soon exercised by inexperienced British district officers. Parallel to this jurisdiction, there was that of the Supreme Court of Calcutta which was originally restricted to the legal affairs of Europeans settled in the territory controlled by the British. The judges of this court were legal luminaries appointed by the British crown. The brightest among them was Sir William Jones who arrived in Calcutta in 1784.[11] He was not only a brilliant law scholar but also a great orientalist who knew Arabic and Persian well and became a master of Sanskrit in India. In a letter written in 1787 he already referred to the similiarities of Sanskrit, Greek and Latin, foreshadowing the subsequent discoveries of comparative philology. Soon after his arrival in India he founded the 'Asiatic Society' in 1784 and started the project of the codification of Hindu law with the help of Indian pandits. Having a Hindu Law Code was of immediate practical importance, because British judges who had to decide cases involving matters of inheritance, etc., could simply refer to this code. Actually this codification was a revolutionary initiative and upset Indian traditions. Earlier the Brahmins as interpreters of Hindu law could adapt it to different circumstances. The published code put an end to this power of interpretation and also to its inherent flexibility. But it universalized the codified law and made it applicable throughout British India. In a way this was also a contribution to nation building. Jones had not conceived of it in this way. To him as a genius of the age of enlightenment codification was simply a matter of the advancement of knowledge.

British courts were spreading in India like wildfire in the late eighteenth century. Providing this new type of jurisdiction was not an altruistic measure, it yielded a substantial revenue from court fees which far surpassed the cost of maintaining the courts. At the same time it helped to enhance the legitimacy of British rule. Indian litigants flocked to these courts, deserting their own judicial institutions. Litigants who could afford to pay the best lawyer were almost sure to win their case before such a court. Becoming a lawyer assured educated Indians of a lucrative career. At a later stage they could even aspire to a position as a judge in a High Court, because the British also followed the rule 'from the bar to the bench' in India, selecting judges from the ranks of the best lawyers who would feel honoured by being addressed as 'Mr. Justice' for which they would gladly forego a higher income as lawyer. Indian Bar Associations which were established even in small district towns served as focal points of an emerging civil society. They also became the breeding ground of Indian nationalism. Almost all leaders of the Indian freedom movement were lawyers. But this happened only at a later stage. At the time when the British began establishing courts in India, they certainly had not thought of the unintended consequences of their policy.

EDUCATION: A NEW UNIVERSE OF DISCOURSE

A similar story of unintended consequences could be told about the spread of British education in India. In the early nineteenth century the provincial governments established only very few government colleges, but those were soon followed by colleges established by different Christian missions. In 1835 the Law Member of the Governor-General's council, Lord Macaulay, had announced the aims of British educational policy in India.[12] Unlike Sir William Jones, he was not in sympathy with Oriental scholarship and despised Indian languages and literatures. To him only English education was acceptable. He wanted to convert educated Indians into perfect gentlemen. Strangely enough, Macaulay's policy was even supported by Raja Radhakanta Deb, the great Sanskrit scholar. Of course, Deb did not share Macaulay's views with regard to Indian languages and literatures, but he thought of 'jobs for the boys'. He knew that only an English education would secure a career for Indians under British rule. This was a realistic assessment and Indians were soon employed in great numbers as subaltern bureaucrats. Colleges proliferated and their syllabi and curricula were copied from those of British colleges. The works of Shakespeare and the philosophy of John Stuart Mill were eagerly read by Indian students. Some of them even surpassed the British civil servants in their intimate knowledge of English literature and their command of the English language.

Unwittingly the British provided the Indians with a new nationwide universe of discourse and with ideas which could be easily turned against them. Indians who read Mill's work 'On Liberty' could not help assessing their own position under foreign rule in terms of this liberal philosophy.[13] Dadabhai Naoroji's famous book *Poverty and Un-British Rule in India* showed this impact of British ideas on Indian nationalists very clearly. Assessed in term of British ideals, British rule in India was 'Un-British'. The new type of education introduced under colonial rule also led to the rise of a lively Indian press. Many newspapers were published in Indian languages. The Indian journalists created a new prose whereas earlier Indian literature was written in verse and was mostly devoted to poetic themes. The novel as a new genre captured the attention of Indian readers. The new prose style enriched many Indian languages. College graduates who did not get a government job often turned into translators who translated English publications into Indian languages. The new universe of discourse was thus extended beyond the narrow circle of those who knew English well. Among the unintended consequences of British rule in India, this was perhaps the most important one. It had an immediate relevance for nation building.

AGITATION: THE RISE OF THE FREEDOM MOVEMENT

Indian nationalism arose among those who shared the new universe of discourse.[14] This nationalism followed two different lines. There was one school of thought which considered British rule as a necessary precondition for India's nation building. These were the liberal constitutionalists who were later on called 'Moderates'. The other school of thought consisted of national revolutionaries who claimed that India had always been a nation and only needed to break the shackles of foreign rule to come into its own again. The 'Moderates' called them 'Extremists'. In order to justify their claim of an 'eternal Indian nation', the national revolutionaries had to delve into a 'useful past' which corresponded to their aspirations. They could turn to the findings of Indologists whose discipline had progressed enormously after its early beginnings in the days of Sir William Jones. The German Indologist, Max Müller, who taught at Oxford, was a friend of many Indian nationalists.[15] He did not hesitate to support their cause publicly. Mahatma Gandhi praised him at a later time and stated that he had learned much about Hinduism from him.[16] Gandhi was a devout Hindu and therefore this statement seems to be rather strange. What could he learn from Max Müller about his own religion? It was 'Hinduism' as a general concept of nationwide relevance which Mueller portrayed and which inspired Gandhi like so many other Indian nationalists. Even before Gandhi, Indian nationalists had produced a new ideology: Neo-Hinduism. It highlighted such elements in the Indian tradition which supported national solidarity such as the Vedanta philosophy which proclaimed that the human soul and the universe are one and that self-realization leads to a recognition of this unity. The divisive nature of the caste system did not fit in with this vision and was rejected by nationalists who espoused this new ideology. Neo-Hinduism, however, could not inspire the Indian Muslims. On the contrary, they had to reject its inclusivism which was incompatible with Islam.

Mahatma Gandhi tried to arrive at an 'overlapping consensus' of Hindus and Muslims in the arena of agitation against injustice and colonial rule. John Rawls who has coined the term 'overlapping consensus' has stressed that this consensus can only be achieved if those who are striving for it do not appeal to 'comprehensive doctrines' such as religious beliefs. In his famous work *The Theory of Justice*, Rawls has devoted a chapter to the right of resistance.[17] A reference to Gandhi and his *satyagraha* is conspicous by its absence in this chapter. Rawls must have known about Gandhi, but he obviously thought of him as a religious leader wedded to a 'comprehensive doctrine'. This is why he did not refer to him. In fact, Gandhi had achieved an 'overlapping consensus' in his first agitational campaigns in South Africa which were jointly supported by Hindus and Muslims. He returned to India during the First World War when political agitation was ruled out under emergency laws. He could only conduct some local campaigns of a 'non-political' nature. It was only after the end of the war that he could win over the Indian National Congress for a nationwide Non-cooperation campaign. He had announced the principle of non-coöperation with the British colonial rulers in his manifesto *Hind Swaraj* in 1909. In this he had argued that the British had not won India by the sword but that the Indians had handed it over to them and that they still kept them in India by co-operating with them. In 1920 this Gandhian message found an enthusiastic response also among the Indian Muslims who resented the terms imposed on the defeated Turkish Caliph by the victorious British. A so called Khilafat movement spread like wildfire in India and Gandhi supported it, because he was glad that he could find a cause on which an 'overlapping consensus' could be based. He did not realize that this cause was subject to the volatility of the pan-Islamic sentiments of the Indian Muslims. When the Turks themselves abolished the office of the Caliph in 1924, the cause was lost and the 'overlapping consensus' disappeared. In fact, many Indian Muslims then turned their attention to communal organizations and spurned any cooperation with the Hindus. With the benefit of hindsight one can state that Gandhi made a mistake by opting for the Khilafat movement.[18] Mohammed Ali Jinnah, the leader of the Muslim League who had been a secular rather than a communal politician had rejected Gandhi's agitational politics and had been marginalized by him. Jinnah held the view that the Khilafat movement was a reactionary one and had not supported it. But when the Muslims were disappointed by the demise of the Khilafat movement, they turned to Jinnah who then emerged as a communal politician with a vengeance. The first steps towards partition were taken at that time when nobody thought of it as yet.

In 1922 Gandhi had terminated his Non-Cooperation movement when it threatened to disintegrate in sporadic violence. While the movement had not reached its immediate goal, it had produced a large number of enthusiastic volunteers who remained full-time politicians. Gandhi was a great fundraiser and managed to support them. When taking over the leadership of the Indian National Congress, he had reorganized it. The boundaries of Provincial Congress Committees (PCC) were redrawn along linguistic lines, because Gandhi wished that Indians should conduct their political debates in their respective mother-tongues rather than in English.[19] He also saw to it that the PCCs recruited more members in rural areas. This prepared the ground for rallying the Indian peasants in the next round of national agitation in the 1930s.

The Indian peasantry, particularly its richer strata, had orginally no reason for siding with the nationalists. In the course of the late nineteenth century the British had passed many tenancy laws from which these strata of the peasantry benefited. In this way the British had hoped to find a new social base for their colonial rule. In the course of the constitutional reforms of the 1930s the British had enfranchised 10 per cent of the Indian people and had seen to it that the dominant strata of the peasantry got the vote. The colonial rulers hoped that they would vote for pro-British agrarian parties rather than for the rebellious Congress party. But the impact of the Great Depression spoiled this plan. Grain prices were halved within a few months in 1930-1, but the peasants still had to pay the old rates of land revenue or rent. Moreover, most peasants were indebted and the moneylenders charged the same usurious interest rates as before or even foreclosed mortgages in order to recover their capital. British monetary policy added to the plight of the peasantry. By maintaining an overvalued currency so as to prevent a 'flight from the Rupee', the British appreciated the amount of rural debt and made the burden of the peasants unbearable.[20] This drove the peasants into the arms of the Congress party which was well prepared to rally them to the cause of nationalism. Since the moneylenders pounced on the peasants, the British tried to control their activities by special legislation. This did not relieve the peasants very much, but made the disgruntled moneylenders also flock to the Congress party. When elections were held in 1936-7 under the new Government of India Act of 1935, the Congress party captured seven out of the nine provinces of British India. These were the Hindu majority provinces, the two Muslim majority provinces Punjab and Bengal were won by regional parties and not by Jinnah's Muslim League.

The new constitution provided for 'provincial autonomy' and the Congress party formed provincial ministries. These ministries resigned at the beginning of the Second World War, because the British refused to announce what they would do about India at the end of that war. Churchill, the great imperialist, could anyhow not be expected to support Indian nationalism. Instead he encouraged his friend Jinnah who emerged as a great leader during the war while the Congress leadership languished in jail. The provincial governments of the Punjab and Bengal did not resign, they remained in office throughout the war and supported the British war effort. Led by local politicians, these governments did not feel that they had to take orders from Jinnah whose Muslim League did not play an important role in their provinces. They agreed that Jinnah could pose as a 'national' spokesman for them as long as he refrained from interfering with their provincial affairs.[21] In order to enhance his 'national' position, Jinnah sponsored the famous Lahore Resolution of the Muslim League of 1940 which became known as the 'Pakistan Resolution' although the word Pakistan was not mentioned in this resolution. It had been coined by Rahmat Ali in 1933 and Jinnah had rejected the Pakistan-idea at that time, because he was then primarily a leader of the Muslims in the Hindu majority provinces to whom 'Pakistan' did not apply. In 1940 he still avoided the word but had opted for its substance. He defended this claim by announcing his 'two-nation' theory according to which Hindus and Muslims are two nations 'by any definition of the term'. He added this because he knew that it would be difficult to define his 'Muslim nation' in territorial terms as millions of Muslims lived in the Hindu majority provinces and were bound to remain there. In subsequent years, he kept his cards close to his chest and never revealed his plans for the territorial demarcation of 'Pakistan'. He hoped that it would at least include the whole of the Punjab and the whole of Bengal although this would have been incompatible with his 'two-nation' theory as substantial parts of the East Punjab and of West Bengal were Hindu majority areas.

During the war, Indian nationalism could not find expression in agitational movements. When Gandhi announced a 'Quit India' movement in 1942, it was nipped in the bud by the British. Gandhi and all other Congress leaders were jailed once more and because Gandhi could not give any direction to the movement, it led to the spontaneous 'August Revolution' of the younger generation.[22] These revolutionaries attacked district headquarters, destroyed railway tracks and committed other acts of sabotage. But the British knew how to deal with such activities and by the end of August they were once more in full control of the country. Gandhi was released from prison in 1944 ahead of the other Congress leaders. By now the British knew that they would win the war. Gandhi was old and would not be able to start an agitational campaign all alone. Gandhi then visited Jinnah and had a round of talks with him. Actually he wanted to call Jinnah's bluff by asking him to spell out his plans for Pakistan. He conceded Pakistan to Jinnah in these talks but hoped that Jinnah would have to admit the absurdity of carving out Pakistan from British India. Jinnah skilfully avoided all concrete details. Finally Gandhi proposed that before partition a treaty should be concluded between the two successor states of British India which would assure their peaceful coexistence.[23] To this Jinnah replied that such a treaty could be concluded only after partition, because otherwise the contracting partners would not exist. Gandhi could not controvert this argument and withdrew, henceforth he avoided any further talks with Jinnah as he must have realized that in matters of constitutional law he could not match Jinnah's legal acumen. By the end of the war, partition seemed to be inevitable unless the British government took a bold step by announcing a road map for granting independence to India and fixing a date for the transfer of power.

PARTITION: THE TRAUMATIC EXPERIENCE OF TERRITORIALITY

In the summer of 1945, Churchill's war cabinet resigned and elections were held. To everybody's surprise the Labour Party won and Clement Attlee became Prime Minister. He was familiar with India as he had chaired the India committee of the war cabinet. He could have taken a bold step now, the more so as India had emerged from the war as a creditor to Great Britain and thus the crucial problem of India's national debt which had been debated before the war did not exist any longer.[24] But Attlee missed his chance and the future of India remained uncertain. In August 1945 President Truman decided to have the atom bomb dropped on Japan. Gandhi was shocked and would have liked to condemn this inhuman act. But he kept quiet and even sent a letter to *The Times* in London, stating that he had not said anything about the atom bomb.[25] He felt that he had to refrain from criticizing Truman in the interest of the Indian freedom movement. The USA and Great Britain might jointly suppress this movement armed with the terrible weapon to which no resistance was possible. Gandhi's non-violent campaigns had always been aimed at an adversary who could be faced and challenged. The bomb made him feel helpless and he did not dare to think of further agitations at this stage.

Instead of providing a road map for India's independence, Attlee ordered that elections should be held in India in the winter of 1945-6. The results of the provincial elections strengthened Jinnah's position. The Congress party again captured the seven Hindu majority provinces, but this time the Muslim League did much better in the Muslim majority provinces and the regional parties declined. The demand for Pakistan became more insistent. In March 1946 a Cabinet Mission was sent to India, consisting of three members of the British cabinet. Again an opportunity was missed to make a statement concerning India's independence. Therefore the mandate of the Cabinet Mission was not clear. It could only make recommendations which were not binding and could be rejected. Jinnah derived great political strength from his veto power.[26] Finally the Viceroy, Lord Wavell, dared to defy him and appointed Jawaharlal Nehru as interim Prime Minister of India in August 1946. After some initial opposition, the Muslim League joined Nehru's cabinet but obstructed its work. Attlee then cut the Gordian knot and appointed Lord Mountbatten as last Viceroy in March 1947. Mountbatten had a clear mandate to prepare India for independence. A date for the transfer of power was set for August 1948. After assessing the situation in India, Mountbatten asked for an earlier date: August 1947. He was afraid that by August 1948 not much power would be left which could be transferred. An Independence of India Act was quickly passed by the British Parliament. It was based on the Government of India Act of 1935.

The final problem was how to respond to the demand for Pakistan. A plan which was suitably called 'Plan Balkan' was sent by Mountbatten to London after he had obtained the consent of the political parties in India. In London this plan was revised in a unexpected manner. Instead of burdening the British with the odious task of partition, the new plan suggested that independence would be granted to the provinces of British India and the princely states. These units could then decide which kind of states they wished to form. Mountbatten showed this plan to Nehru who was furious when he saw it. Mountbatten was surprised at Nehru's reaction. But Nehru saw clearly that this plan could indeed lead to an irreversible balkanization of India.[27] With no central government left, the newly independent units might prefer to go it alone. A partition at the hands of the departing British was to be preferred to this plan. Mountbatten revised the plan accordingly and even Gandhi acquiesced in it although he had earlier referred to partition as the 'vivisection of India'.

With partition the Indian leaders had to face the problem of territoriality for the first time. The freedom movement had been aimed at independence from British rule, it was not inspired by any territorial quest. In the beginning of the twentieth century, India's great poet, Rabindranath Tagore, had coined a term for territoriality: *rashtratantra*.[28] He had argued that Western nations were obsessed with it, but that India was free from this obsession. Jinnah had introduced this 'obsession' by staking a claim for Pakistan, but till the eve of partition he had not discussed the actual boundaries of that state. Mountbatten then asked Jinnah to nominate an impartial person who would demarcate these boundaries and Jinnah opted for a British judge who had no prior knowledge of India.[29] This judge then looked at the census data of the districts of the Punjab and of Bengal and separated the Hindu majority districts from these Muslim majority provinces. Jinnah called this a 'motheaten' Pakistan, but he could not object to the criteria which were formulated according to his 'two-nation' theory. Of course, this partition could not solve the problem of the large Muslim diaspora which remained in India, nor were the princely states included in the terms of reference of the judge who partitioned India. This is why Kashmir later on remained in India although Muslims were in a majority in this princely state. India accepted partition, but it could never accept the 'two-nation' theory as one third of the Muslims of the subcontinent continued to live in India. Mountbatten realized that the traumatic experience of territorial division may cause great unrest. Therefore he decided to grant independence to India and Pakistan first and announce the new boundaries only afterwards. He perhaps hoped that the joy of independence would benumb the people so that they would not feel the pain of 'vivisection'. In this he was mistaken. As soon as the details of the partition were revealed, hordes of refugees stormed across the new borders and there was much bloodshed.

In territorial terms, the two new nation states had different problems. India was riddled with hundreds of princely states which had all become independent in their own right. But as India had inherited a strong central government it was able to incorporate these princely states with a mixture of generosity and coercion. Pakistan included only very few princely states, but it was faced with the territorial absurdity of having two wings which were more than thousand miles apart. Islam was the only common denominator of these two wings. West Pakistan then behaved like a colonial power and imposed its control over East Pakistan which finally seceded in 1971. This was the only revision of the colonial territorial legacy in any colony throughout the world. Everywhere else this legacy has been preserved although many colonial boundaries were of a rather arbitrary character.

In 1948 Mahatma Gandhi had become the most prominent victim of the partition. He did not grasp the full meaning of partition immediately. When he was told that it would also mean the division of the British-Indian army, he could not believe it. But when he saw that this would be a logical consequence of territorial partition, he predicted that the two armies would fight each other – which they soon did. Then the problem of dividing the financial assets of British-India also came up. Being already at war with Pakistan, the independent Government of India was reluctant to transfer Rs. 550 million to Pakistan which would fill the enemy's war chest. Gandhi pleaded for fairness and started his last great fast in order to persuade the Indian government to part with this money.[30] Hindu nationalists regarded this as high treason and one of them assassinated Gandhi on 30 January 1948.

THE REPUBLIC OF INDIA: A DEMOCRATIC NATION STATE

The 'Father of the Nation' was gone, but his 'heir', Jawaharlal Nehru, now guided the nation and saw to it that India would be a democratic nation state. The two men had often differed in their judgement of current affairs and their visions for the future of India. But Nehru had never parted company with Gandhi because he knew that Gandhi was in touch with the Indian people and understood them much better than he could ever do. On the other hand, Gandhi appreciated Nehru's sincerity and his devotion to the cause of the Indian nation.

Unlike Jinnah who became Governor-General of Pakistan and thus continued the viceregal tradition, Nehru remained Prime Minister of India. Under the viceroys there had been no prime minister until Lord Wavell appointed Nehru as interim prime minister at the fag-end of British rule. The Constitution of Independent India contained only a very laconic reference to the office of the prime minister.[31] All powers were vested in the President of India, but it was presumed that he would act on the advice of the Prime Minister and there was a provision that this advice could not be enquired into by a court of law. These rather rudimentary provisions were the foundation of parliamentary democracy in India. It was obviously assumed that the conventions of the unwritten British constitution would also be valid in India. But these conventions had to be established in India – and this was Nehru's great contribution to democratic nation building. He was an enthusiastic parliamentarian and usually attended all of the sessions of Parliament and frequently participated in the debates.

Nehru's contribution to India's political life was crucial, but he could also rely on the Congress party which was a powerful political machine. No other state which emerged from the wave of decolonization which swept Asia and Africa from 1947 to 1960 inherited such a national party. The discipline and cohesion of this party was to a large extent due to Mahatma Gandhi whose followers were still around in the first two decades after independence. Most of them had spent many years in jail during the freedom movement and had proven their worth in this way. Gandhi, however, had never conceived of the Congress as a party, he saw in it a national forum which had achieved its aim with independence and should be disbanded, making way for ordinary political parties.[32] This wish which he expressed shortly before his death was disregarded by his followers who preserved the Congress party as his heritage. For several decades this party would rule India at the centre and in almost all the states. But then regional parties emerged which challenged its dominance.

The regional parties were a product of Indian federalism which had been introduced by the British in the 1930s in the interest of the devolution of power. In this way the colonial rulers had hoped to retain central power while relegating Indian politics to the provincial arena. Nehru hated federalism for this reason, but he retained it after independence. In fact, it has served India well. It provided a democratic framework for regional political aspirations which could have threatened a unitary national state. But even after making headway in various Indian states, regional parties for a long time remained underrepresented in the central parliament. They did not get the number of seats which would have corresponded to the votes they had received. But in recent years this has changed. The two national parties, the Congress party and the Bharatiya Janata Party (BJP) get about a quarter of the votes each whereas the various regional parties win almost 50 per cent of the national vote and the seats in the central parliament now reflect this more or less acurately.[33] Strangely enough, the election results under a majority election system thus approximate the results which would prevail under a system of proportional representation. Such results lead to the emergence of national coalitions headed by one of the national parties which is supported by regional fellow-travellers.

Coalition building requires the shrewd tactics of forging alliances. These tactics can contribute to nation building in a fragmented society as the recent success of Mayawati, the Chief Minister of Uttar Pradesh, has shown.[34] Mayawati is the leader of the Bahujan Samaj Party (BSP) representing the Dalits (Untouchables) who account for about 20 per cent of the population of this huge state. The BSP is the main rival of the Samajwadi Party (SP) which represents the so-called Other Backward Castes (OBC) and also used to attract a large part of the Muslim vote. Muslims have a share of about 17 per cent of the population of Uttar Pradesh. The Brahmins with 10 per cent of the population are also of some importance in this state. They and the members of other high castes (Rajputs, Banias et al.) used to support the BJP which also managed to get some OBC-support. Mayawati was sure of the complete loyalty of her Dalits and could therefore afford to cultivate the Brahmins and the Muslims so as to defeat the SP-government and to marginalize the BJP. In political terms, the hierarchy of the 'caste system' has been completely overturned in this way. As the caste system which is based on the assumption of permanent inequality is incompatible with national solidarity, it must be overcome. Many Indian social reformers have tried their best to do so, but their efforts have not been very successful. The shifts of power in the political arena of a vibrant democracy may accomplish what social reformers have failed to bring about. Democratic nation building has very special features in India, but it seems to be rather successful.

The British legacy which is of great importance for India is due to the unintended consequences of colonial rule. The structure of the British-Indian state was built so as to keep India under imperial control, but in due course this state served as the foundation of a modern democratic nation. The building of that nation progressed in a long freedom struggle against the British. Without this struggle India would not have gained the political maturity which enabled it to become one of the premier nations of the post-war world.

NOTES

1. Hermann Kulke and Dietmar Rothermund, *A History of India*, London: Routledge, 4th edn., 2004, p. 229.
2. Peter Marshall, *The Impeachment of Warren Hastings*, London: Oxford University Press, 1965.
3. Kulke and Rothermund, *A History of India*, p. 235.
4. Ibid., p. 222.
5. Ibid., p. 227.
6. Ibid., pp. 231 ff.
7. *The Constitution of India*, Articles 308-23.
8. Dietmar Rothermund, *An Economic History of India*, London: Routledge, 2nd edn., 1993, pp. 115 ff.
9. Henry Knight, *Food Administration in India, 1939-1947*, Stanford: Stanford University Press, 1954.
10. Dietmar Rothermund, *India: The Rise of an Asian Giant*, New Haven and London: Yale University Press, 2008, pp. 84 f.
11. S. N. Mukherjee, *Sir William Jones: A Study of Eighteenth Century British Attitudes to India*, Cambridge: Cambridge University Press, 1968.
12. Kulke and Rothermund, *A History of India*, pp. 254 f.
13. Lynn Zastoupil, *John Stuart Mill and India*, Stanford: Stanford University Press, 1994.
14. Kulke and Rothermund, *A History of India*, pp. 286 f.
15. Dietmar Rothermund, *The German Intellectual Quest for India*, New Delhi: Manohar, 1986, pp. 47 ff.
16. Ibid., p. 57.
17. John Rawls, *A Theory of Justice*, Cambridge, Mass.: Belknap Press, 1971.
18. Dietmar Rothermund, *Mahatma Gandhi: An Essay in Political Biography*, Delhi: Manohar, 1991, pp. 35 f.
19. Ibid., p. 37.
20. Dietmar Rothermund, *India in the Great Depression, 1929-1939*, Delhi: Manohar, 1992.
21. Ayesha Jalal, *The Sole Spokesman: Jinnah, the Muslim League and the Demand for Pakistan*, Cambridge: Cambridge University Press, 1994.
22. Kulke and Rothermund, *A History of India*, p. 310.
23. Ibid., p. 316.
24. Ibid., p. 317.
25. Rothermund, *Mahatma Gandhi*, p. 107
26. Stanley and Wolpert, *Jinnah of Pakistan*, New York: Oxford University Press, 1984, p. 288.
27. Kulke and Rothermund, *A History of India*, p. 322.
28. Dietmar Rothermund, 'Rabindranath Tagore und seine weltweite Friedensmission', in Bernd Hausberger, ed., *Globale Lebensläufe. Menschen*

als Akteure im weltgeschichtlichen Geschehen, Wien: Mandelbaum, 2006, p. 198.
29. Wolpert, *Jinnah*, p. 332.
30. Rothermund, *Mahatma Gandhi*, p. 127.
31. *The Constitution of India*, Article 74 (1).
32. Rothermund, *Mahatma Gandhi*, pp. 129 f.
33. Rothermund, *India: The Rise of an Asian Giant*, p. 26.
34. Ibid., p. 173.

CHAPTER 11

Max Müller's Science of Language and Religion

MAX MÜLLER'S CENTURY

Max Müller was born at Dessau, Germany, in 1823 and he died at Oxford in 1900. The nineteenth century was his century in which he gained great fame but which also entrapped him. In the twentieth century he was almost forgotten in Europe – though not in India where he was always remembered as an ally in India's quest for a national past. Nirad Chaudhuri's biography of Max Müller is an eloquent testimony to this Indian love of Max Müller. European scholars have only very recently rediscovered him. The Dutch theologian, Lourens van den Bosch, has published an inspiring book in 2002, *Friedrich Max Müller: A Life Devoted to the Humanities.* This emphasis on the humanities puts Max Müller's work in a proper perspective and extracts it from the nineteenth century preoccupation with 'science' as the highest embodiment of human knowledge. Max Müller deliberately called his attempts at analysing the origin and development of human thought and speech a study of the 'science of language' and following this up in the realm of mythology and religion referred to the 'science of religion'. Actually these two 'sciences' were deeply related as we shall see later on. He claimed to have established scientific criteria for his analysis and he even maintained that the 'science of language' was a physical science as it dealt with phenomena which were not subject to voluntary action whereas the historical sciences were concerned with developments determined by the human will.

The physical sciences had proved to be highly successful in the nineteenth century and had set the standard for all other academic endeavours. Evolutionary thought had come to dominate science and philosophy. Herbert Spencer, an engineer turned philosopher, was the prophet of this new thought. He was extremely popular in Victorian England and his ideas spread even in China, India and

Japan in those days. Just like Max Müller he was almost totally forgotten in the twentieth century. Charles Darwin's books on *The Origin of Species* and on *The Descent of Man* promoted evolutionary thought. Spencer popularized Darwin's thought, but it is often forgotten that the famous formula of the 'survival of the fittest' which later on became associated with Darwinism was actually coined by Spencer before Darwin published his findings. Whereas this formula was later on interpreted as a reference to the fierce struggle for survival, Spencer had originally highlighted cooperation as the aim of evolution and to him the most resourceful cooperators were 'the fittest'. Max Müller engaged in spirited debates with both Darwin and Spencer as we shall see later on. In general Max Müller was attracted by evolutionary thought and his science of language and religion was influenced by it, but he believed that a definite threshold divided man from all animals.

The educated Victorians who avidly listened to Max Müller's lectures found in him a friend, philosopher and guide in a world which had felt the combined impact of biblical criticism and modern science. The German theologian, David Friedrich Strauß, had shocked Christian believers by his book on the life of Jesus in which he had called the biblical stories a myth. He had followed this up with a book on Christian dogma in which he had stressed that the best criticism of dogma is its history. These books had been translated into many languages and had led to great debates. Max Müller referred to Strauß and his views, but though he probably agreed with him as far as the criticism of dogma was concerned he did not share his idea of religion as he remained a liberal Christian throughout his life. In this he was akin to many of those who attended his public lectures. However, he displeased his more orthodox contemporaries, some of whom held powerful positions. He thus lost the chance of becoming the Boden Professor of Sanskrit at Oxford in 1860. Colonel Boden, who had endowed this chair, was a pious Christian and had stated in his will that the chair established in his name should help to convert Indians to Christianity. Prof. Monier Williams who finally got the chair was no match to Max Müller as a Sanskrit scholar, but he was an orthodox Christian not known for any liberal views. Actually this loss of a prestigious chair was a blessing in disguise for Max Müller. He now turned with added vigour to his 'science of language and religion'. A special chair of Comparative Philology was established for him at Oxford in 1868. As a crowning event of his career in this field he could deliver the Gifford Lectures at several universities of Scotland from 1889 to 1892. Lord Adam Gifford, a distinguished Scottish judge, had endowed these lectures in his will when he died in 1887. They should be devoted to 'natural theology' and the lecturers should study religion following the strict principles of natural sciences such as astronomy and chemistry. Lord Gifford reflected the spirit of the nineteenth century in this way and Max Müller rose to the occasion. He wrote to a professor at the university of Edinburgh in this context:

> We want to know what Natural Religion has been; that is enough for any man who knows what history means, and what even a Hegelian would have to admit if he knows the true secret of Hegel, that the Rational is only the Real, nay what even the Darwinians will have to learn in time, that Natural Selection is in truth Rational Elimination, and that Development means historical triumph of what is right, or reasonable, or as they now say, 'the fittest.'

These triumphant words sounded like a manifesto of the faith of Max Müller's century. He obviously did not have a deep understanding of Darwin's theory but his words no doubt reflected what Max Müller's contemporaries knew about it. They also revealed his hope that he could reconcile natural theology with evolutionary theory. This made his lectures so attractive at that time. The intellectual atmosphere of the next century was very different.

Max Müller's science of language to which we shall now turn remains only of historical interest. It was based on the advances in this field made by German scholars like Wilhelm von Humboldt, Jacob Grimm, Franz Bopp and many others. Max Müller served as an eloquent interpreter of their ideas in England and furthered philological research in that country by spreading his *Chips from a German Workshop*.

THE SCIENCE OF LANGUAGE

Max Müller's early years at Oxford were spent on the English translation and critical edition of the *Rig Veda* which he finally published in six volumes. This work equipped him with a great storehouse of knowledge on which he could draw for the rest of his life. Even before the last volumes of this great work were published, Max Müller showed in his *Lectures on the Science of Language* in 1861 how well he could use Vedic Sanskrit in order to demonstrate his points. He argued that the science of language is one of the physical sciences, because the original elements of language were not historical products of human will but had come into existence 'naturally' as involuntary expressions of the human mind. But these involuntary expressions were by no means onomatopoeic nor did they consist of mere interjections as some scholars believed. Müller spoke somewhat facetiously of the 'bow-wow' and the 'pooh-pooh' theories of language. The latter theory was favoured by Darwin with whom Müller had a heated debate on this issue. Darwin conceded that he was not a philologist and had adopted this theory at the suggestion of a colleague. In a friendly meeting with Max Müller, Darwin called him jokingly 'a dangerous man'. They agreed to differ. Darwin stated that as he believed that man had originated from lower species he could not believe in a rigid threshold dividing man from animals, whereas Müller was convinced that there was such a threshold and that no animal had ever produced a language as distinct from other means of communication.

With regard to the origin of language Max Müller did not only combat the 'bow-wow' and 'pooh-pooh' theories but also the more sophisticated 'conventional' and 'germinal' ones. According to the 'conventional' theory, the elements of language emerged from deliberations among the speakers of the language. Müller ridiculed this theory which presumed that a kind of congress fixed the language. He was also opposed to the Romantic view held by Friedrich Schlegel and others according to which language germinated in terms of an organic development. Müller stated: 'Language may be conceived of as a production, but it cannot be conceived as a substance that could itself produce.' The laws of this production had to be found out by grammatical analysis and Müller asserted confidently: 'There is no reason to doubt that in the end grammatical analysis will be as successful as chemical analysis'.

The science of grammatical analysis was based on the method of comparison which took a long time to emerge. Müller praised the ancient Indian grammarian Panini for his accurate description of Sanskrit. But, of course, Panini had not produced a comparative grammar, he was interested in what could be termed an 'internal' grammar of his language and for this he adopted admirable standards. For this reason his work proved to be very attractive for the descriptive linguists of the twentieth century. Comparative grammar could arise only from efforts to teach a language to foreigners and this came about only when Greek teachers were asked to teach their language to the Romans. However, even this did not lead to genuine comparison which had to be based on the assumption of the equality of men and their languages. As long as the speakers of foreign languages were called 'barbarians', no progress could be made in this field. Müller asserted: 'Not till the word barbarian was struck out of the dictionary of mankind and replaced by brother . . . can we look even for the beginnings of our science. This change was affected by Christianity.' This assertion points to the connection of the science of language with the science of religion which we have to explore later on.

The fundamental elements of language on which Müller based his analysis were the roots of words. He illustrated this by means of Vedic Sanskrit. He argued that these roots referred originally to repeated human actions. They were general concepts rather than mere percepts, i.e. reflections of momentary perception. Müller insisted that human knowledge is exclusively derived from the impression of the senses, there is no divine inspiration of the concepts of language, these concepts originate from the brain, but they cannot be changed at will. However, there may be synonyms some of which disappear in due course. Etymology serves as a potent tool for the construction of genealogies of languages. It permits to identify roots even if they have been subjected to 'phonetic decay' in the course of time. For Müller 'phonetic decay' and 'dialectical regeneration' were the two processes which change the shape of languages over time. 'Dialectical regeneration' means the continuous supply of new words from local varieties of the respective language, this process as well as that of 'phonetic decay' come to a halt once a language aquires a standardized written form. Furthermore, these two processes do not affect all languages in an equal measure. There are languages like Chinese which consist mainly of roots and do not show traces of agglutinization and amalgamation. At the stage of agglutinization when other elements are added to the roots, the morphology of the language changes. This is even more so when inflection serves as a distinctive tool of grammar and words are amalgamated in such a way that their roots can only be identified by an experienced philologist. The expressive flexibility of language which is gained at this 'higher' stage has a price. The distinctiveness of roots is lost and they shed much of their erstwhile power.

Max Müller's love for clearly identifiable roots is indicated by the choice of the pejorative term 'phonetic decay'. In a more neutral manner one could speak of 'phonetic transformation' and highlight the flexibility of languages affected by it. But there is a deeper reason for Müller's love of roots: they are the pristine evidence of human conceptualization. Müller believes that language and thought are linked with each other. There is for him no thought without language and no language without thought. Later in his life he wrote a book on the science of thought in which he stressed this necessary connection. This is, of course, very onesided and excludes visual imagination as well as processes of abstract, non-verbal thought. Leonardo da Vinci, the paragon of visual imagination, has expressed this very well. He had produced sketches of the human heart, showing the circulation of the blood within the heart so accurately that modern specialists have been amazed at it. Having once built sluice gates and analysed the flow of water controlled by them, he could transfer this knowledge to the working of the heart. Pointing to these sketches Leonardo said: 'Oh writer, how could you describe this object as perfectly as these sketches do. I tell you, don't rely on words unless you are talking to the blind.' This is a challenge which Müller never had to consider. He relied on words, and among them he cherished the roots most of all as they reflected the power of the human mind as he saw it.

The roots were essential for the genealogical construction of languages and were thus at the centre of Max Müller's method of comparative philology. For demonstrating the power of his method he mostly relied on the languages of what he called the Aryan family of languages, but he also applied the same rules to the Semitic family of languages. He was somehow at a loss how to deal with other families of languages which he subsumed under the term 'Turanic languages'. One of these was Turkish whose grammar attracted him very much as the roots were preserved in their pristine originality. Since he could not apply the genealogical method to these languages he resorted to morphology. This permits the philologist to identify the similarity of grammatical forms in languages not related with each other.

Max Müller has recorded an interesting incident of this kind of morphological insight. He met an educated American Mohawk Indian in London who agreed to teach him his language. Müller took these lessons very seriously and he was soon able to correct his teacher when he made a grammatical mistake. The Mohawk Indian was surprised and asked him how he knew this grammatical form, adding that his grandmother used to speak in this manner, but that this form had not be used in recent times.

Learning Mohawk or other strange languages was not Müller's major interest, he always returned to his beloved Sanskrit in which he saw the wellspring of his science of language. When surveying the work of other philologists in the recent past, he lauded their efforts but also described their predicament: 'Languages seemed to float about like islands in the ocean of human speech . . . (until) an electric spark caused the fioating elements to crystallise into regular forms. This electric spark was the discovery of Sanskrit.' And while Sanskrit was the foundation of his science of language, it also served him as an inexhaustible source for his study of comparative mythology which provided him with a bridge between the science of language and the science of religion. He crossed a threshold when he dealt with mythology, because – as he asserted – 'It is the essential character of a true myth that it should no longer be intelligible by a reference to the spoken language'.

COMPARATIVE MYTHOLOGY AS A BRIDGE BETWEEN LANGUAGE AND RELIGION

Max Müller published his essay on comparative mythology in 1856 even before he held his lectures on the science of language. In fact, some of the basic principles of the science of language were sketched in this essay. Müller outlines the transition from the agglutinative to the amalgamated stage of grammar. He equates the latter with the dialectical period which is then followed by the mythic period. He regards this period as a necessary stage in the development of language but he clearly shows that he is not in sympathy with it. He writes: 'it is impossible to conceal the fact that, taken by themselves, and in their literal meaning, most of these ancient myths are irrational and absurd and frequently opposed to the principles of thought, religion and morality'. He refers to a 'disease of language' when writing about this mythic age and alleges that 'language forgets itself' in this period. He feels that by this time the original meaning of words had been forgotten, *nomina* had become *noumina* and as such they had embarked on a life of their own. Being convinced that the concepts of the human brain are derived from the perception of the senses, Müller was puzzled by the appearance of mythical characters which no human being could ever have seen. He attributed the creation of such characters to a loss of etymological consciousnes.

Müller's consolation are those old Indian myths which are linked to natural phenomena such as the rise and the setting of the sun, the glory of the dawn, etc. He finds an echo of the feelings expressed in these myths in the poetry of his contemporary, the Romantic poet William Wordsworth, and quotes his Thanksgiving Ode which begins with the words: 'Hail, orient conqueror of gloomy night! . . .' and ends with 'Once more, heart-cheering sun, I bid thee hail!'. The solar myth is Müller's favourite theme in his interpretation of the hymns of the *Rig Veda*. He refers at length to the mythical story of Pururavas and Urvashi which inspired the Vedic poets as well as Kalidasa, the poet of the classical age of Sanskrit literature. Urvashi, the celestial nymph, is married to King Pururavas but must leave him when she once sees him naked. Urvashi is the dawn and Pururavas the sun. With philological skill, Müller shows the parallel in the Greek myth of Orpheus and Eurydice. Such poetic myths are praised by Müller who is appalled by others which are brutal and immoral.

Victorian audiences were charmed by Müller's comparative mythology, but he was criticized in subsequent years by scholars who objected to his purely philological approach to this subject at a time when the new discipline of cultural anthropology saw mythology in a different light. The founder of this discipline, Edward Burnett Tylor (1832-1917) was initially impressed by Müller's work on comparative mythology and praised it. Müller on his part took note of Tylor's work and they were generally on good terms. With his essay of 1856 Müller was still way ahead of the younger scholar, but in later years Tylor's great work on *Primitive Culture* overshadowed Müller's work in this field. Tylor always treated Müller with great respect, but Andrew Lang (1844-1912) who admired Tylor and published his own massive study of *Myth, Ritual and Religion* in 1887 was not reluctant to take Müller to task for his onesided approach to mythology. Lang had studied classical Greek and had worked on Homer. He appreciated Müller as a philologist and they kept in touch even after Lang had criticised Müller's work on mythology. Lang looked into the social and cultural context of mythology whereas Müller tended to see 'man' as such without taking an interest in the social conditioning of human existence. In his youth Müller had come under the direct influence of German idealism. He was particularly impressed by Friedrich Schelling (1775-1854) whose lectures in Berlin he had attended in 1844 and 1845 when he had also met Schelling personally. Schelling was convinced that mythology represented a necessary stage in the evolution of the human mind.

Müller followed the same line, but he felt that Schelling's characterization of mythology was too vague. It could be improved by making use of etymology. When Schelling's last great work on mythology was published in 1854, Müller was prompted by this book to write his essay on comparative mythology. He did not quote Schelling in his essay, but actually it represented a dialogue with the great idealist philosopher in which he showed that Sanskrit philology provided the concrete evidence which he had missed in Schelling's work. Müller continued this dialogue in his *Contributions to the Science of Mythology* published in 1897. In the meantime the criticism of his etymological approach to this subject had become very strong and he felt that he had to defend his method against his critics. In this defence he stuck to his guns, but in subsequent years the views of his critics prevailed. The new science of cultural anthropology seemed to have more to offer in this field.

THE SCIENCE OF RELIGION

Max Müller provided an introduction to his science of religion in lectures held in 1870 at the Royal Institution in London where he had earlier lectured on the science of language. He published those lectures in 1873 and dedicated them to the American poet and theologian Ralph Waldo Emerson, the leader of the American Transcendentalist movement. Emerson's ideas on nature and religion were akin to Müller's ideas. They had met at Oxford when Emerson was on a lecture tour of Europe. Müller admired him very much. In 1878 Max Müller was invited to deliver the first Hibbert Lectures at Westminister Abbey. Robert Hibbert was a British merchant who had made a fortune in Jamaica. Like Emerson, Hibbert was a Unitarian who believed in an unorthodox faith. The endowment which he established in 1847 was supposed to promote 'the unfettered exercise of private judgement in matters of religion'. Initially the Hibbert Trust granted stipends to students. The idea of funding annual lectures came up only much later. Once Max Müller had attracted a large audience by his first Hibbert Lecture, these lectures became a regular institution and have continued until the present time.

While Müller's earlier lectures at the Royal Institution had referred explicitly to the science of religion, the Hibbert Lectures had the title *On the Origin and Growth of Religion as Illustrated by the Religions of India*. Again, Müller resorted to his treasure trove, the *Rig Veda*.

But in his initial lecture he dealt with ideas of David Strauß, Friedrich Schleiermacher and Ludwig Feuerbach. Müller was obviously impressed by Feuerbach's criticism of religion but mentioned that even Heraklit had referred to faith as a 'holy disease'. Against these critics Müller defended his own definition of religion which to him is a mental faculty of man which enables him to conceive of the Infinite. The quest for an understanding of the Infinite finally turns into a love of god. Müller stresses that the approach to the Infinite is conditioned by the senses which inevitably meet the end of their power of perception. The mental faculty of man which urges him to transcend the limits of perception is a potential energy from which religious ideas emerge. Without this potential energy none of the forms of 'primitive' religions can be explained. In this context Müller deals at length with fetishism which many contemporary scholars described as the earliest form of religion. He denies that and points to Vedic literature in which only the late *Atharva Veda* contains any evidence of fetishism. He also rejects the claim that ancestor worship is the root of religion, a view which was held by Spencer. Müller highlights, of course, the worship of the forces of nature which is illustrated by the hymns of the *Rig Veda*. Once more, he praises the science of language, particularly the method of etymological analysis, which gives access to a better understanding of the earliest vestiges of religion. He rates the achievements of comparative philology in this context more highly than the magnificent contemporary discoveries of archaeologists. Heinrich Schliemann, whose work Müller admired, had found the treasure of Priamos at Troy in 1873 and had excavated the tombs of Mykene in 1876. But Müller argued that even those spectacular discoveries of the material elements of ancient culture did not provide as much insight into the early working of the human mind as comparative philology does.

Demonstrating the uses of the science of language for the science of religion he analyses the origin and the development of the names of gods in the *Rig Veda*. He shows that the Vedic poets addressed different gods, but that they obviously considered the god whom they addressed as the highest god and as such the only god worthy of their attention. Other hymns were addressed with equal devotion to gods of different names. Müller regarded this as different from the later forms of polytheism and coined for this attention to one god the term 'henotheism' (heno = one). As distinct from monotheism which presupposes that there is only one god, henotheism implies devotion to one god without postulating that he is the only one. In this phase of henotheism the general predicates of god are determined.

Müller's description of the later transition from heno to monotheism is less convincing. He argued that with the emergence of early states, monarchy prevailed among men and thus they also believed in monotheism. The religions of India actually did not conform to this rule and in later studies Müller attributed monotheism to the Semitic religious tradition and not to monarchical predilections. In this as well as in some other respects, the Hibbert Lectures mark a transitional period in Müller's science of religion. He returned to this theme ten years later with the Gifford Lectures which have been mentioned earlier. The first cycle of lectures was devoted to the exploration of natural religion. He mainly recapitulated his earlier views and then progressed to the second cycle on physical religion in which he surveyed the gods personifying natural forces such as the sun, etc. He covered new ground when he turned to anthropological religion in the third cycle. The term 'anthropological' did not quite suit his ideas and he would have preferred 'anthropic' but he stated that he avoided it, because he did not wish to introduce a strange neologism. Actually, the designation 'anthropological' was not a misnomer as Müller obviously had taken note of the new discipline of cultural anthropology which was making great progress at that time. He still retained the method of comparative philology but whereas he had earlier been concerned with man's concepts of god, he now turned to man himself and studied the development of the concept of the human soul. He started this third cycle of lectures by discussing the freedom of debate in religious matters. In support of this he quoted Tennyson's verse: 'There lives more faith in serious doubt / Believe me, than in half the creed.' He pleaded for tolerance and objected to the faith in miracles. The existence of god, so he argued, cannot be proven by a faith in him, but the fact that this faith has been universal among men could be taken as a historical proof of god's existence. Similarly the belief in the existence of a human soul is generally found among all human beings. This belief obviously precedes animism as a religious phenomenon as animism is based on the concept of 'anima'. Müller's discussion of animism shows his familarity with the work of Tylor who had coined this term which then became a general designation for primitive religion. Müller also devoted much attention to the cult concerning the dead. This was an important subject as Spencer and many others held that this cult marked the origin of religion. The Vedic concept of 'atman' and the Greek idea of 'psyche' are stressed by Müller. He rejects the theory that the perception of the human shadow or the experience of dreams gave rise to the concept of a human soul. The human soul was conceived of as a necessary counterpart to god according to Max Müller's view. This was very close to the unity of the soul with god, the Vedantic creed which had impressed Müller so much and to which he returned in the fourth cycle of lectures.

This last cycle had the title *Theosophy or Psychological Religion.* Müller emphasized that his use of the term theosophy did not mean that he subscribed to the principles of the Theosophical Society founded by Helena Blavatsky in 1875. He stated that the esoteric doctrines propounded by her were fraudulent and had nothing to do with Indian religion. He used the term theosophy as it was understood by the Greek Neo-Platonic philosophers whom he held in high esteem. In commenting on what he meant by 'psychological religion' he stated that he used this term, because other terms such as 'psychic' and 'mystic' are often misunderstood. His main interest is in the relation between the soul of man and the soul of god. In this context he also deals with the Indian ideas of the migration of the human soul after death. In early Indian texts there is as yet no evidence of the transmigration of souls into other beings nor do these texts refer to a union of the human soul with god. The description of the migration of the soul shows a slow transition from earlier ideas of a sojourn on the moon or in the world of the gods to various indications of a union with god in the Upanishads which are then elaborated in the Vedanta Sutras which are aimed at presenting a system of Vedanta philosophy.

The idea of the union of the soul with god is of utmost importance for Max Müller as he tries to reconcile Vedanta philosophy with the Christian faith in a divine Logos. The lectures on theosophy revealed what he was driving at when pursuing his science of religion. He firmly believed in the Logos as described in the Gospel according to St. John. Logos also meant 'word' but not as a mere sound but as an embodied thought, and finally it also meant god as embodied in Jesus Christ. Müller devoted a great deal of attention to the Jewish philosopher, Philo, who lived in Alexandria and was a contemporary of Jesus. He was an important member of the Jewish community who was well versed in Greek philosophy and a prolific writer in

Greek. He interpreted the Old Testament allegorically and emphasized the divine logos as mediator between god and man. According to Philo, God was unknowable but he influenced the world by his powers which could be witnessed by man. Philo's thought was of great importance for the early Christian philosophers such as Clement of Alexandria, Origines et al. Müller praised Alexandria as the cradle of Christian theology and devoted a considerable part of his last cycle of lectures to this school of thought.

Müller seems to have derived much of his knowledge about early Christian doctrines from the work of the German theologian, Adolf von Harnack, who had published the first volume of his comprehensive history of Christian dogma in 1886. As usual, Max Müller had taken note of the latest German publications in his field. He indicated his indebtedness to Harnack in the preface to the lectures on theosophy. Harnack was a liberal Protestant. He wrote the history of Christian dogma from a critical point of view. According to him Christian dogma had been formulated under the influence of Greek philosophical thought, he considered this to be a negative influence and therefore analysed it with even greater care. Müller benefited from Harnack's insights but did not share his negative view of the influence of Greek philosophy on Christianity, nor did he approve of Harnack's censure of mysticism as irrational. On the contrary, Müller praised Christian mysticism and maintains that there is no difference between that mysticism and other types of mysticism. He pointed out that Bernhard of Clairvaux often described the relations between god and the soul in terms which were similar to those of the Upanishads. He concludes his discussion of Christian mysticism by referring to the medieval theologian Meister Eckhart. For Eckhart creation is an emanation of god and the human souls are embodiments of divine thoughts. Müller discusses his writings at length. He admits that they are often difficult to understand but recommends a study of the Upanishads as a preparation for reading Eckhart.

Again and again Müller returns to the meaning of Logos which he even equates with the Vedic concept of Rta. At the end of his fourth cycle of lectures he even asserts that Christianity achieved its primacy among world religions because it was based on the Logos. The intimate link of Müller's science of language with his science of religion consists of this belief in the divine Logos. This belief also urged him to take an interest in all world religions. The tolerant acceptance of the plurality of religions is as important today as it was in his time. Recently the British theologian, John Hick, has once more highlighted this theme in his Gifford Lectures of 1986-7, held almost exactly one hundred years after Müller's lectures. Hick published these lectures under the title *An Interpretation of Religion: Human Responses to the Transcendent.* He does not seem to be familiar with Max Müller's work, but his lectures could very well indicate a renaissance of Müller's thought which has been neglected for a long time.

The veil of oblivion which shrouded Müller's work after his death did not cover his monumental achievement of publishing 50 volumes of the *Sacred Books of the East.* They are nowadays even available on the internet and provide a wealth of information on the world religions. Müller was not always consistent in recommending his plan. On the one hand he stated that the Sacred Books could become a foundation for a universal religion of mankind, whereas on the other hand he mentioned that it would be of help for Christian missionaries who would have to know more about the religions of those whom they wanted to convert. The publication was supported by the Government of India and by Oxford University Press. Actually, the Sacred Books then sold so well that they did not need to be subsidized any longer. They became a lasting monument to Max Müller's intellectual energy and his great skill of 'academic networking' with which he managed to get together 21 highly qualified authors to share the daunting task of translating and editing those enormous volumes.

A LASTING MONUMENT: THE SACRED BOOKS OF THE EAST

The first evidence of Müller's plan is found in a letter addressed in 1875 to his Oxford colleague, the Sinologist James Legge who was glad to join this enterprise. James Legge (1815-97) had spent about thirty years in Hong kong where he had met a Taiping rebel who had fled from the Chinese mainland. The scholarly rebel helped Legge to translate the Chinese classics. With this treasure trove Legge had returned to Oxford where he finally contributed altogether six volumes to the Sacred Books which prove to be useful to Sinologists even today. Actually, the first of Legge's six volumes was published in 1879 at the same time as Müller's translation of the most important Upanishads and Georg Bühler's volume of the *Sacred Laws of the*

Aryas. With this publication of three major volumes in the first year, the Sacred Books got off to a good start. Georg Bühler (1837-98) proved to be a particularly talented contributor to Müller's project. He edited three volumes including an impressive volume of the Laws of Manu. Young Bühler had met Müller in England soon after taking his doctorate at Göttingen. Müller had recommended him for a post in India where he served as a professor in Elphinstone College, Mumbai. Bühler later on was an educational administrator of the Government of India until his return to Europe in 1880 when he became Professor of Sanskrit at the University of Vienna. In India Bühler had discovered many valuable old manuscripts and deciphered innumerable inscriptions. He was so impressed with the historical sources which he had encountered in India that he warned his European colleagues that they should not refer to India as a country without history any longer.

Next to India and China, ancient Persia had to be represented in the Sacred Books. For this Müller found another amazing young scholar: James Darmesteter (1849-94). He was a French Jew who had taken an interest in ancient Persian early in life and had published a brilliant book on *Ormuzd et Ahriman* in 1877. This work immediately attracted Müller's attention and Darmesteter then translated and edited the first part of the Zend-Avesta for him which was published as the fourth volume of the Sacred Books in 1880. This was followed by the second part in 1883. Darmesteter subsequently visited the Parsis in Mumbai in order to get to know more about their faith. Later on he toured Afghanistan. Müller kept in touch with him and quoted him in his own work. The Pahlavi texts of Zoroasterianism were contributed by Edward William West (1824-1905), a civil engineer and orientalist, who edited altogether five volumes.

Perhaps the most colourful character among the contributors to the Sacred Books was Edward Henry Palmer (1840-82) who translated the Koran for Müller. Palmer was a precursor of Lawrence of Arabia. He had studied Persian and Hindustani at Cambridge and then had travelled with the Bedouins in Palestine where he was called Abdallah Effendi. In 1871 he was appointed Professor of Arabic at Cambridge University. His Koran was published in two volumes in 1880 in the Sacred Books. In 1882 he was sent on another political mission to Palestine.

Thomas William Rhys Davids (1843-1929) had originally studied

Sanskrit in Germany. He had then joined the British colonial civil service and was sent to Ceylon where he became a Pali scholar and participated in the excavation of Anuradhapura. In 1882 he had been appointed Professor of Pali in London and soon became one of the most productive contributors to the Sacred Books. He translated and edited altogether six volumes of Buddhist texts.

In Germany Sanskrit studies had proliferated in the second half of the nineteenth century and Müller could draw on a whole group of excellent scholars who could translate rather special texts for his project. Julius Eggeling (1842-1918) had studied at Breslau and Berlin and had stayed in England since 1866. He was called to the chair of Sanskrit at Edinburgh University in 1875. He contributed five volumes to the Sacred Books, all of them devoted to the *Satapatha Brahmana*. Julius Jolly (1849-1937) edited two volumes on Hindu law and Hermann Jacobi (1850-1937) produced two volumes of Jaina texts. Jacobi had gone to India soon after his doctorate where he spent two years of study with Georg Bühler in 1873-4. Bühler had avidly collected Jaina texts in India and must have inspired Jacobi to edit them. In 1876 Jacobi had become Professor of Sanskrit at Münster and was later on called to chairs at Kiel and Bonn. Hermann Oldenberg (1854-1920) who had studied in Berlin and in 1889 had become Jacobi's successor in Kiel was a pioneer in Buddhist studies but had also worked on Vedic texts. He contributed five volumes to the Sacred Books, these consisted of the Buddhist Vinaya texts, some of which he co-edited with Rhys Davids. But one of Oldenberg's volumes was devoted to Vedic hymns, particularly those to Agni. Müller himself had edited the Vedic hymns to the Maruts and Rudra. George Thibaut (1848-1914) also belonged to the German group of Indologists although he had a French name. He spent some time in England and then became a professor in the Government Sanskrit College at Varanasi in 1875. Presumably Müller had recommended him for this post. He edited three volumes of the *Vedanta Sutras* with the commentaries of Shankaracharya and Ramanuja for the Sacred Books. This was a subject which was particularly close to Max Müller's heart.

India's most famous religious text, the *Bhagavadagita*, had to be represented in the Sacred Books. It was edited by the only Indian in Müller's team: Kashinath Trimbak Telang (1850-93). Telang was one of the early Indian nationalists. He had studied at Elphinstone College, Mumbai. He was a brilliant Sanskrit scholar and had also obtained a law degree. In 1872 he started practising at the High Court in Mumbai of which he later on became a distinguished judge. In 1877 the young lawyer gave a famous lecture in Mumbai in which he criticized the negative impact of British free trade doctrines on the Indian economy. He also took a lively interest in literature and translated Lessing's *Nathan, the Wise*, into his mother-tongue, Marathi. In Mumbai Telang had worked with Georg Bühler who obviously recommended him to Müller for the edition of the *Bhagavadagita*. Telang added to this two additional texts, the *Sanatsujatagita* and the *Anugita*. His introduction to these texts show that Telang was familiar with the methods of comparative philology. He used all kinds of evidence to determine the age of his texts and arrived at the conclusion that the *Bhagavadagita* and the *Sanatsujatagita* were of the same age and were pre-Buddhist whereas the *Anugita* was definitely a later text but probably prior to Apastamba's Dharmasutra which Bühler had dated at about the third century BC. Telang marshalled his evidence with great circumspection and proved to be a master in this field.

At the very end of the great project of the Sacred Books, Müller was joined by Moritz Winternitz (1863-1937), an Austrian Sanskritist who arrived in Oxford at a young age and translated the last two volumes of Müller's Gifford Lectures into German. He also helped Müller with a revised edition of the *Rig Veda* which was reprinted in India, sponsored by an Indian prince, the Maharaja of Vizianagram. In 1894 Müller and Winternitz conceived of a plan of publishing a comprehensive index of the whole series of the Sacred Books. It was to be much more than an index, it should serve as a Manual of Eastern Religions. The final version of this ambitious project had more than 600 pages and kept Winternitz busy for many years. He prepared about 70,000 slips for his alphabetical entries. As Winternitz stated in his introduction, he aimed at a scientific classification of all religious phenomena, but he avoided any reference to theories. He warned the reader that he would look in vain for entries on animism, fetishism, tabu, totemism, etc. The index was finally published in 1910, by that time Winternitz was Professor of Sanskrit at Charles University, Prague. He had left Oxford in 1899, one year before Max Müller's death, but he did not forget the promise he had made to his mentor of completing the index which they had planned together.

Anybody who has ever had to edit even a single volume with contributions of more than a dozen authors knows about the difficulty of getting them to keep their promises. Max Müller managed to see 45 volumes of the Sacred Books through the press before he died and the remaining texts were published soon thereafter. This is a testimony to his abilities but also to the respect shown to him by an international team of authors none of whom had worked under his direct supervision. Many of them were junior to him by some decades, but they were all established scholars in their own right. It also goes to Max Müller's credit that he widened the scope of religions which were documented in the Sacred Book far beyond the Indian sphere which was his immediate field of research. Of course, 32 of the 49 volumes of texts deal with Indian religions, including Buddhism and Jainism. But this was not due to a narrow bias. After all, India had been very productive in the field of religion and had influenced other regions of Asia as well. The inclusion of the Bible in the Sacred Books would have made these series of texts more representative. Max Müller wanted to include it and when the first round of 24 volumes had proved to be very successful and the second round was started in 1885, he had hoped that those who had been against the Bible being classified as a 'Sacred Book of the East' would now ask him to include it. But orthodox Christian exclusivism prevailed.

Inspite of such disappointments, Max Müller's life had been very rich and full of great achievements. Some later Indologists have attributed the fact that he was forgotten so soon after his death to the lack of specific contributions to Sanskrit philology like those of a Bühler, Jacobi or Oldenberg, to mention only a few of the great Indologists of the generation which followed Müller's. But those who criticize him in this way fail to acknowledge that he did a great deal for establishing an international reputation for their discipline and that he encouraged many younger scholars who then surpassed him in terms of their specific work.

BIBLIOGRAPHY

Chaudhuri, Nirad, *Scholar Extraordinary: The Life of Professor the Right Honourable Friedrich Max Müller, P.C.*, New York and Oxford: Chatto & Windus, 1974.

Harnack, Adolf von, *Lehrbuch der Dogmengeschichte*, 3 vols., Tübingen: J.C.B. Mohr, 1886-90.

Hick, John, *An Interpretation of Religion: Human Responses to the Transcendent*, New Haven: Yale University Press, 1989.

Lang, Andrew, *Myth, Ritual and Religion*, 2 vols., London: Macmillan, 1887.

Müller, F. Max, *Essay on Comparative Mythology*, London: Longmans, 1858.

———, *Lectures on the Science of Language*, 2 series, London: Longmans, 1861, 1864.

———, *Chips from a German Workshop*, 4 vols., London: Longmans, 1868-75.

———, *Lectures on the Origin and Growth of Religions as Illustrated by the Religions of India*, London: Longmans, 1878 (Hibbert Lectures).

———, *Natural Religion*, London: Longmans, 1889 (Gifford Lectures).

———, *Physical Religion*, London: Longmans, 1891 (Gifford Lectures).

———, *Anthropological Religion*, London: Longmans, 1892 (Gifford Lectures).

———, *Theosophy, or Psychological Religion*, London: Longmans, 1893 (Gifford Lectures).

Rothermund, Dietmar, 'Max Müller and India's Quest for a National Past', in D. Rothermund, *The German Intellectual Quest for India*, Delhi: Manohar, 1986.

Schelling, Friedrich von, *Philosophie der Mythologie*, Stuttgart: Cotta, 1856.

Tylor, Edward Burnett, *Primitive Culture: Research into the Development of Mythology, Philosophy, Religion, Art and Custom*, 2 vols., London: John Murray, 1871.

van den Bosch, Lourens, *Friedrich Max Müller: A Life Devoted to the Humanities*, Leiden: Brill, 2002.

CHAPTER 12

Rajghat: in Memory of the Mahatma

THE CREATION OF A NATIONAL PLACE OF MEMORY

The Rajghat Samadhi where Mahatma Gandhi was cremated has become the most important national place of memory in India. The Hindu custom of cremating the dead and imersing their ashes into a river actually precludes the transformation of the place of burning the dead into a place of memory. This custom highlights the transient nature of human life and stresses that memory cannot be attached to time and space. There is an exception, however, as far as the 'samadhi' of saints is concerned. 'Samadhi' means a concentration of the mind. It is believed that holy men at the end of their days can leave their mortal body in full consciousness. Although 'samadhi' refers to this process, the term is also used for designating the locality where it has taken place. Small monuments mark such places and they attract worshippers. Calling Gandhi's place of cremation a 'samadhi' makes him a saint which he never claimed to be. But it is only by presuming that he was a saint that this particular place of memory can be justified. It is also treated as a place of worship. Visitors must remove their shoes when approaching the Rajghat Samadhi as they have to do when entering a temple. Most of them also perform a 'pradakshina', a clockwise circumambulation of the monument. This is an ancient ceremony otherwise only performed when visiting a temple. In doing this 'pradakshina' the worshipper personally reaffirms the sacred territorial claim of the temple. Many visitors of the Rajghat Samadhi who have followed the ritual observed there may not be aware of its meaning.

The form of the monument, a plain slab of black marble, was obviously designed according to the wishes of Jawaharlal Nehru who preferred this impressive simplicity. He had first thought of asking an American artist to design it, but there was criticism in Parliament about this[1] and the work was finally entrusted to an Indian artist, Vanu G. Bhuta. The only inscription on the side of the slab of marble are the words 'Hei Ram' which Gandhi uttered when he was shot. A few weeks before his death Gandhi had referred to this end. He had said that the people called him a Mahatma but he may fail the final test of facing his murderer and saying 'Hei Ram', he may be frightened by the murderer and run away.[2] As he did not fail this test, the inscription on the slab of marble can be taken as a testimony to this fact.

There were suggestions to erect a huge statue of Gandhi at the Rajghat Samadhi. Fortunately this was not done as it would have been not in keeping with the memory of the Mahatma. Some members of Parliament (Lok Sabha) recommended the construction of a Gandhi Memorial Library during the debates on the Rajghat Samadhi Act of 1951. But then Nehru intervened in the debate and stressed that the Act was merely intended to look after this place as efficiently as possible, there was a library under the Gandhi Memorial Trust and it would be undesirable to mix up the two. Nehru then added that the committee (empowered by the Act) 'looks after it as a sacred place, non-partisan, non-political, non-propagandist. It is a sacred place which everybody in India holds in reverence'.[3] After Nehru's intervention, all amendments to the Act were withdrawn and it was passed without any objections.

The Rajghat Samadhi Act was in fact a very prosaic piece of legislation. It was introduced by the Minister of Works, Production and Supply and was meant to define the piece of land on which the Rajghat Samadhi was located and to install a Rajghat Samadhi Committee which would act as trustee of the monument. It would be empowered to regulate whatever functions were to be held there. The major part of the text of the Act was taken up by the rules concerning the composition of the committee.[4] It would have 11 members, the Mayor of Delhi would belong to it ex-officio. There would be two members of the Lok Sabha to be nominated by the Speaker and one of the Rajya Sabha to be nominated by its Chairman. There were some un-official members and some civil servants to be nominated by the Government of India. The government also appointed the Minister of Urban Development (earlier Works, Production and Supply) as Chairman of the committee. The government also assigns an annual grant to the committee. In the year 2005-6 this amounted to Rs. 20.5 million (approximately US $ 4,40,000).

With this confirmed legal status, the Rajghat Samadhi has emerged as the central focus of national memory. Every foreign head of government or of state visiting India must pay his respects to the Rajghat Samadhi. He or she usually places a wreath on the marble slab, a gesture which is derived from similar ceremonies elsewhere in the world. But the guests also submit to the Indian ritual of taking off their shoes and doing the proper clockwise circumambulation. Even President Musharraf of Pakistan, the first head of state of his country to visit the Rajghat Samadhi did what he was expected to do.[5] The American Presidents Clinton and Bush were recent visitors. The preparations for President Bush's visit almost caused a major scandal. American security agents took sniffer dogs to the monument to make sure that there were no bomb hidden there. Dogs getting near to the sacred place was considered to be defiling it.[6] The Indian government faced some difficulties in overcoming the resentment caused in this way. Finally Bush's visit was regarded as a success and the dogs were soon forgotten.

Many of the visiting dignitaries also ceremonially planted trees at the Rajghat Samadhi. This reflects an ancient idea which was referred to by Seth Govind Das, a veteran freedom fighter, in the parliamentary debate of 1951. He had mentioned Tapovana (forests of meditation) described in the *Mahabharata* and the Puranas and had recommended that such a sacred grove should surround the Rajghat Samadhi.[7] The foreign diginitaries probably knew nothing about sacred groves but nevertheless participated happily in the nice ceremony of planting their trees.

From a place of memory, the Rajghat Samadhi evolved into a kind of national altar at which politicians or social activists could demonstratively begin or end campaigns and attract popular attention. In March 1977 after defeating Indira Gandhi the members of the new Janata Party took a pledge of joint action at the Rajghat Samadhi. Tibetan freedom marchers also congregated there. Sunderlal Bahuguna who had fasted in protest against the Tehri Dam, solemnly terminated his fast at the Rajghat Samadhi in June 1996. In August 2005 a group of Indian, Pakistani and Nepali peace activists joined a Japanese monk in a ceremonial fast at Rajghat. They commemorated the dropping of the atom bombs on Hiroshima and Nagasaki and prayed for a lasting peace in South Asia. In February 2006 people affected by the demolition of illegal structures around Delhi also held a meeting there in order to draw attention to their plight. This shows that a national place of memory can also serve as a platform for the articulation of protest or for affirming political solidarity. The Rajghat Samadhi Committee sometimes has its problems with such activities as it is pleged to political neutrality. This is not explicitly stated in the Rajghat Samadhi Act, but it can be inferred from Nehru's statement on the 'non-partisan, non-political, non-propagandist' nature of this 'sacred place'. On the other hand it could be argued that Gandhi himself championed political protest and as long as it was articulated in a non-violent manner, he would have supported it. It seems that so far all those who have used the Rajghat Samadhi as a platform for their causes have done this without taking recourse to violence. Much more than the 'command performance' of the foreign dignitaries, this appropriation of the place of memory by groups of civil society contributes to its importance for the nation.

ENACTING THE NATION IN TIME AND SPACE

When Pierre Nora documented the 'Lieux de Mémoire' he did this with the view to confirm French national identity. Enacting the nation by highlighting important conjunctures in time and space would be more effective than abstract references to national history. The nation is an 'imagined community' and imagination is stimulated by tangible evidence. Benedict Anderson[8] who wrote about the nation as an imagined community was obviously influenced by Karl Deutsch[9] who had studied nationalism as a product of social communication, but Anderson did not mention Deutsch in his book. 'Print capitalism' which is highlighted by Anderson is foreshadowed by Deutsch's emphasis on language and the press as essential elements of social communication. Both authors tend to privilege the literary message and do not explain how nationalism can flourish under conditions of widespread illiteracy. Symbolic action rather than an ideology propagated by 'print capitalism' will stir the imagination of the people. Mahatma Gandhi was a master of symbolic action. The epithet 'Father of the Nation' which is applied to Gandhi may often appear to be an element of lipservice, but it does have a real meaning. For many people of the vast nation the consciousness of being 'Indian' was only due to Gandhi's influence. The fate of the indentured labourers transported to Fiji where they worked in the sugar plantations is an interesting case in point. These poor people who had been recruited in the rural areas of northern India were not conscious of being

'Indians'.The common hardship which they had to suffer as indentured servants provided them with a new term which reflected their identity and solidarity. They called themselves 'Girmityas', a Hindi neo-logism derived from the English term 'agreement', i.e. the bond which defined their servitude. It was only when emissaries of Mahatma Gandhi reached Fiji that the 'Girmityas' came to know about their being 'Indians'.[10] This is a very special case, but to a certain extent it is representative of many parts of India where people realized that they belonged to a nation fighting for its freedom only when they came to know about Gandhi's symbolic actions. He was enacting the nation and established its position in time and space. When asked about the message which he wanted to convey to the people, he replied: 'My life is my message'. It was not his intention that this life should end as it did – at the hands of a politically motivated assassin. But even his death was a message as he faced it courageously with the words 'Hei Ram' on his lips.

Rajghat, which commemorates this death also reminds the Indian nation of Gandhi's life. The memory of the historical contours of this life tends to fade with every passing generation. Gandhi himself did not show much interest in history and stressed that truth transcends history.[11] What kind of memory is required which transcends history as experienced by contemporaries or reconstructed by scholars?

HISTORY AND MEMORY

Sir Francis Tuker, a British general who was posted in Bengal at the time of the Partition of India in 1947 published a book under the title: *While Memory Serves.*[12] It is a valuable account of this crucial period by a well informed contemporary witness. The meaning of 'memory' to which Tuker referred in the title of his book is obviously that of his own timebound experience. He wishes to record what he has experienced while he can still remember it. The title also hints at the privilege of the witness who is served by his memory whereas future generations do not share this kind of memory. Of course, he must have also hoped that his record would contribute to a 'master narrative' to be written by future historians.

The memory which served Tuker was in a category different from that located in places of memory. This latter type of memory is not based on personal experience but on an acquired knowledge of the past. It is related to historical consciousness, but whereas this consciousness is mostly based on literary evidence, the knowledge embedded in places of memory is of a different kind. It can be experienced, particularly if the ritual which surrounds the place makes an impression on the mind of the visitor. Going to Rajghat, taking off one's shoes and walking clockwise around the monument is a memorable event. Places of memory are not simply remembered, they create living memory in those who visit them. At the same time, the visitor confirms the relevance of the place of memory just as the people walking around an Indian temple in the prescribed manner reaffirm its sacred territorial claim.

The great attention which historians have devoted to places of memory in recent years is obviously due to the fact that the faith in 'master narratives' has faded. In substituting the study of places of memory for the writing of 'master narratives', these historians have opted for a different approach to historiography. To them history is not a seamless web but a mosaic composed of fragments of memory which must be pieced together in order to form a pattern. Such fragments may not necessarily fit together in a harmonious way; they may reflect contrasts and contradictions. They are an antidote to the unified vision of a 'master narrative'. Indian historiography has not yet paid much attention to places of memory, when it does, Rajghat will certainly be included in the mosaic of Indian places of memory.

NOTES

1. Parliamentary Debates (Lok Sabha), vol. 13, 1951, Col. 10357.
2. 'Harijan', 30 November 1947, in *Collected Works of Mahatma Gandhi*, vol. 90, pp. 87 f.
3. Parliamentary Debates (Lok Sabha), vol. 13, 1951, Col. 10357.
4. The Rajghat Samadhi Act, 1951, §3 (The Rajghat Samadhi Committee).
5. *The Tribune* (Chandigarh), 15 July 2001.
6. *Indian Express*, 21 May 2006.
7. Parliamentary Debates (Lok Sabha), vol. 13, 1951, Col. 10357.
8. Benedict Anderson, *Imagined Communities. Reflections on the Spread and Origin of Nationalism*, London, 1983.
9. Karl W. Deutsch, *Nationalism and Social Communication*, New York, 1953.

10. Dietmar Rothermund, *The Routledge Companion to Decolonization*, London, 2006, p. 207.
11. Dietmar Rothermund, *Mahatma Gandhi: An Essay in Political Biography*, New Delhi, 1991, p. 1.
12. Sir Francis Tuker, *While Memory Serves*, London, 1950.

Bibliography of Dietmar Rothermund

Only books (monographs, textbooks, collected essays) and edited volumes are listed in this bibliography.

BOOKS

The Layman's Progress: Religious and Political Experience in Colonial Pennsylvania, 1740- 1770, Philadelphia: University of Pennsylvania Press, 1961.

Die politische Willensbildung in Indien, 1900-1960, Wiesbaden: Harrassowitz, 1965.

Indien und die Sowjetunion , Köln: Böhlau, 1968.

Grundzüge der indischen Geschichte, Darmstadt: Wissenschaftliche Buchgesellschaft, 1976.

Europa und Asien im Zeitalter des Merkantilismus, Darmstadt: Wissenschaftliche Buchgesellschaft, 1978.

Government, Landlord and Peasant in India: Agrarian Relations under British Rule, 1865-1935, Wiesbaden: Steiner 1978 (translated into Telugu, 1998).

Fünfmal Indien (Panoramen der Welt), München: Piper, 1979 (3rd rev. edn., 1990).

Asian Trade and European Expansion in the Age of Mercantilism, Delhi: Manohar, 1981.

(with Hermann Kulke) *Geschichte Indiens*, Stuttgart: Kohlhammer, 1982 (Later editions: München: Beck, 4th rev. edn., 2010).

The Indian Economy under British Rule and Other Essays, Delhi: Manohar, 1983.

The German Intellectual Quest for India, Delhi: Manohar, 1986.

(with Hermann Kulke) *A History of India*, London: Croom Helm, 1986 (5th rev. edn. London: Routledge, 2010) (translated into Italian, 1991, Turkish 2002, Rumanian 2005, Chinese 2008).

Mahatma Gandhi: An Essay in Political Biography, Delhi: Manohar, 1991.

India in the Great Depression, 1929-1939, Delhi: Manohar, 1992.

An Economic History of India, London: Routledge, 1993 (2nd edn.).

Geschichte als Prozess und Aussage, München: Oldenbourg, 1994.

The Global Impact of the Great Depression, London: Routledge, 1996 (translated into Korean 2003).

Mahatma Gandhi. Eine politische Biographie, München: Beck 2nd edn., 1998.

Delhi, 15. August 1947: Das Ende kolonialer Herrschaft. München: dtv 1998. (translated into Italian, 2000, and into Chinese 2001).

The Role of the State in South Asia and Other Essays, Delhi: Manohar, 2000.

Krisenherd Kaschmir. Der Konflikt der Atommächte Indien und Pakistan. München: Beck, 2002.

The Routledge Companion to Decolonization, London: Routledge, 2006.

India: The Rise of an Asian Giant, New Haven and London: Yale University Press, 2008. (German edition: *Indien: Aufstieg einer asiatischen Weltmacht*, München: Beck, 2008) (translated into Chinese, Arabic and Polish).

Gandhi und Nehru. Zwei Gesichter Indiens, Stuttgart: Kohlhammer, 2010.

Contemporary India, 1947-2011, Delhi: Pearson India, 2013.

BOOKS EDITED

Rabindranath Tagore in Germany: A Cross-Section of Contemporary Reports. Delhi: Max Müller Bhavan, 1961 (rev. and enl. edn., Delhi: Allied Publishers, 2011).

Islam in Southern Asia: A Survey of Current Research, Wiesbaden: Steiner, 1975.

(with D.C. Wadhwa), *Zamindars, Mines and Peasants: Studies in the History of an Indian Coalfield and its Rural Hinterland*, Delhi: Manohar, 1978.

(with E. Kropp, G. Dienemann), *Urban Growth and Rural Stagnation: Studies in the Economy of an Indian Coalfield and its Rural Hinterland*, Delhi: Manohar, 1980.

Die Peripherie in der Weltwirtschaftskrise: Afrika, Asien und Lateinamerika, 1929-1939, Paderborn: Schöningh, 1983.

(with Hermann Kulke) *Regionale Tradition in Südasien*, Wiesbaden: Steiner 1985.

(with John Simon) *Education and the Integration of Ethnic Minorities*, London/New York: Francis Pinter, 1986.

(with Suranjit Saha) *Regional Disparities in India: Rural and Industrial Dimensions*, Delhi: Manohar, 1991.

(with Roderich Ptak) *Emporia, Commodities and Entrepreneurs in Asian Maritime Trade, c. 1400-1750*, Stuttgart: Steiner, 1991.

(with Dagmar Hellmann-Rajanayagam) *Nationalstaat und Sprachkonflikte in Süd- und Südostasien*, Stuttgart: Steiner, 1992.

Indien. Kultur, Geschichte, Politik, Wirtschaft, Umwelt. Ein Handbuch, München: Beck, 1995.

(with Jap de Moor) *Our Laws, Their Lands: Land Use in Modern Colonial Societies,* Münster: Lit, 1995.

Liberalising India: Progress and Problems, Delhi: Manohar, 1996.

(with Subrata Mitra) *Legitimacy and Conflict in South Asia*, Delhi: Manohar, 1997.

Aneignung und Selbstbehauptung. Antworten auf die europäische Expansion, München: Oldenbourg, 1999.

(with Karin Preisendanz), *Südasien in der Neuzeit. Geschichte und Gesellschaft 1500-2000*, Wien: Promedia, 2003.

(with Susanne Weigelin-Schwiedrzik), *Der Indische Ozean. Das afro-asiatische Mittelmeer als Kultur- und Wirtschaftsraum*, Wien: Promedia, 2004.

Index

adult suffrage 78
agglutinization 224
agrarian distress 187
agrarian relations 121, 130, 133 f.
agricultural production 78
Ahmedabad 187
Ajivikas 19, 20
Akbar 28, 30, 73, 85 f., 89, 91
alcabala (tax) 91
Alexander the Great 19
Algeria 146, 148
Allahabad inscription 21
Alliance Against Terror 58
All-India Congress Committee 111
amaranayaka 27
Ambani, Mukesh 197
Anderson, Benedict 242
animism 230
Antulay, A.R. 191
Antunes, Ernesto Mello 151
archers 39, 46
Arkwright, Richard 168
Arms Act 52
Arthashastra 19, 65, 67
Artillery 28, 30, 42, 45 f., 47, 73, 97
Arya 18, 37, 40
Ashoka (Maurya) 19, 20, 21, 41 f., 68
Ashvamedha 39 f.
Atharvaveda 229
atom bomb 55, 60
Attlee, Clement 114 f.
August Revolution (1942) 114
Aungier, Gerald 180 f.
Aurangabad 30
Aurangzeb 29, 74 f.
Azhar, Maulana Masood 58

Babri Masjid 192
Babur 27, 28, 41 f., 49
Bagehot, Walter 164
Bahuguna, Sunderlal 241
Baji Rao I (Peshwa) 180
bakasht 124, 127
Bangalore 45
Bangladesh 55
Bank of England 188
Bayly, Christopher 141
bayonet 51
begar 124
Belgium 145 f.
Bell, Thomas 170
Bengal 18, 21, 31, 40, 77, 111, 163, 167, 169, 170, 174, 243
Bentinck, Lord 164
Bengal Coal Co. 131
Bernhard of Clairvaux 232
Bhagavadgita 102, 235
Bharata Ganarajya 66
Bharatiya Janata Party (BJP) 79
Bhiwandi 165, 192, 196
Bhuinhar 127
Bhuinhar Survey 127
Bhuinyas 133
Bhuta, Vanu G. 240
Bhutto, Zulfiqar Ali 55 f.
Bible 237
Bihar 18, 21
Birsa 129
birth rate 79
Black Cats (National Security Guards) 59
Blanchard, Pascal 158
Blavatsky, Helen 231
Bombay Baroda and Central Railway (BBCIR) 183
Bombay Presidency 167, 179, 181
bonded labour 134
Bopp, Franz 222
Bose, Subhas Chandra 53, 111

Boumedienne, Houari 146
bow, composite 38
Brahmins 18, 65 f., 57, 70
Brazil 154
Brown, Gordon 136
Buddha 19
Buddhism 19, 41, 68 f., 237
Bühler, Georg 233 f., 235, 237
Bukka 27, 72
Burundi 144
Bush, G.W. 241

Cabral, Amilcar 151
Caetano, Marcelo 152
Caliph (Baghdad) 25
Capotorti, Francesco 147
Cartwright, Edmund 169
Castro, Fidel 151
cavalry 24, 25, 42 f. 45, 71
centre-state relations 80
Chaldiran (battle) 45
chanda 122, 127
Chandragupta II 21
Chandragupta (Maurya) 19, 41, 67
chariot 37 f., 40, 66
Charles V. (Habsburg) 86, 92, 95, 97
Charles the Bold (Burgundy) 46, 50
Chattopadhyaya, B.D. 63, 70
Chaudhuri, Nirad 220
Chauri Chaura 104
Chavan, Y.B. 189
Chess 41
China 56 f., 155, 182, 220
Chirac, Jacques 146, 148
Chola dynasty 22 f.
Chotanagpur, Raja of 122
Chota Nagpur Encumbered Estates Act (1876) 131
Chota Nagpur Tenancy Act (1908) 130
Churchill, Winston 100, 112 f., 114
cityness 179, 192, 194
civil disobedience 77, 106, 108
civil service 52
Civil War, American 172, 183
class struggle 121
Clinton, Bill 58, 241
Clive, Robert 30
coal 132
coalition politics 81
collective memory 51 f.
commercial intelligence 175
commercialization 75, 173
Commonwealth, British 139
Commonwealth Immigration Act (1962) 140
Communidade dos Paises de Lingua Portuguesa 153
Communist Party of India (CPI) 189
comparative philology 225, 229 f., 236
Congo 144
Congress, Indian National 106, 179
Congress of the Oppressed Nations (Brussels) 105
Cornwallis, Lord 123
cost plus – formula 188
cotton 17, 31, 166, 171, 178, 183f., 186
country trade 166
court etiquette 91
counterinsurgency 59
Crawford, Arthur 184 f.
Cripps, Stafford 112 f.
Crompton, Samuel 168
Cuba 151
cultural anthropology 227 f., 230
Curacao 142
Cyrus the Great 20

dabbawalas 195
Dange, S.A. 189
Dara Shukoh 47
Darmesteter, James 234
Darwin, Charles 221, 223
Das, Seth Govind 241
Dassalnama 89
Da Vinci, Leonardo 225
decolonization 137, 142, 154
deflation 170, 175
De Gaulle, General Charles 145 f.

de-industrialization 163 f.
Delhi 24
Delhi Sultanate 24, 26, 72
demographic dividend 79
Desai, Morarji 56, 189
De Toqueville, Alexis 146, 148
Deutsch, Karl 242
De Witte, Ludo 145
dhamma 19
dhammamahamatras 19
Dhanbad 130
Dharavi 179, 194 f.
dharmayuddha 39
Dholavira (port city) 17, 18
Din-i-Ilahi 92
disruptive technology 28
Diwan-i-Khass 95
D'Monte, Darryl 192
Dominion Status 113
dragoons 50
Dupleix, Joseph 31, 51
Durrani, Ahmed Shah 49
dynastic Darwinism 48, 74 f.

East India Company 30, 75, 166, 171, 180 f.
Eckhart, Meister 232
economic reforms (1991) 79
Eden, Anthony 139
Eggeling, John 235
elephants 18, 21, 36, 40 f., 67
Elizabeth I, Queen 87
Elphinstone College 182, 234
Elphinstone, Mountstuart 181
Emerson, R.W. 228
Escorial 93 f., 96
Estado da India 85
etymology 224, 228 f.
ex-parte decree 125

Falkland Islands 141
fascism 104
Fatehpur Sikri 93 f.,
federalism 60, 80
Feroz Shah 27
feudalism, military 27, 43, 45, 71
Feuerbach, Ludwig 229
Fiji 242
First World War 32
Fischer, Louis 113
fishermen 180, 194
flying shuttle 169
Forjett, Charles 184 f.
Fortuyn, Pim 143
France 145 f., 158
franchise 110
Freire, Gilberto 152
Frere, Bartle 184, 194
Fujioka Nobukatsu 156 f.

ganasangha 65, 69
Gandhi, Indira 56, 104, 191, 241
Gandhi, Mahatma 32, 77, 81, 100 f. 113, 116, 147, 187, 189, 239
Gandhi-Irwin Pact (1931) 108
Ganges (river) 17
Ganweriwala (city) 18
Geddes, Patrick 195, 197
Gifford, Lord 222
Girangaon 184, 192 f.
girmityas 243
Gladstone, William 101
Goa 150
gold standard 32
Golden Fleece 92
Granada 87 f.
Great Britain 138, 164
Great Depression 32, 77, 106 f., 109, 187
Great Indian Peninsula Railway (GPIR) 182
Grimm, Jacob 222
Guha, Ranajit 123
Guinea-Bissau 151
gunpowder 47
Gupta dynasty 20 f., 68
Gustavus Adolphus 50

handloom weavers 165, 173, 187, 190
Harappa (city) 16, 18
Harappan empire 16 f.

Harappans, mature 16, 18,
Harappans, late 18
Hargreave, James 168
Harihar 27
Harkis 143, 146
Harnack, Adolf von 232
Harshavardhana 22, 69
henotheism 229
Heraklit 229
Herrera, Juan de 95 f.
Hibbert, Robert 228
Hick, John 233
Hind Swaraj 103
Hinduism 102
Hindu rate of growth 76
Hitler, Adolf 112, 190
Hittites 38
Hobsbawm, Eric 80
Hochschild, Adam 144, 157
Home Charges 53
horses 18, 25, 36, 37, 39, 43 f., 47, 57, 71
Hoysala dynasty 27, 71
Humayun 28
Humayun's tomb 94
Humboldt, Wilhelm von 222
Huns 69
Hyksos 38
Hynes, Douglas 165

Ibrahim Lodi 27
Ighilahriz, Louisette 148
Iltutmish 25
imperial preference 187
imperial overstretch 15, 29, 75, 97 f.
imperial social formation 77
import substitution 174
Indian Civil Service (ICS) 32, 75, 183
Indian National Army 53, 112
indirect rule 76
Indonesia 142, 154
Indus (river) 16, 37
Indus civilization 15, 37
industrial enclaves 163
Industrial Revolution 32, 163 f., 168, 170, 173, 175
infantry 31, 51, 75
inflation 163, 171, 186
informal sector 165
Inquisition, Spanish 85 f.
Inter Service Intelligence (ISI, Pakistan) 59
intervention, military 15, 25, 67
iqta 25, 43, 71
Iranis 74
iron ore 18, 131
Irwin, Lord 108

Jacobi, Hermann 235, 237
jagir 73
Jahangir 74
Jainism 19, 71, 237
Jallianwala Bagh 104
jama 74, 89
janapada 64
Japan 107, 112, 114, 154 f.
jati 70
Jawaharlal Nehru Port 196
Jeejeebhoy, Jamshedji 182
Jesus 221
Jharia coalfield 131, 135
Jharkhand 120 f.
Jinnah, Mohammed Ali 114, 117
jiziya 29
Jolly, Julius 235
Joshi, S.M. 189
Juan de Austria 88
judges 76

Kakatiya dynasty 26, 44, 45
Kalam, Abdul 60
Kalidasa 21, 68, 227
Kalinga 19, 68
kamiauti, kamia 133
Kang Sang Jung 156 f.
Kannada 71
Kargil war 57 f., 60
Kashmir 80, 91, 115 f., 117
Kautilya 19, 65 f., 67
Kaye, John 169

Kempe Gowda 45
Khalji, Alauddin 25, 44
Khan, A.Q. 56
khilat 92
King, Martin Luther 147
Kobayashi Yoshinori 156
Kolhan 124
Kolis 180
Kolkata 181
Komagone Takeshi 155
Komori Yoichi 156
Korea 154 f., 156
Korea (North) 57
Krishna III (Rashtrakuta) 23
Krishnadeva Raya 27, 72
Kshatriyas 70
Kulottunga 24
Kumaragupta 21, 68

landless labourers 78
Labour Party (British) 105, 114
Lang, Andrew 227
lawyers 76
League Against Imperialism 105, 111
leasing of ships 31
leather goods 173 f., 194
Le Cour Grandmaison, Olivier 148
Legge, James 233
Leoni, Pompeo 97
Leopold, King of Belgium 144 f., 157
Lepanto (battle) 97
Licchavis 21, 69
lineages 70
linguistic states 81
linkage effects 175
Linlithgow, Lord 112 f.,
Lloyd George, David 32, 101
Logos 231 f.
London 101 f.
long-distance trade 36, 41
Lumumba, Patrice 145 f.
Luso-Tropicalism 152

MacDonald, Ramsey 108 f.,
machine tools 170, 175
Macmillan, Harold 138 f., 145
Madras Presidency 167, 171 f.
Mahabharata 66
Mahasamanta 42
Mahavira 19
Mahmud of Ghazni 23
Malik Kafur 24, 25, 44
Manchuria 155
mansabdars 29, 47 f., 73 f., 89, 91
Manuel I, King of Portugal 95
Manning, Cardinal 102
Maoists 80
Marathas 74, 167, 178, 181
Marco Polo 24
Mariyannu 38, 66
martial races 53 f.
Maruyama Masao 155
Marx, Karl 121, 164, 175
Mary Tudor 86
Mata, Inocencia 153
Megasthenes 67
Mehta, Suketu 179
Meluhha 17
Menon, V.P. 115
Mesopotamia 17, 38
mesta 90
Mehta, Pherozeshah 185
Mehta, Pranjivan 103
mercantilism 166, 168
middle class 79
Migdal, Joel 63, 81
millhands 187
mill lands 193
mill owners 187
Mir Jafar 31
Mittani 38, 66
Mitterand, Francois 147
mleccha 17
Mohawk (language) 225 f.
Mohenjo Daro 16
monetary policy (Mughal) 30
monetary policy (British) 32
moneylenders 107, 125, 131
Mongols 25 f.
Moriscos 87 f.,
Morris, Morris D, 165, 171

Morris, William 103 f.
Mountbatten, Lord Louis 116 f.
Movimento de Forcas Armadas (MFA) 151 f.
Mugabe, Robert 141
Muhammad of Ghor 25, 71
Muhammad Tughluq 26
Müller, Max 102, 220 f.,
Mumbai 178 f.
Münzenberg, Willi 105
Mundari Khuntkattidars 121 f., 129, 133
Mundas 120 f., 126, 128
murid 92
Murten (battle) 50
Musharraf, General Parvez 57, 59, 241
muskets 49 f.
Muslim League 116
Mutiny (1857) 32, 52, 185
mutual deterrent 57 f.
mythology 226, 228

Namboodiripad, E.M.S. 106
nasaq 74
Nationality Act (1948) 139
National Textile Corporation 190
Navarrete, Juan Fernandez de 96
Navi Mumbai 196
nayaks 27, 45, 72
Nixon, Richard 56
Nehru, Jawaharlal 32, 54, 77, 78, 81 f., 100 f., 103 f. 105, 108 f., 116 f., 188, 239 f., 242
Nehru, Kamala 105
Nehru, Motilal 104 f., 108
Netherlands 86 f. 90 f., 141 f., 143
Noel-Baker, Philip 117
Non-Resident Indians (NRI) 81
Nora, Pierre 149, 242
nuclear ambiguity 56
nuclear umbrella 56

Oldenberg, Hermann 235
opium 182
Osborne, John 139

Pakistan 57 f., 114 f., 116 f.
Pall Mall Gazette 102
Pallava dynasty 22
Palmer, E.H. 234
Panini 223
Panipat (battle, 1526) 27
Panipat (battle, 1761) 49
Parliament (British) 32
Parliamentary democracy 78, 116
Parsis 181
Partition of India 115, 196, 243
Pataliputra 20, 21
peasants, peasantry 32, 77
Permanent Settlement (1793) 122, 131
Persian Gulf 23
Philip II of Spain 85 f., 90, 92 f.,
Philo of Alexandria 231 f.
phonetic decay 224
pieds noirs 146
Pindar 39
pir 92
Pitt, William 31
Plan Balkan 115
Plassey (battle) 30
'Platform State' 26
population growth 78
Port Trust (Mumbai) 179, 185, 193
Portugal 85, 90, 150 f., 153, 158, 180
post-colonial studies 137
Powell, Enoch 140
powerloom 169, 190
Prabhavatigupta 21
Prasad, Rajendra 111
Prataparudra (Kakatiya) 26 f., 45
Premchand Roychand 183
princely states 76
print capitalism 242
proportional election system 81
protective tariffs 190
Pulakeshin II (Chalukya) 22
Pumpuhar (port city) 24
Punjab 53 f.
Punjabi Muslims 53
purohit 65

putting-out system 169

qasba 72
Quit India movement 113
Qutbuddin Aibak 25, 71

Radcliffe, Cyril 115
railways 131 f., 175, 178, 185
Rajaraja (Chola) 23, 24
Rajendra (Chola) 23
Rajghat (Samadhi) 239
Rajghat Samadhi Act 242
Rao, P.V. Narasimha 57
Rajputs 74, 86
Rashtrakuta dynasty 23
rathakara 39, 65
ratnin 39 f., 65
real wages 187
Reliance Industries 197
rent 123, 127
Rhys-Davids, William 234 f.
rockets 60
Rig Veda 222, 227 f., 236
Roosevelt, F.D. 112 f.
Round Table Conference 108
Roy, Tirthankar 163, 165, 173
Rta 232
Rwanda 144

sabha 64
sabheya 64
Sacred Books of the East 233 f.
Said, Edward 136
Salazar, Antonio 150
Salisbury, Lord 101
Salsette 180
Salt, Henry 102
Salt March (1930) 106 f.
samadhi 239 f.
Samant, Datta 191
samanta 22, 42, 70
Sambhaji 29
samantachakra 22, 42, 70
Samjukta Maharashtra 188
Samjukta Maharashtra Samiti 189
Samudragupta 21, 26, 68
Sangha (Buddhist) 19
Sanskrit 71, 221, 224, 226, 228, 235, 237
Santals 120, 125 f., 128
Santal Parganas 125 f.
Santal revolt (1855) 125 f.
Sapru, Tej Bahadur 109
Sarkozy, Nicolas 149 f.
Sarvaia de Carvalho, Otello 151
satellites 60
Schelling, Friedrich von 227
Schlegel, Friedrich von 223
Schleiermacher, Friedrich 229
Schliemann, Heinrich 229
seals (steatite) 17
Second World War 32, 52
Seleucos Nikator 41, 67
Selim 46
Shah Ismail (Safavid) 46
Shah Jahan 74, 91
Shankaracharya 69, 235
Shankerseth, Jagannath 182
Shanks, Michael 139
Sharif, Nawaz 67
Shastri, Lal Bahadur 56
Shivaji 29, 180
Shiv Sena 190, 192, 194
Sholapur 165, 183
Sikhs 53
silver 30, 85, 97, 171 f.,
Simone, Abdoumaliq 179
Singh, Manmohan 79
Singhbhum 124
slave, slave society 43, 143
slavery, military 91
Smith, Ian 141
Soares, Mario 152
social bandits 80
software (computer) 179, 197
Soviet Union 56, 58, 105 f.
Specker, Konrad 165, 171
Spencer, Herbert 195, 220 f., 229, 231
spinning jenny 168
Spinola, General Antonio 152

Sri Lanka 23
Srivijaya 23
Stalin, Josef 106
Standard Mill (Mumbai) 188
standing armies 49 f. , 53, 89, 94
state society 15, 63
Stead, William 102
Steel Frame 32
steamships 32, 175, 179
Strauß, David Friedrich 221, 229
Suez Canal 173, 175, 178, 185
Suez crisis (1956) 139
Sufis 92
Sulh Kul 86
Surat 29, 178, 180 f.
Suriname 142
Suvarnagiri 20
Swaraj Party 105
swidden cultivation 120
symbolic action 242

Tagore, Rabindranath 100
Tagore, Satyendranath 183
Taiwan 154 f., 156
Taliban 54
Tamil 71
tank (armour) 53
tanners 194
Tata Consultancy Services 197
Tata Iron and Steel Co. (TISCO) 135
Tata, Jamshetji 186
Taxila 20
tea plantations 128
Telang, K.T. 235 f.
telegraph 32, 175, 179
Telugu 71
Tennyson, Lord 230
tenure holders 124, 131
Terzio 50
textiles 31, 166, 171
textile machinery 184 f., 186
Thackeray, Balasaheb 190
Thane 183
Thatcher, Margaret 141
Thibaut, George 235
Theosophists 102, 231
Thoreau, Henry 102
Tibaldi, Pellegrino 96
Timor, East 153 f.
Tipu Sultan 123
Titian Vecellio 96
Tirumala Nayak 27, 45
Toledo, Don Pedro de 97
Toledo, Juan Bautista de 95 f.
toofangchis 51
Townsend, Meredith 103
trade unions 187, 191
Transfer of Power 80, 138
Tuker, Francis 243
Turanis 74
Turkish (language) 225 f.
two party system 81
Tylor, E.B. 227, 230

Ugra 38
Ulema 86
United Nations 117, 154
USA 33, 58, 81, 107
University of Kolkata 183
University of Mumbai 183
Upanishads 232
urbanity 179
usurpation 25, 72
Uzbeks 46

Vajpayee, A.B. 57
Vakataka dynasty 21
Vale de Almeida, Miguel 153
Van den Bosch, Lourens 220
Vedanta 70, 231, 235
Vegetarian Society 102
Vellut, Jean-Luc 144
Victoria, Queen 32, 182
Vijayanagar empire 24 f., 27, 44 f., 72
vish 65

Wavell, Lord 114, 116
Weber, Max 155

Wellesley, Arthur (Duke of Wellington) 181
wheat 107
Williams, Monier 221
Willingdon, Lord 108
Winternitz, Moritz 236
wool 90, 167
Wordsworth, William 227
worsteds 167

Yamuna 17
yarn 171, 173, 184

zabt 74
zamburak 49
zamindars 74, 122 f., 132
Zia-ul Huq, General 56
Zinni, General Anthony 57